White Wine

D1056105

Quick Reference Card

Instant Wine Identifier

Wine Name	Grape or Place	Wine Name	Grape or Place
Alsace	Place/France	Pinot Grigio/	Grape
Bordeaux	Place/France	Pinot Gris	
Burgundy/	Place/France	Pouilly-Fuissé	Place/France
Bourgogne		Rhine (Rheingau,	Place/Germany
Chablis	Place/France	Rheinhessen)	
Chardonnay	Grape	Riesling	Grape
Chenin Blanc	Grape	Rioja	Place/Spain
Frascati	Place/Italy	Saint-Véran	Place/France
Gewurztraminer	Grape	Sancerre	Place/France
Mâcon	Place/France	Sauvignon Blanc	Grape
Mosel	Place/Germany	Sémillon/ Semillon	Grape
Muscadet	Grape	Silvaner/ Sylvaner	Grape
Müller-Thurgau	Grape	Soave	Place/Italy
Muscat / Moscato	Grape	Verdicchio	Grape
Orvieto	Place/Italy	Viognier	Grape
Pinot Blanc	Grape	Vouvray	Place/France

White Wine Style Finder

If you want a...	Try...	If you want a...	Try...
Crisp, lighter-bodied, dry, unoaked white wine	✔ Soave, Pinot Grigio, Frascati or other Italian white wines ✔ Muscadet ✔ Sancerre ✔ dry German Riesling ✔ Chablis ✔ inexpensive white Bordeaux wines	Fuller-bodied, dry white wine, with oaky character	✔ better California Chardonnays ✔ Australian Chardonnays ✔ white Burgundy wines from the Côte d'Or district ✔ most Pouilly-Fuissé wines ✔ most Rhône Valley whites ✔ some California Sauvignon Blancs ✔ better white Bordeaux wines
Fuller-bodied dry, unoaked white wine	✔ Mâcon-Villages ✔ St. Veran ✔ New Zealand Sauvignon Blanc ✔ Alsace wines ✔ Oregon Pinot Gris ✔ most Austrian whites	Soft, fruity white wine that's not fully dry	✔ inexpensive California Chardonnays ✔ Liebfraumilch ✔ many German Rieslings ✔ many U.S. Rieslings ✔ most U.S. Gewurztraminers ✔ Vouvray

...For Dummies: Bestselling Book Series for Beginners

BUSINESS AND
GENERAL
REFERENCE
BOOK SERIES
FROM IDG

White Wine For Dummies™

Quick Reference Card

Quick Pronunciation Guide to White Wine Names

The stressed syllables, if any, are indicated in capital letters.

Alsace	al zass	Pinot Grigio	pee noh GREE joe
Alto-Adige	AHL toh AH dee jhay	Pinot Gris	pee noh gree
Bordeaux	bor doh	Pouilly-Fuissé	pwee fwee say
Bourgogne	boor guh nyuh	Pouilly-Fumé	pwee foo may
Chablis	shah blee	Puligny-Montrachet	poo lee nyee mon rah shay
Chardonnay	SHAR doh nay		
Chassagne-Montrachet	shah san yuh mon rah shay	Riesling	REES ling
Condrieu	cohn dree uh	Rioja	ree OH ha
Corton-Charlemagne	cor tawn shahr luh mahn	Rueda	roo AE dah
		Rully	roo ye
Entre-Deux-Mers	on truh duh mair	Saint-Véran	san veh rahn
Gewürztraminer	gah VERTZ trah mee ner	Sancerre	sahn sair
		Sauvignon Blanc	saw vee nyon blahnk
Graves	grahv	Sémillon	sem ee yohn
Liebfraumilch	LEEB frow milsh	Soave	so AH vay
Loire	lwahr	Spätlese	SHPATE lay seh
Mâcon	mah kon	Trebbiano	treb bee AH noh
Mâcon-Villages	mah kon vee lahj	Verdicchio	ver DEE key oh
Meursault	muhr so	Vernaccia di San Gimignano	ver NOTCH cha dee san jee mee NYAH noh
Montrachet	mon rah shay		
Mosel-Saar-Ruwer	MOH zel zar ROO ver	Vinho Verde	VEEN yo VAIRD
Müller-Thurgau	MOO ler TER gow	Viognier	vee oh nyay
Muscadet	moos cah day	Vouvray	voo vray
Pays d'Oc	pay ee doc		
Pessac-Léognan	pes sac lay oh nyon		

 TIP

 Rule of thumb for white wine vintages:
Drink young.

IDG BOOKS WORLDWIDE™

...For Dummies: Bestselling Book Series for Beginners

Praise for White Wine For Dummies

"This book is a must if you enjoy the taste of wine! This excellent guide playfully educates amateurs as well as the experts in the pleasures of drinking white wines."
> — Michael Aaron, Chairman, Sherry-Lehmann, world-renowned wine shop, New York City

"*White Wine For Dummies* is an insightful reference guide for the beginning taster or the industry professional who has an appreciation of wine and wit."
> — Lynn Penner-Ash, President/Winemaker, Rex Hill Vineyards, Inc.

"Finally, a book that puts the spotlight exclusively on white wines! Thoroughly enjoyable and easy to read. Every white wine drinker should read this."
> — Terry Robards, Senior Managing Editor, *Wine Enthusiast Magazine*

"Although white wine is a complex subject, this 'Dummies' book totally demystifies the confusion — especially for white Burgundy. It's also a handy reference for food marriages and the authors' white wine recommendations. Reading this book will give wine lovers an excellent new excuse to buy (and drink) more white wine."
> — Allan H. Weitzman, Attorney and Wine Lover

Praise for Wine For Dummies

"[*Wine For Dummies*] is complete and done in an agreeably relaxed style."
> — Frank J. Prial, *The New York Times*

"[*Wine For Dummies*] manages to be smart and totally readable, with something to say to total novices, occasional imbibers and those who have caught the bug..."
> — Irene Sax, *Newsday*

"*Wine For Dummies* offers clear advice and information about wine without a lot of fancy wine language."
> — Jim Wood, *San Francisco Examiner* Food and Wine Critic

"[*Wine For Dummies*] does a remarkable job both as an introduction for the new-comer and a reference work for the more experienced wine drinker."
> — Stephen McFarland, *New York Daily News*

WHITE WINE
FOR
DUMMIES™

by Ed McCarthy
and Mary Ewing-Mulligan MW

IDG Books Worldwide, Inc.
An International Data Group Company

Foster City, CA ♦ Chicago, IL ♦ Indianapolis, IN ♦ Southlake, TX

White Wine For Dummies™

Published by
IDG Books Worldwide, Inc.
An International Data Group Company
919 E. Hillsdale Blvd.
Suite 400
Foster City, CA 94404
www.idgbooks.com (IDG Books Worldwide Web site)
www.dummies.com (Dummies Press Web site)

Library of Congress Catalog Card No.: 96-77704

ISBN: 0-7645-5011-X

Printed in the United States of America

10 9 8 7 6 5 4 3 2

1E/RS/RR/ZX/IN

Distributed in the United States by IDG Books Worldwide, Inc.

Distributed by Macmillan Canada for Canada; by Transworld Publishers Limited in the United Kingdom; by IDG Norge Books for Norway; by IDG Sweden Books for Sweden; by Woodslane Pty. Ltd. for Australia; by Woodslane Enterprises Ltd. for New Zealand; by Longman Singapore Publishers Ltd. for Singapore, Malaysia, Thailand, and Indonesia; by Simron Pty. Ltd. for South Africa; by Toppan Company Ltd. for Japan; by Distribuidora Cuspide for Argentina; by Livraria Cultura for Brazil; by Ediciencia S.A. for Ecuador; by Addison-Wesley Publishing Company for Korea; by Ediciones ZETA S.C.R. Ltda. for Peru; by WS Computer Publishing Corporation, Inc., for the Philippines; by Unalis Corporation for Taiwan; by Contemporanea de Ediciones for Venezuela; by Computer Book & Magazine Store for Puerto Rico; by Express Computer Distributors for the Caribbean and West Indies. Authorized Sales Agent: Anthony Rudkin Associates for the Middle East and North Africa.

For general information on IDG Books Worldwide's books in the U.S., please call our Consumer Customer Service department at 800-762-2974. For reseller information, including discounts and premium sales, please call our Reseller Customer Service department at 800-434-3422.

For information on where to purchase IDG Books Worldwide's books outside the U.S., please contact our International Sales department at 415-655-3200 or fax 415-655-3295.

For information on foreign language translations, please contact our Foreign & Subsidiary Rights department at 415-655-3021 or fax 415-655-3281.

For sales inquiries and special prices for bulk quantities, please contact our Sales department at 415-655-3200 or write to the address above.

For information on using IDG Books Worldwide's books in the classroom or for ordering examination copies, please contact our Educational Sales department at 800-434-2086 or fax 817-251-8174.

For press review copies, author interviews, or other publicity information, please contact our Public Relations department at 415-655-3000 or fax 415-655-3299.

For authorization to photocopy items for corporate, personal, or educational use, please contact Copyright Clearance Center, 222 Rosewood Drive, Danvers, MA 01923, or fax 508-750-4470.

is a trademark under exclusive license to IDG Books Worldwide, Inc., from International Data Group, Inc.

About the Authors

Ed McCarthy and **Mary Ewing-Mulligan** are two wine lovers who met at an Italian wine tasting in New York's Chinatown in 1981 and formally merged their wine libraries and cellars when they married in 1983.

At the time of that fateful meeting, Mary had worked in the wine trade for ten years and had directed the Italian government's wine information bureau for the U.S. She grew up in Pennsylvania and studied English literature at the University of Pennsylvania.

Although employed full-time as an English teacher, Ed held part-time jobs in wine shops to satisfy his passion for wine and to subsidize his rapidly expanding wine collection. Born and raised in New York City, he earned a master's degree in psychology from City University of NY.

Today, Mary is co-owner and director of International Wine Center, a wine school in Manhattan. She and Ed teach classes at the Center — solo and jointly — for wine lovers and for individuals employed in the wine trade. Retired from teaching English, Ed now devotes all of his time to wine, writing articles for *Wine Enthusiast Magazine* and *The Wine Journal,* consulting, and moonlighting at his favorite wine shop.

In 1993, Mary culminated five years of independent study in wine by becoming the only American woman who is a Master of Wine. She earned the title by passing a rigorous professional examination given by London's Institute of Masters of Wine. There are only 206 Masters of Wine in the world, including 14 in America.

In 1995, Mary and Ed co-authored *Wine For Dummies* (IDG Books Worldwide).

When they are not teaching or writing about wine, Mary and Ed take busman's holidays to the wine regions of the world. They admit to living thoroughly unbalanced lives in which their only non-wine pursuits are hiking in the Italian Alps, running, unwinding to Neil Young music, and spending quiet time with Sherry, La Tache, Leoville, Pinot Grigio, Brunello, and Dolcetto — their cats.

ABOUT IDG BOOKS WORLDWIDE

Welcome to the world of IDG Books Worldwide.

IDG Books Worldwide, Inc., is a subsidiary of International Data Group, the world's largest publisher of computer-related information and the leading global provider of information services on information technology. IDG was founded more than 25 years ago and now employs more than 8,500 people worldwide. IDG publishes more than 275 computer publications in over 75 countries (see listing below). More than 60 million people read one or more IDG publications each month.

Launched in 1990, IDG Books Worldwide is today the #1 publisher of best-selling computer books in the United States. We are proud to have received eight awards from the Computer Press Association in recognition of editorial excellence and three from Computer Currents' First Annual Readers' Choice Awards. Our best-selling ...For Dummies® series has more than 30 million copies in print with translations in 30 languages. IDG Books Worldwide, through a joint venture with IDG's Hi-Tech Beijing, became the first U.S. publisher to publish a computer book in the People's Republic of China. In record time, IDG Books Worldwide has become the first choice for millions of readers around the world who want to learn how to better manage their businesses.

Our mission is simple: Every one of our books is designed to bring extra value and skill-building instructions to the reader. Our books are written by experts who understand and care about our readers. The knowledge base of our editorial staff comes from years of experience in publishing, education, and journalism — experience we use to produce books for the '90s. In short, we care about books, so we attract the best people. We devote special attention to details such as audience, interior design, use of icons, and illustrations. And because we use an efficient process of authoring, editing, and desktop publishing our books electronically, we can spend more time ensuring superior content and spend less time on the technicalities of making books.

You can count on our commitment to deliver high-quality books at competitive prices on topics you want to read about. At IDG Books Worldwide, we continue in the IDG tradition of delivering quality for more than 25 years. You'll find no better book on a subject than one from IDG Books Worldwide.

IDG BOOKS WORLDWIDE

John Kilcullen
CEO
IDG Books Worldwide, Inc.

Steven Berkowitz
President and Publisher
IDG Books Worldwide, Inc.

IDG Books Worldwide, Inc., is a subsidiary of International Data Group, the world's largest publisher of computer-related information and the leading global provider of information services on information technology. International Data Group publishes over 275 computer publications in over 75 countries. Sixty million people read one or more International Data Group publications each month. International Data Group's publications include **ARGENTINA:** Buyer's Guide, Computerworld Argentina, PC World Argentina; **AUSTRALIA:** Australian Macworld, Australian PC World, Australian Reseller News, Computerworld, IT Casebook, Network World, Publish, Webmaster; **AUSTRIA:** Computerwelt Österreich, Networks Austria, PC Tip Austria; **BANGLADESH:** PC World Bangladesh; **BELARUS:** PC World Belarus; **BELGIUM:** Data News; **BRAZIL:** Annuário de Informática, Computerworld, Connections, Macworld, PC Player, PC World, Publish, Reseller News, Supergamepower; **BULGARIA:** Computerworld Bulgaria, Network World Bulgaria, PC & MacWorld Bulgaria; **CANADA:** CIO Canada, Client/Server World, ComputerWorld Canada, InfoWorld Canada, NetworkWorld Canada, WebWorld; **CHILE:** Computerworld Chile, PC World Chile; **COLOMBIA:** Computerworld Colombia, PC World Colombia; **COSTA RICA:** PC World Centro America; **THE CZECH AND SLOVAK REPUBLICS:** Computerworld Czechoslovakia, Macworld Czech Republic, PC World Czechoslovakia; **DENMARK:** Communications World Danmark, Computerworld Danmark, Macworld Danmark, PC World Danmark, Techworld Denmark; **DOMINICAN REPUBLIC:** PC World Republica Dominicana; **ECUADOR:** PC World Ecuador; **EGYPT:** Computerworld Middle East, PC World Middle East; **EL SALVADOR:** PC World Centro America; **FINLAND:** MikroPC, Tietoverkko, Tietoviikko; **FRANCE:** Distributique, Hebdo, Info PC, Le Monde Informatique, Macworld, Reseaux & Telecoms, WebMaster France; **GERMANY:** Computer Partner, Computerwoche, Computerwoche Extra, Computerwoche FOCUS, Global Online, Macwelt, PC Welt; **GREECE:** Amiga Computing, GamePro Greece, Multimedia World; **GUATEMALA:** PC World Centro America; **HONDURAS:** PC World Centro America; **HONG KONG:** Computerworld Hong Kong, PC World Hong Kong, Publish in Asia; **HUNGARY:** ABCD CD-ROM, Computerworld Szamitastechnika, Internetto online Magazine, PC World Hungary, PC-X Magazin Hungary; **ICELAND:** Tolvuheimur PC World Island; **INDIA:** Information Communications World, Information Systems Computerworld, PC World India, Publish in Asia; **INDONESIA:** InfoKomputer PC World, Komputek Computerworld, Publish in Asia; **IRELAND:** ComputerScope, PC Live!; **ISRAEL:** Macworld Israel, People & Computers/Computerworld; **ITALY:** Computerworld Italia, Macworld Italia, Networking Italia, PC World Italia; **JAPAN:** DTP World, Macworld Japan, Nikkei Personal Computing, OS/2 World Japan, SunWorld Japan, Windows NT World, Windows World Japan; **KENYA:** PC World East African; **KOREA:** Hi-Tech Information, Macworld Korea, PC World Korea; **MACEDONIA:** PC World Macedonia; **MALAYSIA:** Computerworld Malaysia, PC World Malaysia, Publish in Asia; **MALTA:** PC World Malta; **MEXICO:** Computerworld Mexico, PC World Mexico; **MYANMAR:** PC World Myanmar; **NETHERLANDS:** Computer! Totaal, LAN Internetworking Magazine, LAN World Buyers Guide, Macworld Netherlands, Net, WebWereld; **NEW ZEALAND:** Absolute Beginners Guide and Plain & Simple Series, Computer Buyer, Computer Industry Directory, Computerworld New Zealand, MTB, Network World, PC World New Zealand; **NICARAGUA:** PC World Centro America; **NORWAY:** Computerworld Norge, CW Rapport, Datamagasinet, Financial Rapport, Kursguide Norge, Macworld Norge, Multimediaworld Norge, PC World Ekspress Norge, PC World Nettverk, PC World Norge, PC World ProduktGuide Norge; **PAKISTAN:** Computerworld Pakistan; **PANAMA:** PC World Panama; **PEOPLE'S REPUBLIC OF CHINA:** China Computer Users, China Computerworld, China InfoWorld, China Telecom World Weekly, Computer & Communication, Electronic Design China, Electronics Today, Electronics Weekly, Game Software, PC World China, Popular Computer Week, Software Weekly, Software World, Telecom World; **PERU:** Computerworld Peru, PC World Profesional Peru, PC World SoHo Peru; **PHILIPPINES:** Click!, Computerworld Philippines, PC World Philippines, Publish in Asia; **POLAND:** Computerworld Poland, Computerworld Special Report Poland, Cyber, Macworld Poland, Networld Poland, PC World Komputer; **PORTUGAL:** Cerebro/PC World Portugal, Mac*In/PC*In Portugal, Multimedia World; **PUERTO RICO:** PC World Puerto Rico; **ROMANIA:** Computerworld Romania, PC World Romania, Telecom Romania; **RUSSIA:** Computerworld Russia, Mir PK, Publish, Seti; **SINGAPORE:** Computerworld Singapore, PC World Singapore, Publish in Asia; **SLOVENIA:** Monitor; **SOUTH AFRICA:** Computing SA, Network World SA, Software World SA; **SPAIN:** Communicaciones World España, Computerworld España, Dealer World España, Macworld España, PC World España; **SRI LANKA:** Infolink PC World; **SWEDEN:** CAP&Design, Computer Sweden, Corporate Computing Sweden, Internetworld Sweden, it.branschen, Macworld Sweden, MaxiData Sweden, MikroDatorn, Nätverk & Kommunikation, PC World Sweden, PCaktiv, Windows World Sweden; **SWITZERLAND:** Computerworld Schweiz, Macworld Schweiz, PCtip; **TAIWAN:** Computerworld Taiwan, Macworld Taiwan, NEW ViSiON/Publish, PC World Taiwan, Windows World Taiwan; **THAILAND:** Publish in Asia, Thai Computerworld; **TURKEY:** Computerworld Turkiye, Macworld Turkiye, Network World Turkiye, PC World Turkiye; **UKRAINE:** Computerworld Kiev, Multimedia World Ukraine, PC World Ukraine; **UNITED KINGDOM:** Acorn User UK, Amiga Action UK, Amiga Computing UK, Apple Talk UK, Computing, Macworld, Parents and Computers UK, PC Advisor, PC Home, PSX Pro, The WEB; **UNITED STATES:** Cable in the Classroom, CIO Magazine, Computerworld, DOS World, Federal Computer Week, GamePro Magazine, InfoWorld, I-Way, Macworld, Network World, PC Games, PC World, Publish, Video Event, THE WEB Magazine, and WebMaster; online webzines: JavaWorld, NetscapeWorld, and SunWorld Online; **URUGUAY:** InfoWorld Uruguay; **VENEZUELA:** Computerworld Venezuela, PC World Venezuela; and **VIETNAM:** PC World Vietnam.
3/24/97

Dedication

We dedicate this book to all the budding wine lovers of the world, with the wish that they will find a white wine or two (or more) that captures their fascination and opens to them a whole new world of experience and pleasure.

Acknowledgments

One of the things we love the most about the publisher of *White Wine For Dummies*, IDG Books Worldwide, is the ability to turn our thoughts and manuscript into a book in what to us is record time! We acknowledge, with deep respect and gratitude, the team responsible for this feat — President John Kilcullen, Milissa Koloski, Kathy Welton, Sarah Kennedy, Stacy Collins, our project editor, Kathy Cox, and our copy editor, Suzanne Packer, as well as the wonderful folks in Production and Proofreading. We love the Dummies concept of taking difficult, technical subjects and turning them into readable prose that removes the intimidation factor from the subject. We're happy that we can be part of this concept.

We acknowledge Paul Hart and Jan Jacobsen of Rex Hill Vineyards, Karen Hinsdale, and Wendy Lane for their generous and unselfish support of our writing. We also acknowledge all of the wonderful people in the wine trade, who share our passion for this incredible beverage, and who have helped us in so many ways to write this book.

We would also like to thank Margaret Stern of Stern Communications; Mario Cordero and Tricia Chimento of Remy Amerique, Inc.; Jeff Pogash of Schieffelin & Somerset Co.; David Wagner of Banfi Vintners; John W. Gay of Rosemount Estates; Barbara Scalera of Winebow Inc.; Jose Fernandez of Southcorp Wines, USA Inc.; Kimberly Charles of Kobrand Corporation; Bill Sciambi of Lauber Imports; Derry Golding of Jordan Winery; Brian Larky; Paula Ramsey of Valckenberg International, Inc.; Christine Deusen and Nina Brondmo of Clicquot, Inc.; Mary Marshall of Paterno Imports; J. Boutari and Son, S.A.; Miguel A. Torres, S.A of Torres Wines, Barcelona, Spain; Rainer Karl Lingenfelder; Lynn Penner-Ash of Rex Hill Vineyards; Kerry Godes of Kendall-Jackson (Cambria); John R. Shafer and Doug Shafer of Shafer Vineyards; Kathleen Talbert of Talbert Communications and Marsha Palanci of Cornerstone Communications/Palace Brands Company for sending us labels for use in this book. We only wish we had room to use them all.

Publisher's Acknowledgments

We're proud of this book; please register your comments through our IDG Books Worldwide Online Registration Form located at: http://my2cents.dummies.com.

Some of the people who helped bring this book to market include the following:

Acquisitions, Development, and Editorial

Project Editor: Kathleen M. Cox

Acquisitions Editor: Sarah Kennedy, Executive Editor

Copy Editor: Suzanne Packer

Technical Reviewer: Tim Hanni, MW, Beringer Vineyards

General Reviewers: Tom Mathews, Gloria R. Wilson

Editorial Manager: Kristin A. Cocks

Editorial Assistant: Ann Miller

Production

Associate Project Coordinator: Regina Snyder

Layout and Graphics: E. Shawn Aylsworth, Brett Black, Elizabeth Cárdenas-Nelson, Cameron Booker, Linda Boyer, Dominique DeFelice, Patricia R. Reynolds, Anna Rohrer, Kate Snell

Proofreaders: Nancy L. Reinhardt, Rachel Garvey, Nancy Price, Dwight Ramsey, Robert Springer, Carrie Voorhis

Indexer: Sherry Massey

General and Administrative

IDG Books Worldwide, Inc.: John Kilcullen, CEO; Steven Berkowitz, President and Publisher

IDG Books Technology Publishing: Brenda McLaughlin, Senior Vice President and Group Publisher

Dummies Technology Press and Dummies Editorial: Diane Graves Steele, Vice President and Associate Publisher; Mary Bednarek, Acquisitions and Product Development Director; Kristin A. Cocks, Editorial Director

Dummies Trade Press: Kathleen A. Welton, Vice President and Publisher; Kevin Thornton, Acquisitions Manager

IDG Books Production for Dummies Press: Beth Jenkins, Production Director; Cindy L. Phipps, Manager of Project Coordination, Production Proofreading, and Indexing; Kathie S. Schutte, Supervisor of Page Layout; Shelley Lea, Supervisor of Graphics and Design; Debbie J. Gates, Production Systems Specialist; Robert Springer, Supervisor of Proofreading; Debbie Stailey, Special Projects Coordinator; Tony Augsburger, Supervisor of Reprints and Bluelines; Leslie Popplewell, Media Archive Coordinator

Dummies Packaging and Book Design: Patti Crane, Packaging Specialist; Lance Kayser, Packaging Assistant; Kavish + Kavish, Cover Design

♦

The publisher would like to give special thanks to Patrick J. McGovern, without whom this book would not have been possible.

♦

Contents at a Glance

Table of Contents

The 5th Wave

By Rich Tennant

"WHAT DO YOU MEAN YOU FORGOT THE WHITE WINE?! YOU KNOW DARN WELL I CAN'T SERVE FISH WITHOUT WHITE WINE!"

Introduction

"I'll have a glass of white wine, please." Not very long ago, thousands of people across America uttered that request every day in bars and restaurants. But no longer. Now, most people say "I'll have a glass of Chardonnay, please," referring to a specific type of white wine made from the Chardonnay grape.

Have wine drinkers come a long way, baby — or have they merely taken, in the words of the Boss, "two steps up and three steps back"?

Most people who are associated with the wine business tell you that wine drinkers' more specific preference for Chardonnay over any old white wine is real progress. Wine drinkers are "trading up" (in the lingo of the business) to "premium wine."

But we can't help wondering: How many people order Chardonnay not because they specifically want it, but because that's the hip wine to order? Or because Chardonnay is the only white wine they know? How will wine drinkers ever learn about all the other wonderful white wines of the world if Chardonnay remains the one white wine that bars and restaurants automatically serve?

(In other words, can being in a rut possibly ever be a good thing?)

These ruminations of ours fashioned the mission of this book:

- ✔ To expand the narrow (and narrowing) view of white wine
- ✔ To broaden awareness of the almost-endless array of white wines that exists
- ✔ To offer suggestion upon delicious suggestion of white wines worth knowing (many of them even Chardonnays)

We happen to believe that one of the nicest things about wine is its variety. The world of white wine has more than enough fascinating wine regions, grapes, wine styles, and individual wines to keep us all entertained for the rest of our lives. White wine definitely needn't be boring.

How to Use This Book

White Wine For Dummies is a book that you can take along with you when you buy wine; it's small and yet it's full of recommendations on types of wines to try, which vintages to buy, and which producers to look for.

But this book is far more than a buyer's guide. You can use this book to learn about white wine from ground zero: discover how wine is made, what the major white grape varieties are, which wine regions of the world specialize in white wine, and what the major types of white wine are. Even if you never set eyes on a glass of white wine, this book can help you develop a broad base of knowledge about white wine.

This book addresses white table wines only — that is, those white wines of the sort that you would drink with a meal. We do not cover sparkling wines (wines with bubbles, such as Champagne), nor do we cover sweet dessert wines, such as Sauternes, or *fortified* white wines (wines with alcohol added), such as sherry.

Part I: A Course of White Wine

The five chapters in this first part of the book provide fundamental information about white wine in general and lay the groundwork for the more specialized chapters that follow.

In **Chapter 1,** we explain what white wine is and how it differs from red wine; we also describe the range of aromas, flavors, textures, and other taste characteristics that white wines can have. If you're a novice, by all means don't miss this chapter. But even if you already have some knowledge of white wine, you might want to review Chapter 1 just to assure that we're all using the same vocabulary.

Chapter 2 tackles the issue of why individual white wines taste the way they do, explaining how growing conditions and winemaking techniques can shape the style of a white wine. Judging from the number of times that we wrote "Turn to Chapter 2 for an explanation of these terms" in subsequent chapters, we imagine that you'll be turning there often!

A frequent question on wine lovers' lips — "What grape is this wine made from?" — is the topic of **Chapter 3**. An even dozen white wine grapes — and the types of wines they make — are described here. In **Chapter 4,** we name what we consider the seven most important types of white wine in the world and describe them in some detail. Just knowing that the chapter is there can give you the same sense of security as having a leather-bound set of classic novels on your bookshelf.

Chapter 5 is dedicated to the eternal issue of what wine to have with dinner. You might be surprised to discover how versatile white wine is with food.

Part II: A World of White Wine

We wouldn't exactly describe this section of the book as armchair travel — maybe more like wine glass travel. Eleven countries of the world are important for white wine production, and we drop in on all of them to see which grape varieties they use, how they name their wines, and who the best producers are. This is the part of *White Wine For Dummies* where you'll find solid advice that you can carry to the wine shop.

Our emphasis in these chapters is practical information, of the sort that you can actually use. Many of the wine suggestions that we make in these chapters therefore fall into the reasonably priced category — less expensive wines that wine drinkers can actually afford to buy. We sprinkle these practical recommendations with tips on more expensive wines — and occasionally even legendary, exorbitantly priced wines — in order to paint a picture of the full range of white wines that exists. We mark our personal favorites with a ♟, and note especially good values with a ¢.

The first three chapters of Part II deal with the wines of the United States. California Chardonnay gets its own chapter, **Chapter 6,** in deference to the huge market share it enjoys among white wines. **Chapter 7** covers Sauvignon Blanc and other white wines from California, while **Chapter 8** explores the white wines of the Pacific Northwest and of New York.

The white wines of Australia, New Zealand, and South Africa might not have a whole lot in common tastewise, but they all come from Southern Hemisphere countries, and they're all covered in **Chapter 9.**

If fame and status interest you, *allons, enfants* to **Chapters 10 and 11,** where we delve into the wines of France. (In other words, simply go to those chapters for a look at some of the world's great white wines.) The intricacies of the white wines of Burgundy demand a whole chapter themselves; other important French wines, such as Sancerre, white Bordeaux, and the wines of Alsace share the spotlight in the next chapter.

The final three chapters of Part II describe the white wines from European countries other than France: the all-important wines of Germany in **Chapter 12;** Italian white wines in **Chapter 13;** and the white wines of Spain, Portugal, Austria, and Switzerland in **Chapter 14.**

Part III: The Part of Tens

We know some people who turn to this last section of most . . .*For Dummies* books first, for quick answers to questions they didn't even know they had. The chapters in this section of our book answer questions — but they also make recommendations, and they even give you homework assignments.

Chapter 15 lists and describes ten white wines that you might not be familiar with but, in our humble opinion, you should be. **Chapter 16** has the answers to the questions you didn't know you had; we're also secretly hoping that one or two of our answers deal with issues that you really have been wondering about but could never get a straight answer on. **Chapter 17** has the homework assignments: ten wine-tasting exercises that make you a better wine-taster, enhance your knowledge and appreciation of white wine, and qualify you for the position of neighborhood wine guru.

Part IV: Appendixes

When you need to remember exactly how to pronounce *Bienvenues-Bâtard Montrachet* or any other mouthful of a white wine name, you can find the answer quickly in the **Pronunciation Guide, Appendix A.** The **Glossary, Appendix B,** carries definitions of all the technical terms that we use anywhere in the book (although we hope we explain ourselves so well that you don't have to turn there very often). The **Vintage Chart, Appendix C,** is a short one for white wine, because most white wines are bought young and consumed quickly; but when you purchase a special bottle, you might want to consult the Vintage Chart.

Icons Used in This Book

Everyone who writes about wine has his or her own favorite wine producers and wines. Because two of us wrote this book, however, we have at least twice as many favorite wines. You find them all marked with this symbol.

Intimidation and snobbery take all the fun out of wine — unless, of course, you're the one who's intimidating (in which case: sorry, we're busy that evening). Defuse ignorant wine snobbery by learning the facts about issues that others might try to snow you on. Those issues are marked with this icon.

One of the important factors distinguishing wine from other alcohol beverages is that wine is a mealtime beverage. Where you see this icon, you find suggestions of foods to try with the wine you happen to be reading about. (All Pavlov had was a silly bell.)

Some people love wine because they love the way it tastes, but others love wine because they find it intellectually stimulating. If you're in that second group, be sure to read the behind-the-scenes technical information we mark with this symbol.

When we particularly want to drive a point home, we mark the paragraph with this symbol. Often the point is something that we mention elsewhere in the book but that bears repeating.

The space limitations of a portable reference book don't permit us to go into as much detail as we'd like on some aspects of white wine. When we know that we've already covered a particular subject in more detail in our full-sized book, *Wine For Dummies* (published by IDG Books Worldwide, Inc.), we use this symbol to suggest that you turn there for more information.

Although we have tried to make white wine as easy and confusion-free as possible, a few pitfalls and potholes are inevitable. Keep your eye out for the "Caution" sign, so that you can steer clear of these problem areas.

Fun or interesting or useful white wine information of a miscellaneous sort is marked by this symbol.

Part I
A Course of White Wine

In this part . . .

RRRiiight this way, folks! Inside this tent is everything necessary to turn a 98-pound white wine novice into a sophisticated oenophilic connoisseur whose mere presence in a restaurant is enough to make the sommelier tremble with intimidation!

- ✔ Meet the seven wonders of the white wine world!

- ✔ Gain an instant, magic sixth sense for knowing which white wine to serve with which food!

- ✔ Become intimate with the most influential white grape varieties in the world!

Okay, you're right. We're getting carried away. But at least one phrase is true: *white wine novice.* Even if you have never tasted white wine, you can learn about it painlessly in the chapters that follow. And if you already enjoy white wine with some frequency, there are still those rich and famous grape varieties to rub taste buds with. . . .

Chapter 1

Beyond the Red Horizon

*W*hite wine brought us together. A mutual acquaintance who was deep into the hobby of wine and food matchmaking invited each of us to Chinatown, where we and half a dozen other wine lovers tasted dozens of wines with a multicourse Chinese dinner, seeking to discover the best wines for the food. Every one of those wines was a white wine.

Some cuisines of the world naturally seem better suited to white wines than to red wines. White wines cool down spiciness, refresh your mouth between tastes of slightly sweet foods, and are versatile enough for meals that have a cacophony of flavors. (White wines also do not stain your teeth purple — a fact we were both very grateful for that evening.)

At that particular dinner, every wine worked magic with every scrumptious dish. (Of course, the company helped.)

Even red wine lovers agree that sometimes white wines do the job just perfectly.

What White Wine Is

White wine is the most fundamental type of wine there is. White wine is simply grape juice (most wine grapes have pale, "white" juice; the "red" color comes from the skins) whose fruit sugar has changed into alcohol through a natural process called *fermentation*. The agents of change are microorganisms called *yeasts*, tiny life-forms related to the yeasts that cause breads to rise.

Any wines without red or pink color are technically *white wines.* Most white wines manage to avoid that red or pink color by being made from so-called white grapes, which have no red pigmentation in the first place. ("White" grapes are actually greenish, golden, or slightly pink.)

A white wine can also come from the juice of red grapes, provided that the red grapeskins are not allowed to soak in the pale juice and color it. Without soaking up color from the skins, the juice — and the wine made from that juice — would be white.

The Personality of White Wines

White wines come in all shapes and sizes — figuratively speaking, of course. Some white wines are mild-mannered, easy-to-drink beverages that you can enjoy without fuss. Others are full-flavored, complex wines of the sort that provoke wine lovers to furrow their brows and scribble their impressions after every sniff and every sip.

Chemically speaking, white wines are more simple than red wines because they lack certain substances that red wines absorb from their red grapeskins. The most important of these substances is *tannin,* a bitter-tasting compound that helps red wines to age. Red wines with a lot of tannin go beautifully with steak. You probably won't catch members of the beef lobby drinking white wine.

Because white wines lack tannin, generally speaking (we look at a few exceptions in Chapters 5 and 6), you can chill them more than red wines. When you drink a white wine very cold — as cold as you'd drink a can of soda — you don't get all the flavor out of it that you would at a less-cold temperature, but at least it doesn't taste unpleasant, as most red wines do when chilled.

Whites are the wines of warm weather and sunshine. They are friendly, sociable wines that you can offer to your friends without worrying about whether your friends will like them or not — everyone enjoys at least an occasional glass of white wine. White wines are natural *apéritif* wines, that is, wines to drink before your meal. They're also wonderful *with* your meal if you're having fish, poultry, pasta, salad, or grilled vegetables — to name only a few enticing possibilities.

Back in the days before political correctness, winemakers used to describe their white wines as feminine and their red wines as masculine. (Now, of course, they choose different characterizations, out of respect for their wines.) Still, the stereotype persists that women prefer white wine and men prefer red wine. One wine salesman of the sort who would never get caught drinking anything but red wine explained to us once that women prefer white wine because it doesn't tint their teeth, it has fewer calories than red wine, and it doesn't stain their clothes if they spill it. We're still waiting for those sales statistics he promised to send us as proof. In our experience, women and men enjoy both red and white wines, depending on the food and the occasion.

A White Is a White Is a White (Not!)

We're frequently tempted to compare wines to human beings because, among wines as among people, no two are exactly alike. (In fact, in the world of wine, there are not even identical twins!)

White wines differ from one another in

- ✔ Their *color*
- ✔ Their *aromas* and *flavors*
- ✔ Their *body* (that is, their perceived weight in your mouth)
- ✔ Their *texture* (how they feel in your mouth, such as silky, thick, creamy, crisp, and so on)
- ✔ Their *quality* (how all these characteristics measure up, in the opinion of experienced wine-tasters)

With all those variables at issue, how could any two white wines ever possibly be identical?!

Color me yellow

Sometimes the difference between one white wine and another is evident just by looking at the two wines. At one end of the spectrum, white wines can be almost colorless, like water; at the opposite end are wines that are deep yellow or even amber. White wines can be straw-colored, greenish yellow, golden, or orange-yellow. (But they're never literally white.) Whatever the hue, their *intensity* of color — that is, how saturated they are with color — can be pale, medium, or deep.

Some white wines are deeper in color than others because they were born that way. The type of grape that made the wine and the growing conditions of the grapes, such as the summer temperature, are two factors that determine a wine's color.

But sometimes a deep color in a white wine can result from age or poor storage. If a white wine looks unusually dark to you, taste it carefully to decide whether it is fresh. If the wine has a slightly cooked smell or if it seems *flat* when you smell it — that is, dull and lacking any fresh, *primary aromas* (aromas of the grape) — you probably have a poor bottle or a too-old white wine.

If two white wines are both young, but one is deeper in color than the other, you can expect the darker wine to be more intensely flavored and the paler wine to be lighter in body and less intense — and you will generally be right.

Yes, we have no bananas

The white wines of the world have a wide range of aromas and flavors, depending on

- ✔ What grape made the wine (different types of grapes have different inherent aromas)
- ✔ Where the grapes were grown (variables such as the type of soil or the climate can affect the flavor of the grapes, and therefore the wine made from those grapes)
- ✔ How the wine was made (winemaking techniques can bring out the natural grape aromas in a wine, or hide them)

We take a close look at each of these factors in the next two chapters, explaining some of the specific effects that grape variety, climate, or winemaking can have on a white wine.

White wines commonly have aromas or flavors reminiscent of lemons, apples, peaches, pears, apricots, pineapple, figs, melons, fresh herbs, butter, smoke, toast, green grass, hay, asparagus (really!), roses, honeysuckle, honey, butterscotch, lanolin — we could go on and on.

The easiest way of talking about all these aromas and flavors — and a good way to inspire your scent receptors when you're not sure exactly what you're smelling in a white wine — is to group individual scents or flavors into families of aromas. For example, if a white wine smells like peaches, it has a fruity aroma; if it smells like green beans, it has a vegetal aroma.

How young is young?

 White wines have a shorter production cycle than red wines do, and they are therefore available in wine shops at a younger age. White wines made in Northern Hemisphere countries, where harvest usually occurs from August to October, are released for sale as early as January or February of the next year. Southern Hemisphere white wines, whose grapes are harvested from March to May, are often released before the end of the calendar year.

The wines that are released for sale very young are usually fresh, simple wines (such as many Italian whites; see Chapter 13) that should be drunk within the first year or two of their lives — before they lose that freshness. More "serious" white wines (such as the best white Burgundies, described in Chapter 10) are not usually released for sale by the winery until 18 months or two years after the harvest.

To figure out how old a white wine is, look at its vintage date — and don't forget to consider whether the date represents a Northern or a Southern Hemisphere autumn.

The families of aromas and flavors that white wines typically exhibit include

- **Fruity aromas:** citrus fruits (lemon, lime, orange, and grapefruit), tree fruits (apple, pear, peach, and apricot), tropical fruits (melons, pineapple, papaya, guava, and lychee fruit); berry aromas are unusual in white wines

- **Floral aromas:** roses, honeysuckle, jasmine, and mixed flowers

- **Vegetal aromas:** green grass, hay, asparagus, and green beans

- **Earthy aromas:** mushrooms, chalk, flint, mineral, and wet stone

- **Woody aromas:** vanilla, toast, smoke, charred wood, and coffee

- **Caramelized aromas:** honey, butterscotch, and caramel

- **Nutty aromas:** almonds, hazelnuts, and malt

- **Animal-like aromas:** lanolin and cat pee

What you smell is what you taste

Flavors are really aromas that you "smell" in your mouth when you taste a wine. To detect a wine's scent, or aroma, you inhale the wine's aroma molecules through your nose. When you taste a wine, those same aroma molecules vaporize in your mouth and travel up a rear nasal passage to your olfactory nerves.

When we say aromas and flavors again and again, instead of just one or the other, it's not because we're trying to pad our word-count; it's because aromas and flavors are the same thing.

We realize that drinking a wine whose smell is reminiscent of cat pee is not high on anyone's agenda. So before you decide that this whole wine-tasting business sounds entirely too kinky for you, you should know this: If you stick to the most popular types of wine, you'll encounter mainly just fruity and woody aromas, with an occasional foray into the floral or vegetal families of smell and taste. The chalk, wet stone, lanolin — and a few aromas we didn't mention, like diesel fuel and wet dog — make their appearance mainly in unusual wines that you won't run into unless you want to. (And would you believe that, in the right wine, those smells can be fascinating?!)

All of these aromas are natural aromas that exist in a wine because of the grapes, the soil, and chemical transformations that occur in the winemaking process. No one ever adds essence of roses or almonds or anything else to a wine (unless the wine is a *flavored wine* and says so on the label). The one exception is woody aromas, which can come naturally from oak barrels that are used as containers for the wine, or could also be added (see "Barrel-aging" in Chapter 2).

How dry I am

Most white wines fall into the category of *dry* wines, that is, not sweet. (White dessert wines are sweet, of course, but we don't cover dessert wines in this book.)

But within the category of dry white wines, many wines do have some slight sweetness that is perceptible to some people. (No official boundary exists between sweetness and dryness, and everyone perceives sweetness to different degrees.) Some white wines, such as many inexpensive California wines and many German wines, are *off-dry*, meaning that they are mildly sweet. Their sweetness comes from the natural sweetness of the grapes themselves (see "Sweetening techniques" in Chapter 2).

The descriptors for different levels of sweetness are (in decreasing order of dryness): dry, medium-dry, medium-sweet, and sweet. The term off-dry is a generalized term for wines that fall between dry and sweet.

Of crispness and flabbiness

As a child, one of us took a bologna sandwich on soft, commercial white bread to school every day for lunch. One day, another child offered to share her potato chips — and we discovered the importance of texture in food. With the crisp potato chips layered between the bologna and the bread, the sandwich was transformed from a soft, pasty glob into a crunchy delight that crackled with every bite. (To this day, we like to put potato chips inside soft sandwiches.)

Just like solid food, wine too has texture. To talk about texture in a liquid might seem ridiculous: A liquid can't crunch like a potato chip, or stick to your teeth like a bologna sandwich. But consider the texture of cola. When cola is ice-cold and poured from a freshly opened bottle, it crackles with carbonation in your mouth and may even seem a bit sharp (those bubbles can feel like edges that cut your mouth). When the soda is warm and flat, it feels limp and lifeless, like a globby bologna sandwich.

If a white wine has bubbles, like Champagne, those bubbles give texture to the wine, just as they do in soda. But the white wines we're talking about here are not sparkling, bubbly wines like Champagne — they're wines that are *still,* that have no bubbles. What makes these wines snap, crackle, and pop?

After water, which constitutes about 80 to 90 percent of most wines, the main *components* (ingredients) of white wine are

- ✔ **Alcohol:** Alcohol constitutes about 9 to 14 percent of the wine (with most white wines in the 11 to 13.5 percent range).
- ✔ **Acid:** Acid constitutes less than one percent of the wine, generally from 0.5 to 0.7 percent.
- ✔ **Grape sugar:** Wines that are not sweet contain small amounts of unfermentable sugar from the grape, which constitutes 0.1 to 0.2 percent of the wine. Some wines that

do not taste sweet to most people contain as much as 0.5 percent grape sugar, and wines that are mildly sweet *(off-dry,* in wine lingo) contain 1 to 2 percent sugar.

Alcohol, acid, and sugar are what give white wine its substance and weight. (Wine professionals call these components *structural elements* because they are building-blocks of wine.)

The texture of a white wine depends on the relationship of these three ingredients to one another. Alcohol and sugar both make a white wine feel soft and smooth in your mouth, while acid makes the wine feel crisp. For instance,

- White wines that are relatively low in alcohol and high in acid, such as many Italian white wines, taste crisp, firm, and lively.

- White wines that are low in acid relative to their alcohol or sugar content taste soft and round, or even *fat,* as wine lovers might say.

- In the extreme, low acid causes a wine to taste *flabby* — a characteristic no more positive in wine than in people.

Another characteristic of wine that derives from the relationship of a wine's structural elements is *balance.* When a white wine's acid, alcohol, and sugar exist in such a relationship to each other that none of the three elements stands out obtrusively, that wine is said to be *well-balanced.* When a wine has an excess of any of its major components, it is said to be *out-of-balance.* Because everyone has personal thresholds for perceiving alcohol, acid, and sweetness, the judgment of balance or imbalance in a wine is subjective. (One person's "flabby, unbalanced wine" might be the next person's "balanced wine.")

Body beautiful

Besides differing in color, in aroma and flavor, and in texture, white wines can vary in body, from light-bodied to full-bodied.

The amount of alcohol in a white wine is the main determinant of the wine's body: The more alcohol, the fuller and heavier you perceive the wine to be in your mouth. A wine's *extract* — all the solids dissolved in the wine, such as sugar, acids, minerals, and so on — also contributes to the perception of body.

Although full-bodied white wines are often soft and fat in texture and light-bodied wines are often crisp and lean, body and texture don't always correlate so neatly. For example, a number of soft white wines are light-bodied; some German whites, especially the less-expensive wines like Liebfraumilch *(LEEB frow milsh)* exemplify this style (see Chapter 11). And a number of crisp wines (like some California Sauvignon Blancs) are full-bodied.

When in doubt about a wine's body, don't forget that there is such a thing as *medium-bodied* (not full-bodied yet not light-bodied) — which most white wines are!

Drinking Versus Tasting

Most of the time, when you have a glass of white wine you just *drink* it — meaning that you don't pay particular attention to any of the wine's fine points, such as its body or texture. You might notice a flavor or two in the wine, or you might notice that it's dry, and certainly you have an opinion on whether you like it or not, but that's about all. And nothing's wrong with that.

But if you want to learn about wine and become better attuned to all the variations that exist among the wines of the world, invest a little time and attention in *tasting* wine — thoughtfully observing the visual, olfactory, and taste characteristics of a wine. (Tasting two wines side-by-side is particularly valuable because the characteristics of each wine offset the traits of the other.)

Wine-tasting technique

Here's a quick review of wine-tasting technique:

- ✔ **See the wine:** Tilt the glass and look at the color against a white background (a napkin or piece of white paper works just fine) to judge its hue and intensity

- ✔ **Smell the wine:** Holding the base of the glass on the table, rotate the glass so that the wine swirls (this procedure releases the wine's aromas) and then bring the glass to your nose and take a thoughtful whiff of the wine's aromas. Repeat as necessary, giving your nose a chance to recover occasionally.

✔ **Sip the wine:** Take a medium-sized taste of the wine (probably more than you normally sip) and move the wine around your mouth; then draw air into your mouth to release the flavors of the wine. Hold the wine in your mouth (alternately moving it around, aerating it, and just holding it still) for about ten seconds, all the while thinking about characteristics such as dryness, sweetness, texture, body, and the wine's flavors.

If you have never before tasted wine this way, ease into the complicated part — the stage when the wine is in your mouth — by deciding before each sip to focus on only one or two aspects of the wine: dryness and body on the first sip, for example, and then texture, and then flavors. Just be aware that with every sip, concentration becomes a bit more challenging. (Which is why professional wine-tasters always spit each sip — a practice that we definitely do not recommend at the dinner table!)

What you observe in the wine is probably minimal at first, but with experience you can begin to identify all sorts of wonderful subtleties that make every wine different from the next.

Range of characteristics

With practice, you can observe that even if two white wines are identical in some characteristic (they share the same flavors, for example, or they have exactly the same amount of sweetness in laboratory tests), no two white wines have precisely the same *combination* of characteristics (see Table 1-1).

Table 1-1 The Range of Characteristics of Dry White Wines

Characteristic	Low	High
Aromas and Flavors	not intense	intense
Texture	crisp	soft, round
Body	light weight	full-bodied
Sweetness	bone dry	slightly sweet

Test your taste

Why take *our* word on wine variations? To appreciate just how different white wines can be, taste three dry white wines side-by-side, and compare them according to their flavor intensity, texture, body, and sweetness. (See our book *Wine For Dummies* from IDG Books Worldwide, Inc. for in-depth information about wine tasting.) Here, we suggest types of white wine that illustrate various points of the range:

- ✔ As examples of the lightest, crispest, dryest end of the range, try a Soave (pronounced *so AH vay,* from Italy; see Chapter 13) or a Muscadet (pronounced *moos cah day,* from France; see Chapter 11).

- ✔ As examples of the middle of the range, try a Pouilly-Fumé *(pwee foo may)* or a St. Veran *(san vehr an),* both from France, or a Chardonnay from the Pays d'Oc *(pay ee doc)* area of southern France.

- ✔ As examples of the fullest, softest, most intense end of the range, try a Gewürztraminer *(gah VERTZ trah mee ner)* from the Alsace region of France, or an American Gewürztraminer wine that's labeled as "dry"; or try a Chardonnay from California (see Chapter 6) or from Australia (see Chapter 9).

Chapter 2

Accounting for Taste

*S*ome people take beauty as it comes. They can walk into a beautifully decorated room and simply enjoy being in that room, without trying to understand the artistic influences that contribute to the room's style. They can relish the food of a brilliant chef without dissecting the dish into its ingredients. They can savor a glass of scrumptious white wine and not wonder why the wine tastes exactly the way that it does.

Other people want to analyze, dissect, understand, and get to the bottom of things. We hope that you are one of the analyzing types, because we're about to launch into an explanation of why white wines taste the way they do.

Climate as Style

If wine were a manufactured beverage, the people who make wine would have complete control over the style of wine that they make. Pull out the recipe for medium-bodied, dry white wine with ripe apple and lime flavors and a hint of jasmine, and that would be exactly what you get. (What's more, the wine would be the same every time.)

But wine is an agricultural product. Before anyone can make wine, someone has to grow the grapes. And the amount of sunshine, heat, wind, rain, clouds, drought, or hail that visit the grape vines each summer — affecting the crop — are obviously not in mankind's control. Thanks to the whims of Mother Nature, every white wine is different from every other white wine, and every white wine is different every year.

The vintage game: was it a very good year?

Most wines carry a vintage date on them to indicate the year the grapes were harvested — because most wines are made from the crop of a single year's harvest. The vintage year on the bottle not only helps you figure out how old the wine is, but also serves as a reminder that every wine varies from year to year, at least a little. When no vintage year is on a wine, that wine was probably blended from wines that came from more than one year; naturally enough, such wines are known as non-vintage wines. The whole point of blending across vintages is to even out the quality and taste of the wine so that the wine seems the same this year as it did two years ago. For more information on vintage-dating of wines and other wine-labeling issues, see our book *Wine For Dummies,* from IDG Books Worldwide, Inc.

The *style* of any white wine — that is, the set of characteristics through which a wine manifests itself — depends on the *climate* of the wine region where the grapes grow (that is, the region's general pattern of heat, rain, wind, and so on) as well as the *weather* in that region in any given year (the annual variation of climatic forces). And Nature, not mankind, runs that game.

The ripeness card

The card that Nature plays (or holds) is ripeness. Like other farmers, grapegrowers pray for a large crop of perfectly ripe, healthy fruit every year. When their dreams fall short, it's usually because the grapes didn't ripen as much as the growers had hoped, or the grapes ripened too fast so that the flavors aren't right, or the crop is very small because of quirks of the weather.

Over the centuries, people have learned to plant vineyards for wine only in those locations where the climate and soil give better-than-even odds that the grapes will ripen sufficiently. But ripeness is relative. Some vineyards enjoy so much sunshine and heat each year that they routinely produce soft, plump grapes bursting with sweet juice — while vineyards in other regions manage to ripen their grapes only to the minimum level necessary to make wine.

The ripeness level of the grapes influences the ultimate style of the wine. Here's how that happens: The juice of very ripe grapes has a lot of sugar and not a lot of fruit acid (because grapes trade off acidity for sugar as they ripen); after fermentation, when all the grape sugar has changed into alcohol, the wine from very ripe grapes is higher in alcohol and lower in acid than a wine from less-ripe grapes. And the amount of alcohol and acid in a white wine affects the body and texture of the wine. (See the section "Of crispness and flabbiness" in Chapter 1.)

Hot makes full; cool makes light

The climate of the vineyard therefore dictates the style of a white wine:

- ✔ Vineyards in hot, sunny climates produce very ripe grapes, making full-bodied, soft white wines.
- ✔ Cool vineyards produce less-ripe grapes that make wines with pronounced acidity and relatively low alcohol — that is; light-bodied, crisp white wines.

(Turn to Chapter 1 for an explanation of body, crispness, and softness.)

Winemaking as Style

Although Nature dictates the character of the raw material for every wine, human beings have quite a lot of leeway in deciding what kind of wine to make from that raw material.

When a winemaker confronts a typical batch of white grapes that have been harvested at a normal level of ripeness, his options include

- ✔ Turning the grapes into either dry wine (that is, not sweet) or off-dry wine (that is, slightly sweet)
- ✔ Turning the grapes into a crisp wine or a soft wine
- ✔ Making a white wine that is oaky (that is, having flavors or other characteristics that come from oak wood) or unoaked

Certain kinds of grapes and certain climates favor one style or the other. For example, Riesling (*REES ling*) grapes are hardly ever made into an oaky wine, because most winemakers agree that the combination of Riesling and oak just doesn't taste very good. But every winemaker exercises some control over the final style of the wine.

Beyond simple ripeness: nudging Nature along

If you're inclined to see things as strictly black or white, you may have the idea that grapegrowers are victims of the climate, powerless to control the forces of Nature that prevail upon their region. Actually, grapegrowers do have some control over how their fruit ripens — provided that the growers are not too greedy. By limiting the number of grape bunches on each vine, for example, growers can improve the ripeness of each bunch. And by training the shoots of their grapevines into certain positions, growers can increase the amount of sunlight that hits the grapes. Besides enhancing ripeness, techniques like these improve the flavors of the grapes and make the grape juice more concentrated, that is, richer in all sorts of trace minerals and chemicals that improve the quality of the wine made from that juice. When a grapegrower is more focused on quantity than quality, however, and tries to produce the maximum crop possible, the grapes that result often make dilute, poor quality wines.

Now and then we hear of contests in which several chefs are given an identical set of ingredients and challenged to make the best dish possible from those ingredients. In the end, naturally, no two dishes are the same, because each chef applies his or her personal creativity to the task. If someone were to give several winemakers identical batches of grapes and challenge them to make the best wine possible, the winemakers would each come up with a different wine, based on their own ideas of what a good wine is (and, of course, their skill).

Best wine or best seller

In the real world, the winemaker's goal is not necessarily to make the best wine possible. The goal of most winemakers is to make the best-*selling* wine possible. Winemaking is at least as much a business as it is an art. Most winemakers today turn their grapes into whatever style of wine sells well in their markets.

We realize that the situation we just described isn't very romantic. In case you've been harboring notions of impassioned winemakers dedicating their careers to making the greatest wine the world has ever known, please let us assure you that such winemakers do exist — but the fact is that their wines are in the minority, because those wines are usually made in small quantities. And in some ways, that's just as well. After all, if every winemaker were an artist rather than a business person, there would be no such thing as inexpensive, decent-quality wine for everyday enjoyment. (Just as if every novelist were an artist, there would be nothing to read on airplanes.)

Tasteful techniques

Crisp or soft? Dry or off-dry? Oaky or unoaked? Winemakers have various ways of obtaining the style they desire in their white wine, whichever style that is.

You don't really need to know anything about these wine-making techniques to enjoy white wine. But the more you drink wine, the greater the odds that you'll encounter some of this wine-making lingo, either on the labels of wine bottles, in the language that retailers use when they sell you wine, or in articles about wine — or even from your wine-loving friends. When you need to know what the lingo means, check the sections that follow.

Malolactic fermentation

Also known as ML, *malolactic fermentation* is a process that makes a white wine softer than it would otherwise be. ML is caused by a special strain of (benevolent) bacteria that

- Reduces the total acidity of the wine, and
- Changes the harshest acid in the wine (malic acid) into a softer acid (lactic acid)

The ML process not only makes the wine softer, but also subdues the fruit character of the wine and can sometimes contribute buttery flavor.

Many Chardonnay wines undergo ML, as do some Sauvignon Blancs, especially those that are oaky. But white wines that are meant to be crisp and have direct fruit flavor — like German Rieslings, or Sancerres, or Muscat-based wines — do not undergo ML because ML diminishes the impression of fruit in the wine. (See Chapter 3 for information on grapes like Chardonnay, Muscat, and Sauvignon Blanc; see Chapter 4 for a discussion of wines like German Riesling and Sancerre.)

Barrel-aging (oak-aging)

Barrel-aging involves putting a wine into oak barrels for a period of time between fermentation and bottling. The purpose is twofold: to extract aromas and flavors from the barrels and to expose the wine gradually to a small amount of oxygen, which facilitates all sorts of chemical changes that influence the wine's aroma, flavor, and texture. (Tank aging, in comparison, protects the wine from any contact with oxygen.) In a nutshell, the effects of barrel-aging in white wines are

- Oaky flavors in the wine, such as vanilla, smokiness, toastiness, or — in the extreme — an overtly woody aroma, like a carpenter's workroom

- A deeper, more golden color than the wine would otherwise have

- Diminished fruitiness in the aroma and taste of the wine

- Sometimes, the presence of oak tannin in the wine, which gives the wine firmness and — depending on the amount of tannin — can contribute bitterness and/or a mouth-drying character (for more about tannins and wine firmness, see Chapter 1).

Because oak-aging diminishes fruitiness, just as ML does, wines that are meant to have fresh, vibrant fruit character, such as crisp Sauvignon Blancs or Rieslings, do not generally age in oak. Chardonnays usually do.

The smaller the oak barrel and the newer it is, the more that it influences the wine. For fine white wines, many winemakers use small, 60-gallon barrels of French oak; they use each barrel three to five times (that is, for three to five harvests) before replacing it, the barrel's oakiness diminishing with each use. ("New" oak generally refers to the first year usage.)

Because many of the finest, most expensive white wines of the world spend some time in oak barrels, oak-aging has become a popular buzzword. But most inexpensive (under $10) wines that claim to be oak-aged never saw the inside of a barrel. To get an oaky flavor in these white wines, winemakers soak oak chips in the wine. The wine extracts flavor and tannin from the chips, but to a rather crude degree (and the subtle effects of the oxygen exposure in barrels don't occur). Just remember that oak doesn't always mean oak barrels.

Barrel-fermentation

Barrel-fermentation involves putting grape juice into oak barrels and letting the juice change into wine while in the barrel. Afterward, the wine usually stays in the barrel for a period of barrel-aging. White wines that are barrel-fermented, as opposed to simply being barrel-aged, generally taste less oaky, even though they spend more time in oak. The reasons are rather complicated, but the effect is obvious: the oak flavors are well-integrated in the wine rather than tasting as if the oak had just been added on to the wine. Other effects of barrel-fermentation include a rich, creamy texture in the wine, diminished fruitiness, relatively deep color, and some tannin in the wine.

Lees-contact

Lees is another popular buzzword, although less popular than oak. *Lees* are the residue of white wine fermentation — solid matter such as dead yeast cells and grape pulp — that falls to the bottom of the wine.

If a winemaker does not separate the lees from the wine, but instead leaves the wine in contact with its lees during the wine's aging period (usually a few months), chemical changes occur in the wine. White wines can develop slightly nutty flavors from lees-aging; they become more complex, and sometimes their texture becomes richer. Because lees-contact encourages ML (see the section "Malolactic fermentation" earlier in this chapter), the process is generally used only for wines that also undergo ML.

The compound effect of the lees-contact and ML is a diminished degree of fruitiness in the wine, softer and less-crisp texture, and flavors such as nuttiness and butteriness that do not derive from the grapes themselves. Lees-stirring (literally stirring the lees up into the wine instead of letting them sit at the bottom) exaggerates the effect of lees-contact.

Sweetening techniques

You won't find many winemakers boasting about which techniques they use to make a white wine slightly sweet, for one simple reason: Sweetness is not chic these days. Yet, believe it or not, many of the best-selling white wines in America (such as inexpensive Chardonnays) actually are slightly sweet.

A winemaker who wants to make a white wine that's slightly sweet has two ways of doing so:

  ✔ The first method is to block the fermentation before it is complete. When the winemaker stops the fermentation (usually by filtering the yeasts out of the wine), some of the natural grape sugar remains in the wine; naturally, the wine is also slightly lower in alcohol than it would be if all the sugar in the juice had been converted into alcohol.

✔ The second method is to ferment the wine completely so that it is dry, and then to add back a small amount of unfermented juice from the same grapes. The juice sweetens the wine and dilutes the alcohol level as well.

Although adding sugar to the grape juice is quite a common technique, it is not a method of making the wine sweet. Instead, that technique increases the alcohol content in the wine, because the added sugar ferments into alcohol.

Nature versus Nurture

Who has final say regarding the style of a white wine? The winemaker who crafts the wine? Or Nature, who dictates the growing conditions of the grapes? (If you like the wine in your glass, whom should you toast in gratitude?)

One axiom of the wine business is that even the most talented winemaker on earth cannot make good wine out of poor grapes. Score one point for Mother Nature.

But there's no denying that, whatever the condition of the grapes, the winemaking process happens after the grapegrowing process and leaves an indelible mark on the wine. Score one point for the winemaker.

In the end, winemaking is a collaborative effort between the winemaker and Nature. The most important thing is that, in the glass, you can taste the contribution of both parties.

Is oak always a virtue?

So many popular white wines are oaked these days that it's easy to think that oaky white wines are inherently better than unoaked wines. In fact, the issue of oaky white wine versus unoaked white wine is merely a stylistic choice — a choice of the winemaker in making the wine and a choice of the wine drinker in buying the wine. Frankly, unoaked white wines (fermented and aged entirely in stainless steel tanks) are often easier to enjoy with food than oaky whites. And in unoaked white wines, you can taste the character of the grape more clearly than you can in an oaky wine. At the moment, the pendulum of fashion favors oaky whites — but you know how pendulums swing. . . .

Chapter 3

Grape Expectations

*W*e're both very picky about fabrics. When we go through shop-by-mail catalogs, we always check to see what the fabric is before we decide to order a particular jacket or blouse. In stores, we've been known to turn clothes inside-out looking for the little label that tells us exactly what stuff the garment is made from. When we know what fiber a piece of clothing is made from, we figure that we have a good idea of how it will feel when we wear it and how it will perform after it's washed or dry-cleaned.

Grape varieties are to wines what fiber content is to clothing. If you know what grape (or what combination of grapes) a wine is made from — and if you know something about that particular grape — then you have some idea of what the wine might taste like. You can build up a working knowledge of the world's white grape varieties by trying wines made from each of the varieties one by one every Saturday night for two years. Or you can take a shortcut, by reading on.

Variety Is the Spice of Wine

The plant world loves variety. Dozens of different varieties of roses, lilies, apples, and tomatoes exist — as do a few hundred varieties of white grapes for making wine.

A *variety* in the plant world is a subdivision of a *species* — a category of plants that share certain characteristics. Most wine grapes — red or white — belong to a species called *vitis vinifera* (see Chapter 9 of *Wine For Dummies*).

At the beginning of time, probably very few grape varieties existed, but new varieties were born through evolution or the spontaneous mutation of existing varieties. For about the past 100 years, people have propagated new varieties by cross-breeding existing varieties — much as people cross-breed roses to make ever more gorgeous, hardy, and sweet-smelling types. Cross-bred roses are called hybrids; most cross-bred grapes are simply called *crossings;* in wine, *hybrid* is a term reserved for grape varieties cross-bred between two different species — a fairly unusual occurrence. (The best known hybrid grape is Seyval Blanc.)

The "in" and the "out" of wine grapes

Some varieties of white grapes are popular, fashionable, and always have a date on Saturday night. Other varieties of white grapes are downright obscure. The popular varieties, like Chardonnay, usually have their names plastered all over the labels of the wines that are made from them. (If a winemaker is using a chic grape, he wants you to know that he is.)

The fact that winemakers and wine drinkers favor certain white grape varieties over others is not surprising. Some grapes are considered *noble* varieties in the eyes of wine experts, because they have made truly great wines in the past and are capable of making truly great wines forever in the hands of skilled wine-makers. The popular grape varieties are usually noble grapes.

But not every noble grape variety is popular. Take Riesling *(REES ling),* for example: Although Riesling is clearly a noble grape, capable of making extremely fine wines, its wines are low on the totem pole of popularity with wine drinkers, at least at present. Riesling's lack of popularity is probably due to the fact that Riesling wine is best when it is not oaked (see Chapter 2), and unoaked white wines are far less popular these days than oaky whites.

In case you need to impress your wine-snob boss or sister-in-law, here's our current list of the "in" and "out" grapes among the most important varieties, as well as the grapes on their way up the ladder of popularity, based on popularity of the wines made from those grapes.

In	Out	Moving Up
Chardonnay	Riesling	Viognier
	Chenin Blanc	Pinot Gris
	Müller-Thurgau	Sauvignon Blanc
	Muscat	Sémillon
	Gewürztraminer	

Do you get the impression that Chardonnay has placed a glass ceiling between itself and the other varieties? That's how very powerful Chardonnay is on the international wine market.

The strong and the gentle

A number of characteristics distinguish one white grape variety from another. For one thing, each variety looks different from other varieties, at least to the trained eyes of specialists. Some "white" varieties, such as Pinot Gris, actually are pinkish in color, for example. And each variety has its own distinct leaf shape. More importantly (because you can't really taste a grape's color or leaf shape), each variety has specific flavor compounds that end up as aromas and flavors in the wines made from that grape.

For a good understanding of how grape varieties differ from one another in general, refer to *Wine For Dummies,* Chapter 9, particularly the section "How the Grape Done It."

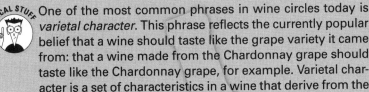

Variety/Varietal

One of the most common phrases in wine circles today is *varietal character*. This phrase reflects the currently popular belief that a wine should taste like the grape variety it came from: that a wine made from the Chardonnay grape should taste like the Chardonnay grape, for example. Varietal character is a set of characteristics in a wine that derive from the wine's grape variety. Not every white wine can have distinct varietal character, because sometimes a wine is a blend of several grape varieties, and sometimes winemaking techniques such as oak-aging can overpower varietal character.

Some white grapes are considered *aromatic* varieties because they have very intense aroma and flavor compounds that leave an unmistakable mark on the wines made from those grapes. The wines made from aromatic white grapes are quite fragrant and flavorful — like literal translations of the grape in the glass. (The Italian white wine called Moscato d'Asti, for example, smells and tastes exactly like the Muscat grape, an aromatic variety.)

Winemakers who are using an aromatic grape generally go with the (grape's) flow and let the grape speak out clearly in the wine, instead of fighting the grape's flavors with oak or malolactic fermentation (see Chapter 2). Because aromatic white grapes have enough to say on their own, the wines made from them are usually unblended wines — that is, no other grape is used in the wine.

The most common aromatic grape varieties are

- Muscat
- Gewürztraminer
- Riesling
- Viognier
- Chenin Blanc
- Sauvignon Blanc

Of these, the Sauvignon Blanc grape presents a big exception to the norm of making unoaked, unblended wines from aromatic grapes. Although some Sauvignon Blanc-based wines — such as Sancerre, Pouilly Fumé, and New Zealand Sauvignon Blanc — are in fact unoaked and unblended, others such as some white Bordeaux wines and many California Sauvignon Blanc wines include the Sémillon grape in their blend and/or are oaked.

The opposite of an *aromatic* white grape variety is — well, there's really no precise name for the group of white grapes that do not fall into the aromatic category. *Non-aromatic* doesn't work because these grapes do have aromas and flavors, just less assertive aromas and flavors. We just call them *other* white grapes. Most white wine grapes fall into this category (way too many to list).

The *varietal* aroma (that is, the aroma and flavor inherent to the grape variety) of these other white grapes is not strong. Therefore, these grapes often end up in wines that taste more of oak and other flavors derived from winemaking processes such as ML (see Chapter 2) than they taste of the grapes themselves. Or these grapes end up in wines that are made from a combination of grape varieties, such that no specific grape character is evident. Most Chardonnay-based wines provide perfect examples of winemaking technique superseding varietal character; white wines from the Rhone Valley in France (see Chapter 10), or white wines like Orvieto and Frascati from central Italy, are examples of blended whites lacking singular varietal character.

The acid question

Another important trait that distinguishes one white grape variety from another (and one white wine from another) is the amount of natural acidity each variety tends to have. Because the acidity of grapes drops during ripening, while sugar content rises, the issue of acidity is conversely the issue of how much sugar each variety tends to produce, and therefore how much alcohol tends to be in the wine from that variety.

Grapes that are relatively high in acidity generally make crisp, light- to medium-bodied white wines with well-defined varietal aromas and flavors (see Chapter 1). High-acid grapes include

- ✔ Riesling
- ✔ Sauvignon Blanc
- ✔ Chenin Blanc
- ✔ Trebbiano

Grapes that are relatively low in acidity generally make soft, medium- to full-bodied white wines, with ripe fruit or earthy aromas and flavors. Lower-acid grapes include

- ✔ Gewürztraminer
- ✔ Sémillon
- ✔ Chardonnay
- ✔ Pinot Gris
- ✔ Pinot Blanc
- ✔ Muscat

The crooked bottom line on varietal character

All the generalizations we make about the characteristics of individual grape varieties are true in theory — but they're not absolutely true in every vineyard. The particular climate and soil of each vineyard, as well as the farming techniques that each grower uses, influence the nature of every grape variety that grows in that vineyard. For example, although the Chardonnay grape tends to be low in acid compared to Sauvignon Blanc and Riesling, a Chardonnay wine can be very crisp (refreshing in acidity) if the grapes are grown in a cool climate; France's famous Chablis wine, made entirely from Chardonnay in the place called Chablis, is an example of such a situation.

The *wine* made from a particular crop of grapes reflects not only the characteristics of its particular grapes, but also the climate, soil, and farming practices that influenced the grapes, and the winemaking techniques used in turning the grapes into wine. There *is* a line connecting grape characteristics to wine flavor and style — but it is a crooked line.

Considering how few Sure Things exist in this life, however, we think that a working knowledge of grape varieties is valuable for anyone who wants to understand wine better. The next section, "Who's Who in White Grapedom," contains descriptions of the major white grape varieties.

Who's Who in White Grapedom

We don't like to eat the same thing every night, and we don't like to drink the same thing every night. Unfortunately, most people in the business of making white wine don't share our feelings. They're all in a rut. Chardonnay, Chardonnay, Chardonnay. We're tempted to be lazy and describe just one white grape variety here (Chardonnay), then take the rest of the day off; most of the wines that you encounter are made from that grape anyway. But we refuse to let the world of white wine begin and end with the Chardonnay grape. A full dozen of the most important white wine grapes are described in this section.

The grape varieties are listed alphabetically, for easy reference (so guess which grape comes first? Chardonnay!). We describe the characteristics of each grape and the style of wine made from that grape, and we name a few examples of wines made from each grape. Don't forget, though, that the grape's characteristics are just the starting point for each wine; some wines won't taste anything like what you might expect from reading our description of the grape. (Maybe they'll taste better!)

Table 3-1 (later in this chapter) summarizes the characteristics of wines made from each grape.

From grape to wine

Every wine starts as a grape variety (or two, or three) — but ends up tasting of the grape *plus* growing conditions *plus* winemaking technique. The grape is the starting point, just like the fiber that makes a garment.

grape variety	=	fiber
grape variety grown in specific circumstances	=	fabric
wine	=	garment

In the end, it's the quality and style of the garment that matters, not just the fiber.

Chardonnay

Pronunciation: SHAR doh nay

Where grown: Everywhere, especially the U.S. (California, Oregon, Washington, New York), France (Burgundy region and south of France), Australia, Chile, South Africa, New Zealand, and elsewhere

Chardonnay wines with other names: Bourgogne Blanc, Mâcon, St. Veran, Pouilly-Fuissé, Chablis (if from France), Puligny-Montrachet, Chassagne-Montrachet, and many more.

Depending on whom you ask, you can get two very different answers to the question, "What is the varietal character of the Chardonnay grape?" Winemakers who grow the grape in cool climates say that apple is the dominant fruit flavor of Chardonnay, sometimes lemon, and that earthy aromas and flavors such as mushroom are common, along with mineral characteristics. Those who grow the grape in other climates tell you that Chardonnay is rich in tropical fruit flavors — such as pineapple, mango, and papaya — as well as peach.

Who's right? Unfortunately for you when you're buying a bottle of Chardonnay, both statements are right. Wines from the Chardonnay grape taste very different when the grape is grown in different places — not to mention when the wine is made in different ways — and you just have to pay attention to the fine print if you want to know in advance what you're getting.

Frankly, we don't think it matters all that much whether Chardonnay *juice* tastes like apple or pineapple, because by the time you drink the *wine,* that juice has lost most of its primal flavor. What you taste in most Chardonnays is spicy, toasty, or smoky oak (turn to Chapter 2 to read about the use of oak in making white wine), sweet alcohol, and butterscotch or butter, derived from the winemaking techniques. If you're lucky, you'll taste some lemon or apple or pineapple underneath all that. (Sweet, oaky, butterscotch pineapple juice — lucky you!)

One of the famous expressions about Chardonnay juice is that it is the perfect "blank canvas" that winemakers can fashion into just the type of wine they want to make. These days, that type of wine is sweet, vaguely fruity, and screaming with alcohol — not exactly our cup of tea.

Okay, enough griping. Just because we believe that a lot of Chardonnay wine these days isn't very good shouldn't turn you off to the grape. The Chardonnay grape is probably the most noble white grape in the world. The greatest white wines in the world — those from the Burgundy region of France, described in Chapter 10 — are made entirely from the Chardonnay grape. And considering the enormous popularity of California Chardonnay wines, the grape must be doing something right in the U.S., too.

Specific winemaking techniques aside, the Chardonnay grape produces wines that are medium in acidity, but full-bodied with high alcohol from ripe, sweet grapes. Whatever the fruit flavors, the wine tends to be broad in the mouth, and dry, with a smooth, silky texture (see *Wine For Dummies,* Chapter 2, for more about wine-tasting). If the grapes come from a cool growing region like Chablis in France or Anderson Valley in California, the wine can be medium bodied rather than full, and its acidity can be quite crisp. Look for these characteristics when you drink Chardonnay, and you'll be able to distinguish the Chardonnay from the winemaking. Figure 3-1 shows a label from a good California Chardonnay wine.

Figure 3-1: Label from a California Chardonnay wine. In France, the Chardonnay grape makes white Burgundy wine.

Chenin Blanc

Pronunciation: shen in blahnk

Where grown: France (Loire Valley), South Africa, California, Texas, and elsewhere

Chenin Blanc wines with other names: Vouvray, Anjou, Saveuniéres, Saumur, Steen

You will rarely encounter a wine that has the grape-name *Chenin Blanc* on it. In those parts of the world where the Chenin Blanc grape is held in high esteem, specifically the Loire Valley of France, wines are named not for the grape but for the specific locale where the grape grows (such as Vouvray). And in those parts of the world where wines are named after the grape variety that makes them, the Chenin Blanc grape is not held in high esteem.

In France's Loire Valley, the Chenin Blanc grape makes every kind of white wine imaginable: sparkling wine, dry wine, medium dry wine, and luscious sweet dessert wine. The type of wine depends on the location of the vineyard and how good the weather is in a particular year — in other words, the ripeness of the grapes. The still (non-sparkling) wines are medium-bodied and flavorful with honey, apple, and floral nuances; their very high acidity is balanced by a rich, almost oily texture (and by some sweetness in those examples that are not fully dry).

In California, Chenin Blanc is most commonly used (often in combination with other grapes) to make light-bodied, floral, slightly sweet wines with crisp acidity. Chenin Blanc could be a silent player in your Chardonnay, and it's almost certainly part of any inexpensive wine that is labeled *generically,* that is, without the name of a grape variety or a place name.

In South Africa, Chenin Blanc is one of the most common white grape varieties. There, it's called Steen, and the wines are generally off-dry, crisp, and inexpensive.

See Chapter 7 of *Wine For Dummies* for more information than you ever wanted to know about how wines are named.

Gewürztraminer

Pronunciation: gah VERTZ trah mee ner

Where grown: France (Alsace), Germany, U.S. (California, New York, Washington, Oregon), British Columbia, and elsewhere

Gewürztraminer wines with other names: No major wine names

The Gewürztraminer grape makes an outrageously perfumed, flavorful wine that is completely unique among white wines. Think of the heady perfume of fresh roses and the exotic, perfumey flavor of fresh lychee fruit (the canned version gives you similar flavor to a lesser degree). Imagine a soft, fat wine that fills your mouth with those flavors and yet is dry and spicy, with a slightly bitter, earthy undercurrent of flavor. That's Gewürztraminer.

In the Alsace region of France, where the best Gewürztraminer wines come from, the wine is dry. Much of the wine labeled Gewürztraminer in the U.S., however, is made in an off-dry, weak-flavored version that is to real Gewürztraminer what a dimestore reproduction is to a real painting by Van Gogh. In some cool growing regions of California and the Pacific Northwest, however, some very good Gewürztraminers are made. (See Chapter 6 for our specific suggestions.)

If you have never tasted a dry Gewürztraminer, plan to. You might hate it, because it is entirely too flavorful for some people. But you just might fall in love.

Müller-Thurgau

Pronunciation: MOO ler TER gow

Where grown: Germany, New Zealand, Austria, Canada, England, Oregon, and elsewhere

Müller-Thurgau wines with other names: Liebfraumilch, Riesling-Silvaner

This grape was born in 1882 by crossing two other grapes, presumably Riesling and Silvaner although no one is absolutely sure. Because this grape is easy to grow and ripens early (important in cool climates), Müller-Thurgau claims a rightful place among white grapes of the world. But no one will ever claim that its quality is superior.

If you have ever drunk Germany's popular wine called Liebfraumilch, you've tasted Müller-Thurgau (although Liebfraumilch can have other grapes blended in): light bodied, slightly floral, moderate in acidity, and slightly pungent. In Austria, where the grape is usually called Riesling-Silvaner, the wine from Müller-Thurgau can be richer and more interesting.

Muscat

Pronunciation: moos caht

Where grown: Italy, France (Alsace), Austria, and elsewhere

Muscat wines with other names: Muskateller, Muskadel (Muscadelle is a different grape)

Muscat is one of the important white wine grapes in the world, but we can't mention most of the wines made from it because they're either sparkling (like Asti) or dessert wines (like Muscat de Beaumes de Venise) — neither of which we cover in this book (see our book, *Wine For Dummies,* for more information). That leaves us with Moscato d'Asti (a less sparkling version of Asti), dry Muscats from Alsace, and some very fine dry Muscats from Austria.

To understand the Muscat grape, pop open a *fresh* bottle of Asti (ask your retailer how long he has had it; if he says anything more than six months, go to a store with a higher turnover). That flowery, perfumey, fruity flavor is what the Muscat grape tastes like. The experience is worth more than any words we could use to describe the grape.

Actually, two different varieties of Muscat grape exist, and one is considered finer than the other because its flavors are more elegant and less heavy (that's the one you'll taste when you open your Asti). Considering that non-sparkling, non-dessert Muscat-based wines are fairly uncommon, though, we'll leave the details on the two varieties for another time.

Pinot Blanc

Pronunciation: *pee noh blahnk*

Where grown: France (Alsace), Italy, Germany, Austria, California, and elsewhere

Pinot Blanc wines with other names: Pinot Bianco *(pee noh bee AHN coh),* Weissburgunder *(VICE bur gund er)*

This grape belongs to the Pinot family of grapes (its siblings are a red grape called Pinot Noir and a pink grape called Pinot Gris) that originated in the Burgundy region of France. It grows all through northeastern Italy, where the wine name is Italianized to Pinot Bianco; in Germany and Austria, where the name is Germanized to Weissburgunder ("white burgundy"); in the Alsace region of France; and in California (where a lot of so-called Pinot Blanc is really a different grape, but you can find some of the real thing, too; see Chapter 7).

The Pinot Blanc grape doesn't contribute much aroma or flavor to the wines made from it, but it provides enough ripeness to give its wines a fairly high level of alcohol, and it gives fairly high acidity, too. The result is usually a dry, crisp, full-bodied white with neutral flavors, maybe a slight nutty character. Versions from Alsace can be slightly softer and sometimes ever so slightly off-dry. Figure 3-2 shows a label from an Italian wine made from the Pinot Blanc grape.

PRODUCE OF ITALY
Estate bottled by:
Schlosskellerei Turmhof TIEFENBRUNNER Srl.
Entikkar-Kurtatsch, Cortaccia (BZ) ITALY

T I E F E N B R U N N E R

1995

Pinot Bianco Alto Adige

Denominazione di Origine Controllata

750 ML NET CONTENTS   DRY WHITE WINE   ALCOHOL 12.5% BY VOL.

Figure 3-2: Label from an Italian Pinot Bianco.

Pinot Gris

Pronunciation: *pee noh gree*

Where grown: France (Alsace), Italy, Germany, Austria, U.S. (Oregon, California), and elsewhere

Pinot Gris wines with other names: Pinot Grigio *(pee noh GREE joe),* Tokay, Rülander

The Pinot Gris grape is much darker-skinned than most other "white" grapes that make white wine — in fact, it's pink or gray in color, hence the name "gray Pinot." *(Gris* is French for *gray.)*

Pinot Gris gives not only more color to its wines than does Pinot Blanc, but also more aroma and flavor. The differences are quite apparent if you compare a Pinot Gris wine with a Pinot Blanc wine from Alsace (see Chapter 11). Italy's popular Pinot Grigio wine, however, has only a tad more personality than Pinot Bianco; Pinot Grigio is usually light to medium bodied and fairly neutral in flavor, belying the reputation of the Pinot Gris grape as a source of richly flavored, full-bodied wines.

Pinot Gris wines from Oregon or California are typically fruitier than the Italian and French versions and sometimes are slightly oaky. Figure 3-3 highlights an Oregon Pinot Gris wine.

Figure 3-3: Label from an Oregon Pinot Gris.

To experience the range of styles that wines from the Pinot Gris grape have, try the Pinot Gris wine-tasting exercise in Chapter 17.

Riesling

Pronunciation: *REES ling*

Where grown: Germany, France (Alsace), Austria, Australia, U.S. (Washington, Oregon, New York, California), Canada, and elsewhere

Riesling wines with other names: White Riesling, Rhine Riesling, Johannisberg Riesling

High acidity and a wealth of fascinating aromas — from flowers to fruit to earthy and mineral scents to honey — are two of the most defining characteristics of the Riesling grape. Riesling from warm enough (but not too warm) climates, such as the Alsace region of France, can reach a high level of ripeness, producing wines with fairly high alcohol content to balance the high acidity, when the wine is vinified dry. Riesling is often vinified as a low-alcohol, off-dry wine, however, to accentuate the wonderful juiciness of its flavors.

The Riesling grape makes the finest dessert wines in the world. Even in off-dry or sweet styles, good Riesling wine manages to be firm and gutsy, with plenty of character.

Over the centuries, grapes other than true Riesling have come to be called Riesling. European labeling regulations decree that only the real thing, wines made from the Riesling grape, can use the name Riesling (compared to the similarly named Welschriesling, Laski Rizling, or Olaz Rizling grapes often found in Eastern European wines); but no such regulation exists for buyers in the U.S. The three names listed at the beginning of this section, however, are accepted synonyms for the real Riesling grape. Figure 3-4 shows a label from a Riesling wine from the Pfalz region of Germany.

WEINGUT

Dr·Bürklin-Wolf

1994
Forster
Riesling

Alc. 11%
by vol.

Pfalz   e 750 ml

Qualitätswein b. A. · L. A. P. Nr. 5 142 043 11 95
Produce of Germany · D-67157 Wachenheim

Estate Bottled

Figure 3-4: Label from a German Riesling wine.

Sauvignon Blanc

Pronunciation: saw vee nyon blahnk

Where grown: France (Bordeaux, Loire Valley), U.S. (California, Washington), New Zealand, South Africa, Chile, Italy, and elsewhere

Sauvignon Blanc wines with other names: Bordeaux Blanc, Graves, Pessac-Leognan, Sancerre, Pouilly-Fumé, Fumé Blanc

Some wine critics believe that the Sauvignon Blanc grape is less noble somehow than Chardonnay, Riesling, and even Chenin Blanc. Yet when wine lovers tire of Chardonnay, they frequently turn to Sauvignon Blanc as their alternative, rather than to wines from the other two grapes.

Sauvignon Blanc is one of the most personality-laden grapes: its aromas and flavors are vivid and forthright — grass, herbs, minerals, and tart fruits when grown in cool climates; melons, figs, ripe citrus, and peaches when grown in warmer climes. It is versatile, making crisp unoaked wines with plenty of flavor (the stylistic opposite of most Chardonnays), or wines that are rounded by oak, with fruit character muted by the winemaking (rather in the style of Chardonnay). Its high acidity makes it well-suited to food. Figure 3-5 shows a label from a popular New Zealand Sauvignon Blanc.

Figure 3-5: Label from a favorite Sauvignon Blanc wine from New Zealand.

Sémillon

Pronunciation: *sem ee yon*

Where grown: France (Bordeaux), U.S. (Washington, California), Australia, Chile, South Africa, and elsewhere

Sémillon wines with other names: Bordeaux Blanc

The Sémillon grape is much less known among wine drinkers than Sauvignon Blanc, although many a Sauvignon Blanc wine actually relies on Sémillon as a blending partner.

Sémillon's lower acidity and more generous body complement Sauvignon Blanc very well, such that the blend is usually more complex and higher in quality than either wine alone. Bordeaux's greatest dry white wines are composed of about 50 percent of each grape. (And Bordeaux's great dessert wines, such as Sauternes, are almost entirely Sémillon.)

In Australia, Semillon often combines with Chardonnay to make a wine called SemChard; some American producers have adopted this practice. Australia's Semillons (pronounced *SEM eh lon* there) without the Chardonnay can be extraordinary, especially when they are aged.

Apart from Australia, however, Sémillon is not common as a varietal wine. A few varietal Sémillons exist in California and Washington (see Chapters 7 and 8), and they can be quite good, graced by a delicate aroma of mustard seed.

Trebbiano

Pronunciation: *treb bee AH noh*

Where grown: Italy, France (Provence, Gascony, and elsewhere), Portugal, South Africa, Argentina, and elsewhere

Trebbiano wines with other names: Frascati, Orvieto

Trebbiano is a workhorse grape that produces large quantities of crisp, neutral-flavored white wine — just the style of white wine favored in Italy, because wines of this style are refreshing with food but do not compete with the food's flavor. Besides being the dominant grape variety in Orvieto, Frascati, Trebbiano di Romagna, and many Tuscan white wines, Trebbiano is a blending grape in Soave and Verdicchio wines.

Called Ugni *(oo nyee)* Blanc in France, Trebbiano is the raw material for Cognac and Armagnac brandies. This grape is also grown throughout the south of France, where it appears in many Provence white wines.

Viognier

Pronunciation: vee oh nyay

Where grown: France (Rhone Valley, southern France), California

Viognier wines with other names: Condrieu, Chateau Grillet

Wines made from the Viognier grape are rather chic these days — an ironic fact, considering how little Viognier is grown in the world. The grape's flavor and aroma are certainly intriguing, and the soft style of most Viognier wines is easy to enjoy. Like Gewürztraminer, Viognier adapts well to the fascinating smells-sweet-but-tastes-dry style of wine. Some producers of Condrieu wine, from the northern Rhone Valley of France (see Chapter 10), are using oak to make more serious and mainstream wines based on Viognier.

What's What in White Winedom

Although the grape's characteristics are the starting point for each wine, each wine has its own characteristics determined by the many factors that go into producing it. Table 3-1 summarizes the chief characteristics of each wine. Try some and see if your taste buds agree.

Table 3-1	Characteristics of Wines Made from Various White Grapes			
Wine	**Acidity**	**Sugar (Alcohol Level)**	**Aromas/ Flavors**	**Wine Style**
Chardonnay	Medium to low	Fairly high	Apple, citrus, earth, and mineral in cooler climates; melon and tropical fruits in warmer climates	Usually oaked; often full-bodied, sweet, soft, and toasty; sometimes dry, crisp, and earthy

Wine	Acidity	Sugar (Alcohol Level)	Aromas/ Flavors	Wine Style
Chenin Blanc	High	Varies significantly with the climate	Honey, floral, wet straw, melon	Unoaked, crisp wines with rich texture; inexpensive versions are light-bodied, fruity, and off-dry
Gewürztraminer	Low	High	Roses and other flowers, lychee fruit, delicate spice	Generally not oaked; usually full-bodied, soft, and very flavorful; often sweet, but the dry versions are far more intriguing
Müller-Thurgau	Medium	Low to medium	Slightly floral and pungent	Not oaked; fruity, light-bodied, and crisp
Muscat	Medium	Medium	Very floral and fruity	Very fragrant and flavorful, light-bodied; not oaked; sometimes made in a high-alcohol dessert wine style
Pinot Blanc	Medium to high	Fairly high	Fairly neutral, almondy	Dry, crisp, medium- to full-bodied; sometimes (but not usually) oaked

(continued)

Table 3-1 *(continued)*

Wine	Acidity	Sugar (Alcohol Level)	Aroma/ Flavors	Wine Style
Pinot Gris	Medium to low	Fairly high	Peach-pit, orange peel	Generally not oaked; Italian versions are dry, crisp, and not very flavorful; Alsace versions are full-bodied, rich, flavorful, and dry; U.S. versions are medium-bodied, fruity, and occasionally oaked
Riesling	High	Low to medium	Floral; fruity, especially peaches and a touch of lime, apricots; steely; honeyed	Generally light- to medium-bodied; crisp wines with pronounced fruitiness, sometimes times dry and sometimes off-dry
Sauvignon Blanc	Crisp	Medium	Herbal aromas in cooler climates; melons, figs, and pears in warmer climates	One style is unoaked, crisp, lean, and zesty; another style is oaky, rich, and fuller
Sémillon	Low	Medium	Herbal, mustard seed, figs, honey, lanolin, wax	Medium-bodied, soft, not very flavorful; can be oaked or unoaked

Wine	Acidity	Sugar (Alcohol Level)	Aromas/ Flavors	Wine Style
Trebbiano	Medium to high	Low	Neutral; sometimes pear	Crisp, low-flavor, unoaked wines
Viognier	Low	High	Floral, apricots, peaches	Dry but aromatic, medium-bodied wine; usually not oaked

Chapter 4
The Seven Classic Types of White Wine

- -

In This Chapter

▶ Role models for famous grapes

▶ Why most classic types of wine are European

▶ The original Chardonnay-based wine

▶ California shapes a new protoype

- -

*T*rends come and go, but the classics remain. Whatever the art form, the classics provide the backdrop against which every future generation of artists measures its work. The classics also provide a solid foundation for study of that art form.

In the wine world, the classics are the types of wine that have been around the longest — those types that have survived over the centuries and have inspired countless winemakers in all parts of the world. We describe seven classic kinds of white wine in this chapter so that you can become familiar with them, even if you have never tasted them.

Genesis: Europe

Most of the types of wine that are considered classic are European wines, because the Europeans had a big head start in making wine. All the best varieties of wine grapes — varieties that today grow in vineyards all over the world — originated in Europe, and Europeans therefore had the first shot in discovering (and defining) the potential of each variety.

But here and there in other countries, winemakers have created new interpretations of European grape varieties that amount to new classic styles. (In addition to California Chardonnay, which we do include in our group of classic wine types, Australian Semillon represents a unique and original style from that grape, for example.)

In naming our seven classic types of white wines, we're not necessarily naming the seven best types of white wine in the world, or even our seven favorite types of white wine. What these seven kinds of wine represent are stylistic models — role models that winemakers emulate (or defy) in producing the white wines that you drink.

Of course, the best examples of each category of classic white wine also happen to be excellent. For students of wine, homework can be delicious!

The descriptions that follow are meant to give you a broad idea of the nature of each of the classic types of white wine. Specific information about the wines that make up each classic type follows, in Part II of this book.

White Burgundy: The Mother of All Chardonnays

Are the white wines of the Burgundy region of eastern France the greatest dry white wines in the whole world? Many wine critics think so. Certainly they are the most influential type of white wine ever, judging by the promulgation of the Chardonnay grape, the grape of white Burgundy, to the four corners of the wine world.

White Burgundy wines are the original Chardonnays. With a few exceptions too trivial to mention, every white wine of the Burgundy region is made 100 percent from the Chardonnay grape. The quality and style of these wines have inspired winemakers all over the world to grow Chardonnay themselves and make Chardonnay wine. (The Chardonnay-based wines made elsewhere in the world are quite different from those of Burgundy, however; for an example, turn to the section "California Chardonnay" near the end of this chapter.)

Because European wines are typically named not for their grape variety but for the locale where the grapes grow, white Burgundies are not called Chardonnay. Some of them are called *Bourgogne Blanc,* literally white Burgundy; others carry the names of specific districts or villages, or even vineyards — according to the source of grapes for each wine. If we were to count up all the names of white Burgundy wines, we'd probably end up with somewhere between 125 and 150 different wines.

(See Chapter 7 of our book, *Wine For Dummies,* published by IDG Books Worldwide, Inc., for more about how wines are named.)

Every one of these 125 to 150 wines is a white Burgundy and is made from Chardonnay (except, of course, those few exceptions). But obviously not every one of them is of inspirational quality. The wines from the best vineyard sites, from the finest producers, however, are legendary.

The most legendary white wines of Burgundy include, as a few examples

- ✔ Montrachet *(mon rah shay)*
- ✔ Corton-Charlemagne *(cor tawn shahr luh mahn)*
- ✔ Batard-Montrachet *(bah tar mon rah shay)*
- ✔ Chevalier-Montrachet *(sheh vah lyay mon rah shay)* and the slightly less exalted Puligny-Montrachet *(poo lee nyee mon rah shay)*
- ✔ Chassagne-Montrachet *(shah san yuh mon rah shay)*
- ✔ Meursault *(muhr so)*

Figure 4-1 shows a label from a White Burgundy wine.

These wines are all made by simple, traditional methods such as fermenting the grape juice in oak barrels and allowing the wine to sit on its fermentation lees for many months before bottling. (See Chapter 2 for an explanation of these winemaking techniques.) They are full-bodied, rich wines with creamy texture and amazingly complex aromas and flavors suggestive of honey, apple, nuts, spice, vanilla, earth, and toast. Although

Figure 4-1: A label of a Puligny-Montrachet wine from Burgundy.

the aromas and flavors of these wines are complex and concentrated, these wines are not particularly fruity. Even in their most full-bodied, expressive manifestations, white Burgundies are subtle wines that keep wine lovers coming back, glass after glass, to discover nuances that lurk in hiding.

Some other white Burgundies — especially most of the wines from Chablis *(shah blee)* and the Mâcon *(mah kon)* district (see Chapter 10 for an explanation of the districts of Burgundy) — are produced in stainless steel rather than oak. As a result, these wines lack the smoky, toasty nuances of oak-aging, but they are rich in mineral and earthy flavors. Chablis, a wine from a cool, northerly growing area, is quite crisp and lighter in body than most other Burgundies; Mâcon wines are medium- to full-bodied but slightly less complex and subtle than many other Burgundies.

The greatest white wines of Burgundy are produced in tiny quantities and are, therefore, extremely expensive. Because weather in the region varies considerably from year to year, quality varies from vintage to vintage. Quality also varies significantly from producer to producer. These pragmatic issues — price, availability, and consistency of quality — make white Burgundy the most challenging type of white wine to buy. But most serious wine lovers — and winemakers all over the world — believe that the rewards of good white Burgundy are absolutely worth the effort.

Turn to Chapter 10 for more detailed explanation of specific types (and names) of white Burgundy wine, as well as our all-important recommendations of producers of great and good white Burgundies.

White Burgundy wine at a glance

Where from: The Burgundy region of eastern France

Grape variety: Chardonnay

Style of wine: Two distinct styles: rich and full-bodied but firm with complex but fairly subtle aromas of honey, toast, smoke, nuts, and earth; and crisp, less-fleshy, with mineral nuances

Price range: $6 to $600

Recent good vintages (very fine vintages are in bold): 1995, 1994, **1992**, 1990, **1989, 1986,** 1985

Where to turn for more specific information: Chapter 10

King Riesling of Germany

Among the types of great white wine in the world, German Riesling and white Burgundy are opposite poles, equally great but completely different from one another stylistically.

Wines from the Riesling grape variety grown in Germany's best vineyards are excellent wines by any of the standards typically used to evaluate quality in wine — such as concentration of flavor, depth, complexity, length, and balance. (See Chapter 2 of *Wine For Dummies* for an explanation of all of these attributes of wine.) Germany's Rieslings are highly individual wines that express their grape variety — Riesling — interpreted through the soil and climate of each vineyard.

Because Germany's wine regions sport a wide variety of soils and climatic nuances and because the weather in Germany is highly variable from year to year, German Rieslings vary quite a lot from one example to the next.

In some areas, such as parts of the Mosel-Saar-Ruwer *(MOH zel zar ROO ver)* region, Riesling often expresses itself as a light-bodied wine with an indescribable floral-fruity aroma, all delicacy and freshness on the palate.

In other areas, such as the warmer Pfalz *(fallz)* region, Riesling is medium-bodied and firm, with mineral aromas intermingling with ripe fruit character suggestive of peaches and lime. Depending on the ripeness of the grapes each year, any wine might be made in a fully dry style, an off-dry (slightly sweet) style, or a sweet style. (Late-harvested Rieslings made from very ripe grapes are Germany's particular claim to fame, but they fall beyond the scope of this book.)

Whichever part of Germany they come from, German Rieslings share the fundamental characteristics of the Riesling grape:

- ✔ High acidity that gives the wine a sense of freshness, no matter how old it is
- ✔ Vibrant fruit aromas and flavors ranging from lime to peach to dried apricots
- ✔ A vivid intensity of flavor

Because these wines are not oaky (if they are made in oak casks, the casks are old and have no oak flavors to impart) and they do not undergo malolactic fermentation (see Chapter 2), they are crisp wines that express their flavors frankly and forthrightly. German Rieslings age remarkably well, developing unusual but not unpleasant petrol aromas with several years of age.

Unfortunately, German Riesling is not in vogue these days among wine drinkers outside of Europe, who prefer the soft and oaky style of white wine. But a classic type it remains.

German Riesling wine at a glance

Where from: The wine regions of Germany, especially the Mosel-Saar-Ruwer, Pfalz, and Rheingau regions

Grape variety: Riesling

Style of wine: Unoaked, crisp wines that range from bone-dry to very sweet, from light-bodied to medium-bodied, from floral and fresh-fruity to earthy and suggestive of dried fruits

Price range: $10 to $35

Recent good vintages (very fine vintages are in bold): 1995, 1993, **1990, 1989,** 1988

Where to turn for more specific information: Chapter 12, "A League of Their Own: Germany's White Wines"

Sancerre and Pouilly-Fumé: Sauvignon Blanc, Loud and Clear

The Sauvignon Blanc grape grows in about a dozen different countries around the world, but no vineyard area has as great a stake in that grape as the easternmost part of the Loire *(lwahr)* Valley region of France.

The towns of Sancerre and Pouilly-sur-Loire, on opposite banks of the upper Loire River, practically in the dead-center of France, give their names to two types of wine — Sancerre *(sahn sehr)* and Pouilly-Fumé *(pwee foo may)* — that have come to epitomize Sauvignon Blanc in the minds of most wine lovers. In the particular climate of this area (warm summers, cold winters) and the soils of the hillside vineyards (mainly limestone, with varying amounts of clay, gravel, or flint), Sauvignon Blanc expresses its full-blown pungency of aroma, crisp acidity, and mineral-laden flavor.

Both Sancerre and Pouilly-Fumé are made entirely from the Sauvignon Blanc grape. (Some red and rosé Sancerre wines exist, both made from the red Pinot Noir grape.) With a few exceptions, both Sancerre and Pouilly-Fumé are not oak-influenced and do not undergo malolactic fermentation (see Chapter 2), resulting in high-acid, aromatically intense wines that smell and taste only of the grape (influenced, of course, by the particular growing conditions of each vineyard).

Individual examples of these wines range from light-bodied to medium-bodied, depending on the vintage year and the producer, and they are bone-dry. Typical aromas and flavors include green grass, tart green fruit (most British wine books say *gooseberries,* but we must confess that we have never met a gooseberry), sometimes a smoky gunflint aroma (like cap guns that children use), or a cold, stony character. Sancerre is typically considered crisper, lighter in body, and more herbaceous than Pouilly-Fumé, which is usually categorized as smoky and slightly fuller — but in fact these characterizations depend on the grower and the vintage.

Sancerre and Pouilly-Fumé are such unique wines that words do not do them justice. Imagine the crispest, dryest white wine possible, with pronounced aromas and flavors that remind you of all sorts of things that are green. Better yet, try a bottle. In Chapter 11, you find our recommended wines.

Because Sancerre and Pouilly-Fumé are such direct expressions of their grape, they are most enjoyable young, while their flavors are fresh and vivid.

Sancerre and Pouilly-Fumé wine at a glance

Where from: The eastern vineyards of the Loire Valley wine region of France

Grape variety: Sauvignon Blanc

Style of wine: Dry, very crisp, light- to medium-bodied unoaked wines with pronounced aromas and flavors that range from green grass and other herbaceous scents to tart fruit and mineral scents

Price range: $10 to $40

Recent good vintages (very fine vintages are in bold): 1995, 1993, **1990, 1989**

Where to turn for more specific information: The section, "The Crisp White Wines of the Loire Valley" in Chapter 11

White Bordeaux: The Beauty of Blending

The Bordeaux region of western France produces plenty of unremarkable, even poor, white wine. But like the little girl with the curl in the middle of her forehead, when it is good, it is very, very good. The best white wines of the Bordeaux region, in fact, are so good — and so unique — that they have spawned a school of admirers among winemakers in California.

Classic white Bordeaux wines are made from a blend of two grapes, Sauvignon Blanc and Sémillon. The proportions vary from producer to producer (from *château* to *château,* as they say in Bordeaux), but many of the best wines feature approximately 50 percent of each grape.

The combination of Sauvignon Blanc and Sémillon is nothing short of brilliant. The lean, high-acid, herbal-scented, and quick-to-mature Sauvignon Blanc wine perfectly complements the round, lower-acid, lanolin-and-fig-scented, slow-to-develop wines of the Sémillon grape. The resulting blend is refreshing and tasty when young, if slightly austere, and it blossoms into a rich, smoky, honeyed wine after it has had a chance to mature in the bottle. To enhance the smoky/toasty characteristics of the Sémillon grape and to make the blend more complex when it is young, most producers ferment the wine in oak barrels.

Despite the beauty of this grape blend, a handful of serious producers have chosen to make their white Bordeaux wine exclusively from the Sauvignon Blanc grape — with great success. These wines tend to rely heavily on oak to round out the edges of Sauvignon Blanc's flavor. Although these wines differ from the blended versions in the nature of the raw material, their quality and style are consistent with the wines blended from Sauvignon Blanc and Sémillon.

Almost every white Bordeaux that could be considered a classic, prototypical wine hails from the Graves *(grahv)* district of Bordeaux, especially the Pessac-Leognan *(pes sac lay oh nyon)* area of the Graves district. Plenty of other wines that are technically also white Bordeaux come from other parts of the large Bordeaux region. Some of them are made entirely from the Sauvignon Blanc grape without any oak, resulting in fresh, crisp, light-bodied wines; others are made entirely from Sémillon.

White Bordeaux wine at a glance

Where from: The Bordeaux region of western France, especially the Graves district and its Pessac-Leognan subdistrict

Grape Variety: Sauvignon Blanc and Sémillon, often in approximately 50-50 proportions

Style of Wine: Medium- to full-bodied, with firm acidity and relatively austere, herbal flavors when young, overlaid with smoky oak; evolves to a richly textured wine with complex aromas/flavors of honey, toast, and lanolin

Price range: $10 to $90

Recent good vintages (very fine vintages are in bold):
1994, 1993, 1992, 1990, **1989,** 1988, **1987, 1985**

Where to turn for more specific information: The section, "Bordeaux Also Comes in *Blanc,* " in Chapter 11

Aristocratic is a word that comes to mind when wine lovers taste a well-aged, classic white Bordeaux. The wine is rich, complex, and flavorful without overly obvious, vulgar fruitiness; full yet elegant and refined in its style, with glints of honey in its flavor and glints of gold in its color, like so many royal jewels.

Chapter 11 provides more information on white Bordeaux wine and offers specific recommendations on wines worth trying.

The Taste of Alsace

White Bordeaux, white Burgundy, and (white) Sancerre are specific types of wine (each with a certain range of quality and style variations). But Alsace is not a specific type of wine, technically speaking. Alsace is a place in eastern France where people make wine — many wines, most of them white and most of them named after their grape variety. Alsace Riesling, Alsace Gewurztraminer, Alsace Tokay-Pinot Gris, and Alsace Pinot Blanc are types of wine; Alsace itself is just the place.

To lump all these different types of wine together and declare the wines of Alsace, collectively, a classic white wine type is a bit unorthodox. But we taste such a strong family resemblance among all the white wines of Alsace, and we consider each of the wines such a unique interpretation of its grape variety, that we could not logically single out any one wine. Better unorthodox than illogical.

The wines of Alsace come from a long, narrow strip of vineyards along the border of France and Germany. These vineyards are separated from the rest of France by the Vosges *(voejhe)* Mountains, which block most rain, making Alsace one of the driest wine regions in France. Soils are varied throughout the hills where the grapes grow, suiting different grape varieties in different places.

Alsace wines are, for the most part, made entirely from the grape variety named on the label. The one exception is Alsace Pinot Blanc wine, which often contains some wine from another grape variety known as Auxerrois *(aus ser whah)*. Wines from the best vineyard sites and made from what local authorities consider the best grape varieties (Riesling, Gewürztraminer, Pinot Gris, and Muscat) are entitled to be designated as *grand cru* wines—that is, wines of higher status, and usually higher price .

Naturally, every wine of Alsace tastes different from every other wine of Alsace, depending on its grape variety, the soil in the vineyard, the winemaker, and the weather that year. What each wine has in common with the others is considerable, however:

- ✔ All the white wines of Alsace practice the creed of vivid fruit character, unencumbered by oak or malolactic fermentation (see Chapter 2); what you smell in an Alsace wine is the grape variety (filtered by the soil and climate of Alsace), and what you taste is the grape variety (similarly filtered).

- ✔ The white wines of Alsace are all fairly high in alcohol and quite full-bodied for white wines (Alsace Pinot Blanc tends to be the lightest of the wines). With the exception of the late-harvested dessert-wine styles, Alsace wines are dry.

- ✔ And then there is that unique Alsace aroma. We are as much at a loss to describe the aroma as all the writers before us who have tried. *Earthy* is a satisfactory descriptor because the aroma surely derives from the earth, but it's more than earthy: a bit spicy, a bit chemical-like, sort of minerally. To a greater or lesser degree, all the wines of Alsace have this distinct but indescribable aroma.

Alsace's version of every grape variety it grows is distinctly different from other wines of the same grape grown elsewhere:

- Alsace Riesling typically is more full-bodied and powerful than dry German Riesling.

- Alsace Gewürztraminer combines exotic fruit and flower aromas with dry flavor and rich texture in such a way that it sets the standard for Gewürztraminer all over the world.

- Alsace Pinot Gris is richer and more flavorful than any other Pinot Gris anywhere.

- Pinot Blanc from Alsace expresses far more character than the grape typically is capable of giving.

Alsace wines are each, and all, a classic wine type.

Chapter 11 lists our favorite producers of Alsace wines, as well as describing the individual types in more detail.

White Alsace wines at a glance

Where from: The Alsace region in northeastern France, near the Franco-German border

Grape variety: The wines are *varietal wines,* each named for its variety; the main grape varieties are Riesling, Gewürztraminer, Pinot Gris, Muscat, and Pinot Blanc.

Style of wine: Dry, full-bodied, with rich texture and intense aromas and flavors specific to the grape variety, as well as an earthy aroma characteristic of the region

Price range: $8 to $35

Recent good vintages (very fine vintages are in bold): 1995, **1994, 1990, 1989**

Where to turn for more specific information: The section, "The *Dry* White Wines of Alsace" in Chapter 11

Chardonnay Wine from California

From a historical perspective, California Chardonnay wine shouldn't be included among the world's classic types of white wine. Chardonnay from California began its rise to prominence only in the early 1970s; the white wines of Burgundy, in comparison, were commercially important 300 years ago. But in their short history of making Chardonnay, California winemakers have managed to redefine the grape's possibilities and forge an original style of wine that is already a classic.

The Chardonnay grape grows in every nook and cranny of California's vineyards, from the hot Central Valley to cool regions such as Carneros, the Santa Maria Valley, and Mendocino. Naturally, the quality of the wines varies according to where the grapes grow, and so does the style of the wines. Furthermore, California Chardonnay wines as a group have been in constant stylistic flux ever since they were born.

Nevertheless, Chardonnay wines from California do consistently have certain characteristics that could be pegged as representative of "The California Style." (See Figure 4-2 for an example of a California Chardonnay wine label.)

 ✔ California Chardonnay wines are quite full-bodied and high in alcohol, with pronounced aromas and flavors, generally of tropical fruits (pineapple, ripe citrus, and mango) but sometimes of apple, earth, and herbs, if the grapes come from a cooler climate.

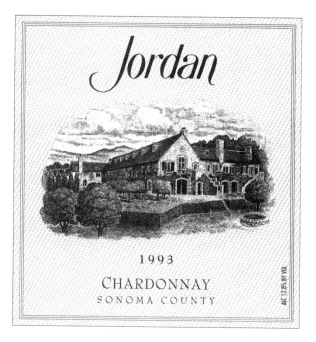

Figure 4-2: An example of a California Chardonnay wine label.

✔ California Chardonnay wines are almost always oaked — sometimes ineptly, resulting in harsh, bitter oak flavor; often wholeheartedly, resulting in strong butterscotch flavors; and sometimes judiciously, resulting in creamy texture and smoky/toasty aromas that accent the wines' fruit.

✔ Although just about every California Chardonnay would claim to be a dry wine, many of them, in fact, taste noticeably sweet to experienced tasters.

The sweetness, high alcohol, and pronounced fruitiness all add up to a big, voluptuous mouthful of flavor. Nothing subtle or suggestive here. (This full-blown style of California Chardonnay has its counterpart in Australia.)

Because they are so full-bodied and flavorful (not to mention their sweetness), California Chardonnays are temperamental partners for food. Rich foods such as lobster, flavorful or rich sauces, and dishes with fruit (such as island cuisines) are likely matches.

In Chapter 6, we recommend many dozens of California Chardonnays in three separate price ranges.

California Chardonnay wine at a glance

Where from: California

Grape Variety: Chardonnay (75 to 100 percent)

Style of Wine: Full-bodied, high in alcohol, often rather sweet, and very flavorful; aromas and flavors suggest tropical fruits, citrus, ripe apple, or other fruits, as well as toasty or butterscotch flavors derived from oak

Price range: $4 to $44

Recent good vintages (very fine vintages are in bold): 1995, 1994, **1993, 1992, 1990**

Where to turn for more specific information: Chapter 6 of this book

Venerable Vouvray

If it weren't for the town of Vouvray *(voo vray)* and its neighboring vineyards, the Chenin Blanc grape would not be considered one of the noble white grape varieties of the world; and if it weren't for Chenin Blanc, the wine of Vouvray would not be considered a classic type of wine. In other words, the grape and the place were made for each other, and together they are both important.

The Vouvray district is on the Loire River, in northwestern France, near the city of Tours. In the fairly cool climate and limestone-based soil of Vouvray's vineyards, the Chenin Blanc grape ripens sometimes less, sometimes more — and the style of Vouvray wine that is made varies according to the grapes' ripeness. The highest-quality Vouvray wines are considered to be those that are made as very sweet dessert-style wines; but even limiting the discussion to dry and semi-dry wines (the scope of this book), Vouvray is still a classic wine type.

To capture the full essence of Chenin Blanc in their wine, the producers of Vouvray do not oak their wine, nor do they practice malolactic fermentation (see Chapter 2).

Vouvray is always high in acidity, thanks to the Chenin Blanc grape. The crispness of its high acidity is balanced, however, by a rich, almost oily texture. Honeyed flavors enhance the wine's richness — as does sweetness, in those versions that are not dry. The result is a fascinating point-counterpoint of flavor: rich yet crisp, unctuous yet lean.

The most inexpensive Vouvray wines are much less exciting to taste than those of the best producers; run-of-the-mill Vouvray is a pleasant enough off-dry wine with floral aromas. For suggestions on reliable producers of Vouvray, turn to Chapter 11.

Other Loire Valley wines made with the Chenin Blanc grape — and therefore similar types of wine to Vouvray — include Savennieres *(sah ven nyair),* Saumur *(soh muhr),* and Anjou *(ahn jew).*

Vouvray wine at a glance

Where from: Vineyards in the vicinity of the town of Vouvray, in the central part of France's Loire Valley wine region

Grape variety: Chenin Blanc

Style of wine: Can be dry, medium-dry, or medium-sweet (and a sweet dessert-wine version also exists). Unoaked, with very high acidity and rich texture; aromas/flavors suggestive of flowers and honey

Price range: $6 to $17

Recent good vintages (very fine vintages are in bold): 1995, **1990, 1989**

Where to turn for more specific information: The section, "Vouvray — home of Chenin Blanc" in Chapter 11

Chapter 5

White Wine with Fish — and More

*T*hanks to the movies, wine drinkers already know which wine goes best with illicit seduction (Demi Moore serves Pahlmeyer Chardonnay in *Disclosure*) and which wine best culminates dangerous feats of international espionage (Bond always drinks Bollinger Champagne). But we suspect that neither sexual harassment nor espionage is on your menu for next Saturday night. And the movies just don't have much advice to give regarding a good wine for turkey burgers, do they?

In the sections that follow, we offer some guidelines that help you choose which white wines to serve with the foods that you like to eat — on all those evenings when life fails to imitate art.

Setting the Scene

Matching wine with food is one of the most fun aspects of wine, as well as one of the tastiest. Wine comes alive at the table, enlivening the food, the conversation, and the company. And contrary to what some people think, matching wine and food is fairly easy.

Before we launch into a specific discussion of white wines and the foods that go with them, we offer some preliminary pointers on the business of matching wine with food. Keep these points in mind when you choose the wines to accompany your own meals:

  ✔ Any effort at perfectionism in matching wine and food — that is, finding precisely the perfect wine for a particular dish — is useless. The possible combinations of foods and wines are more numerous than all the individual wines in the world, all the individual foods, and all food dishes — in other words, practically infinite. Mealtime is a lot easier and more pleasant when you settle for a merely good match instead of reaching for the gold.

✔ **What you like is what counts.** If a particular type of wine tastes good to you with a dish that the experts say is wrong for that wine, don't worry. Not everyone has the same taste — and *your* taste is what you have to live with.

✔ **Matching wine and food always involves guesswork.** When you (or anyone else) choose a wine to go with a particular dish, you make the match-up mentally first, in your imagination. You guess how the food will taste, you guess how the wine will taste, and you guess how the two might interact. (The only way to avoid guesswork is to make a specific recipe and drink it with the specific wine — same vintage, producer, grape variety, and region — recommended to accompany that recipe. Of course you might not *like* that combination, per our preceding point.)

✔ If you eat the foods you like and drink the kinds of wine you like, you will very seldom encounter a food-and-wine disaster, in which the two taste absolutely horrible together.

Matching food and wine is a pursuit whose end goal is enjoyment. An open-minded attitude and a sense of adventure accomplish that goal far better than the highest knowledge of the subject coupled with an obsessive need to make the perfect match.

Is the Answer Always "White"?

We know that you like white wine — at least we assume you do, based on the fact that you're reading this book. But we must tell you, right at the start: Some foods just don't go very well with white wine. (We'd state *unequivocally* that some foods do not go with white wine, except that our second pointer in the preceding section, the one about personal taste, is fresh in our minds at the moment.)

White wines encompass such a range of styles — from super light and elegant to super rich — that white wine is a plausible accompaniment to *most* types of foods. But we, speaking for our own personal tastes, exclude the following foods from our repertoire of white wine dishes (knowing full well that some people disagree with us):

- ✔ Venison and boar (some boors don't improve with *any* wine)
- ✔ Simple beef dishes such as prime rib or plain hamburger
- ✔ Hearty beef stews
- ✔ Strong-flavored birds such as squab or duck

Certain other foods could go well with white wine, but the match-ups are tricky. Such foods include

- ✔ Very spicy, fiery dishes
- ✔ Very flavorful, pungent aged cheeses
- ✔ Rich pâté

Most other foods provide sure footing for white wines. We can't imagine a food that's too delicate for white wine, and, at the opposite end of the spectrum, even extremely rich and flavorful foods can find their match with certain types of white wines.

Approaches to Food-and-Wine Pairings

You know what food you plan to serve for dinner. Now how do you begin to figure out which wine to serve?

Your goal is to find a wine that

- ✔ Makes the food taste better than it otherwise would
- ✔ Tastes better with the food than that wine would taste alone

The best wine-and-food matches are about transformation: The characteristics of the wine transform the food, and the characteristics of the food transform the wine. The whole success of the match-up revolves around those two sets of characteristics, the wine's and the food's.

And what characteristics are those? Well, not color; the color of the food has no particular impact on the wine's taste. (At least that's one aspect you don't have to think about!) The weight of the dish and the weight of the wine — how light each is, or how heavy and rich — is a relevant characteristic, however, as is texture of the food and the wine, and the flavor of each partner in the pairing. Flavor involves two aspects: intensity of flavor and the nature of the flavors.

Your first step in choosing a wine, then, is to think about these questions:

- How flavorful is the food?
- How delicate or heavy is the food?
- What flavors dominate the dish (for example, spicy flavors, or bitter flavors, or earthy flavors like mushrooms, and so on)?
- What kind of texture does the food have?

The second step is to consider which wines you have (or could buy) that resemble the food in flavor intensity, weight, flavors, or texture — or that contrast with the food on any of those points in a way that seems interesting.

Pairing flavor intensities

Half the trick in matching white wines with food is to heed the issue of the food's flavor intensity. Some white wines have very little flavor and they can easily be overwhelmed by a flavorful dish. And some white wines have so much flavor that they can easily overwhelm a delicate dish.

In most cases, you are wise to choose a wine whose flavor intensity matches that of the dish, rather than to seek an interesting contrast between the wine and food:

- White wines with fairly neutral flavors — such as most Italian whites, Muscadet, French wines based on the Ugni Blanc (Trebbiano) grape, inexpensive white Bordeaux wines, most Pinot Blanc-based wines, and inexpensive Chilean whites — are candidates for matching with dishes that are rather bland in flavor.

- Moderately flavorful types of white wine — such as Sancerre, Oregon Pinot Gris, most German wines, white Burgundies, Spanish and Portuguese white wines, whites from France's Rhône Valley, and most South African whites — are likely partners for moderately flavorful dishes, such as chicken, veal, or pork dishes that don't have intensely flavored sauces.

- The most flavorful types of white wine — California Chardonnays and Sauvignon Blancs, Gewürztraminers, Australian Chardonnays and Semillon-Chardonnay blends, New Zealand Sauvignon Blanc, and Vouvray, to name a few — have the odds in their favor for matching with very flavorful dishes.

Pairing weights

Nearly as important as flavor intensity is the relative weight of the wine and the food. Again, in most cases, a similarity of weight between the wine and food is desirable — a light-bodied white wine with light dishes, a full-bodied white with heavier dishes.

You might sometimes choose to serve a light wine with a heavy dish — contrasting, rather than matching, the weight of the food and the wine — but in such cases the wine is likely to take a back seat to the food, setting off the food at its own expense, rather than remaining an equal partner in the pairing:

- ✓ Light-bodied white wines include most Italian whites, delicate German wines, inexpensive white Bordeaux wines, Muscadet, and some Sancerre wines.

- ✓ Medium-bodied white wines include Pouilly-Fumé, Pouilly-Fuissé, South African whites, inexpensive California Chardonnay wines, better white Bordeaux wines, most Côte d'Or white Burgundies, premier cru and grand cru Chablis.

- ✓ Full-bodied white wines include better California Chardonnays, most Alsace whites, Australia Chardonnays and Semillon-Chardonnays, Rhône Valley whites and the best Côte d'Or white Burgundies.

Turn to Chapters 6 through 14 for descriptions of all these types of wine.

Pairing flavors

We consider the relative flavors of the food and wine much less important than the relative weight and flavor intensity of the food and wine. If the flavors of the food and wine are similar — herbal accents in the wine and herbal flavors in the food, for example — or if the flavors contrast nicely — a lemony-tasting wine with a buttery dish, for example — the meal is certainly enhanced. But failing to match or contrast flavors won't ruin the food-and-wine combination the way an imbalance of relative flavor intensity does. The flavors themselves are just the icing on the cake.

Types of flavor that you are likely to find in foods, and some wines with similar flavors, are

- ✓ **Herbal flavors:** Sauvignon Blanc wines, especially from the Loire Valley; Alsace Pinot Blanc; and Soave

✓ **Earthy flavors:** White Burgundies, especially Mâcon wines (Mâcon-Villages, St. Veran) and Chablis; Sancerre and Pouilly-Fumé; and Alsace whites

✓ **Fruity flavors:** California Chardonnays and Sauvignon Blancs, German Rieslings, most Alsace whites, and young Riesling wines

✓ **Vegetal flavors:** New Zealand Sauvignon Blanc wines, many Napa Valley Sauvignon Blanc wines, Chilean Sauvignon Blancs, and Gruner Veltliner wines from Austria

✓ **Smoky flavors:** Most oaked white wines, such as California and Australian Chardonnays, white Burgundies from the Côte d'Or, and better white Bordeaux wines

Pairing texture

The issue of texture represents more icing on the cake of food-and-wine pairing. Textural similarities — such as a creamy white wine with a creamy dish — can add an extra dimension of interest to a particular food-and-wine combination, as can textural contrast — such as a crackling crisp wine with a creamy dish. The relative textures of the wine and food are certainly worth considering when you're attempting to match a wine with a particular dish — but only after you have considered the more important issues of flavor intensity and weight.

For more about the concept of texture in wine, turn to Chapter 1.

Concrete suggestions

If the theory of food-and-wine pairing leaves you uninspired and what you really want are some specific suggestions, here's where you can turn:

✓ Turn to Chapter 19 of our book *Wine For Dummies* to read about some classic food-and-wine combinations.

✓ Look for the Wine and Dine icon in Chapters 6 through 14, to learn which foods go well with the various types of wine discussed in each chapter.

✓ Ask for help from your wine merchant; retailers routinely advise their customers on wines to accompany specific meals or dishes.

The Particulars of White

Some white wines have characteristics beyond their weight, flavor intensity, texture, and specific flavors that must be taken into consideration when you pair the wines with food. What would otherwise be a very good white-wine-and-food match-up can be sabotaged by hidden sweetness in the wine or bitterness from oak. (Maybe espionage is on your menu after all!)

The sweetness issue

Excluding dessert wines, the majority of white wines in the world are categorized as *dry*, that is, not sweet. Therefore, wine drinkers often assume that if they steer clear of German whites and Rieslings (the wines most notorious for sweetness — but many of which, ironically, are dry), the white wine they select will be dry. As if!

In reality, the line between dry and sweet in white wine is

- ✔ Arbitrary
- ✔ A matter of individual perception
- ✔ A favorite hockey puck in the game of wine marketing

Some experts claim that sweetness below .5 percent in a wine is not detectable to most humans, while other experts argue that any sweetness above .2 percent is in fact detectable. (Your own ability to detect sweetness might fall somewhere in between; everyone has individual thresholds at which various tastes can begin to be detected.) In any case, the *perceived* sweetness of a wine reflects more than just the wine's measurable sweetness level — it depends on the balance of acid, sweetness, and alcohol in the wine.

- ✔ High-acid white wines taste *less sweet* than their numbers indicate.
- ✔ High-alcohol white wines taste *sweeter* than their numbers.

Furthermore, because many wine drinkers actually like some sweetness in their wines but would never admit it, wine labels frequently proclaim wines to be dry when, in fact, they taste somewhat sweet.

For anyone accustomed to drinking sweet soft drinks or fruit juice with dinner, none of this talk about sweetness really matters. But wine lovers accustomed to drinking wine with their dinner can find the unexpected sweetness of a supposedly dry white wine to be disruptive to the food pairing.

White wines with some sweetness — most California white wines, Vouvrays, Liebfraumilch and some other German whites, some Rieslings, and some Gewürztraminers, for example — are best paired with dishes that have some element of sweetness themselves, such as fruit and sweet vegetables such as carrots, or have sweet sauces such as barbecue sauce or many Asian sauces.

The oak issue

Some white wines that are aged in oak have noticeable *tannin* — a bitter-tasting substance more commonly associated with red wines, which take tannin from their grapeskins. White wines can absorb tannin from the oak barrels as they age.

White wines with tannin can be difficult matches with any dishes that have their own bitter flavors (such as dishes with walnuts or bitter green vegetables), because the effect of bitter-upon-bitter can be too strong. Salty dishes can taste unpleasant with a tannic wine, and acidic dishes (a dish with a strong lemon influence, for example) can make wine tannins taste very sharp.

Fortunately, most white wines that are heavily oaked — such as most California Chardonnays — are somewhat sweet, too; their sweetness counterbalances their own bitterness and neutralizes, to some extent, the effect of tannin on the food. Nevertheless, very oaky white wines are more difficult to pair with food than discreetly oaked or unoaked whites.

The acid test

White wines that are high in acidity can be a particular pleasure with food. Crisp acidity in a wine refreshes the mouth, stimulates the flow of saliva, and leaves you ready for another bite. The next time that you drink a crisp white wine (such as a Muscadet, a Sancerre, a Soave, or a Pinot Grigio) with food, notice whether the bottle becomes empty sooner than you expected. In our experience, crisp white wines are so easy to enjoy with food that they seem to evaporate into thin air!

Most crisp white wines fall into the light-bodied, low flavor-intensity category. To the extent that you aim for a harmonious, balanced match between your wine and your food, your opportunities to drink these wines are infrequent. On evenings when you choose not to give much thought to your wine-and-food pairing, however, crisp white wines are a good, all-purpose choice.

Almost all white wines from Italy fall into the high-acid category. Leave it to the Italians to make wines that are easy with food!

Warmer is richer

A final issue that affects the way a white wine works with food is the wine's temperature. Any white wine that is served very cold (cold enough to cause condensation on the outside of your wine glass) tastes lighter and less flavorful than it would at a warmer temperature — regardless of how rich or flavorful the wine otherwise is.

Try serving white wines chilled rather than cold; between 58° and 62°F is the best range. Fine white wines especially deserve the proper temperature, so that their subtleties and complexities can show. About 30 minutes in the refrigerator should be all it takes.

Part II
A World of White Wine

In this part . . .

We sometimes wonder what Jules Verne's Phileas Fogg drank on his 80-day voyage around the world. He probably didn't enjoy half as many different types of white wine as you find on the pages of the chapters that follow, because the wine world was very small in his day.

Wine drinkers today have so many choices in white wine that it's almost too much of a good thing. And that's exactly why this part of the book should be valuable. For every type of wine that we describe, we list our recommended producers and/ or specific wines that you can buy.

Some of our very favorite wines are a little pricey, we admit, but you can find plenty of recommended wines under $10 a bottle or even lower. Just remember not to linger too long in any one wine region: the whole world of white wines beckons!

Chapter 6

California Chardonnay

*T*he story of California Chardonnay is the story of the evolution in drinking habits of an entire nation.

For most of America's history, sweet, alcohol-fortified wines prevailed over regular "table" wines. Those who did drink dry table wines were mainly immigrants who carried their European winemaking traditions with them to the U.S. — and they tended to drink dry *red* wine rather than white wine. As recently as 20 years ago, vodka and gin — not wine — were the dry white alcoholic beverages of choice in the United States. What white wine Americans *did* drink was usually a semi-sweet wine blended from anonymous grapes and sold mainly in large glass jugs. Then America discovered Chardonnay.

Varietal Wines Discover America

The first domestic white wines that we ever drank (longer ago than we care to admit) had names such as Chablis (sometimes called "Golden Chablis" or "Mountain Chablis"), Rhine Wine, and Sauterne. These wines all tasted the same — rather bland, high in alcohol, and fairly sweet. They were the product of inexpensive, easy-to-grow grape varieties such as French Colombard and Thompson Seedless (the latter also known as Sultana) that were grown in the hot San Joaquin (Central) Valley in California.

But a transformation was under way in post-World War II America. People started flying to Europe, and many of them discovered the European tradition of enjoying dry wine with meals. And the wines they enjoyed were usually better than the domestic jug wines available back home. Demand for dry wine in America increased.

An even more important development for *white* wine consumption has been the growing health-consciousness of many Americans during the past 20 years. As fish, poultry, vegetables, and pasta became more popular, and heavier cuisines based on red meat less popular, Americans turned to dry white wines as their wines of choice. By the early 1980s, Chardonnay — the one dry white wine that seems to suit so many wine-drinkers' tastes — became America's wine.

The growth of Chardonnay in America exemplifies the trend toward *varietal wines,* wines named after the (usually noble) grape varieties from which the wines are made (see Chapter 3 for a discussion of grape varieties).

Generic versus varietal, or what's in a name?

American wine producers, mostly European immigrants, "borrowed" the names of popular European white wines — such as Chablis, Rhine, and Sauterne (actually, the French spell it Sauternes) — when they named their domestic white wine blends. In fact, the European wines that carry those names are far different from the similarly named, inexpensive, domestic wines in the U.S. (For one thing, the European versions are made in prestigious wine regions for which the wines are named; for another thing, they are made from noble grape varieties such as Chardonnay, Riesling, Sauvignon Blanc, and Sémillon.)

Wine writers refer to these inexpensive, domestic wines as *generic* wines because their names are neither legitimate place names (as most European wine names are) nor grape variety names.

Today, all the finest white wines in the U.S. are made from noble grape varieties and most of them — such as Chardonnay, Sauvignon Blanc, and Riesling — are *varietal* wines, that is, they are named after their grape varieties.

California Chardonnay — the Ruling Queen

The most popular dry wine in the United States is Chardonnay, especially California Chardonnay. The only serious contender at present — of any color — is White Zinfandel (but that's really a slightly sweet pink wine made from red Zinfandel grapes).

One of the reasons Chardonnay has become so popular in the United States — in addition to the fact that people like the way it tastes — is simply that Chardonnay is a white wine! Many American wine drinkers prefer white wine to red because

✔ Most Americans did not grow up in a wine-drinking culture, and new wine drinkers find white wine easier to drink than red wine because it is less tannic and austere.

✔ With much of the food Americans eat today, white wine goes better than red. Chardonnay, for example, is delicious with poultry (especially chicken) all kinds of seafood (especially lobster), salmon, other fish in light sauces, veal, and ham. Chardonnay is also fine with creamy cheeses such as Brie or Camembert.

Chardonnay, probably as a grape variety and certainly as a wine, originated in France (in fact, there is a village named Chardonnay in the Burgundy region of France). Many wine connoisseurs maintain that the greatest examples of Chardonnay still come from the Burgundy region; these wines have names such as Montrachet *(mon rah shay)*, Meursault *(muhr so)*, Corton-Charlemagne *(cor ton shahr luh mahn)*, and Pouilly-Fuisse *(pwee fwee say)*. See Chapter 10 for more information on these French Chardonnay-based wines.

Two California pioneers of Chardonnay in the post-World War II era were Fred and Eleanor McCrea, who released their first Chardonnay from their Stony Hill Vineyard at Spring Mountain (in the Napa Valley wine region, north of San Francisco) in 1952, and James Zellerbach, who planted the variety at his Hanzell Vineyards in Sonoma Valley (near the coast, north of San Francisco) the same year. But it was not until the 1970s, when the wine boom hit California and hundreds of new wineries opened, that Chardonnay really began to achieve its current popularity as a white wine.

Chardonnay around the world

Chardonnay is the wine world's most popular white grape variety. Just about every country that produces wine produces a Chardonnay. In addition to the U.S., Chardonnay is especially prevalent in France, Australia, Chile, and South Africa, and is becoming increasingly popular in Italy.

The California style

California's wine-growing regions are generally warmer and dryer than France's — therefore, California Chardonnay wines tend to differ from French wines made from the Chardonnay grape (see Chapter 10). Even if many of the better California wineries grow Chardonnay in the coolest vineyard areas of the state (or buy their grapes from cool areas), soil differences and winemaking techniques make the wines taste distinctly different from French wines. In fact, Australian Chardonnays (see Chapter 9) resemble California Chardonnays more than the French versions do.

In general, California Chardonnays are made from very ripe grapes and thus have a high alcohol content. They are usually more full-bodied than their French counterparts, with more assertive flavors and more fruitiness. Logically, California Chardonnays should be fairly low in acid because their grapes are so ripe, but in fact many producers add acid to the juice so that the wine ends up being firm in acidity.

California Chardonnays vary somewhat in style, especially at different price levels. The least expensive wines tend to have the most obvious flavors, while the most expensive wines have subtler flavors. (Subtlety of flavor is a valued characteristic for serious wine lovers — perceiving "hidden" characteristics in the wine is half the fun!)

The better California Chardonnays are made 100 percent from the Chardonnay grape variety. But the less expensive brands often exercise their legal right to blend 25 percent of other grapes in their Chardonnay to keep production costs low. (Chardonnay is the most expensive white grape in California.) Depending on which grape is used for that blending, the "Chardonnay" can have flowery aromas, or a distinctly peachy flavor, or even an herbal character.

Nearly all California Chardonnays are oaky. The better wines are aged in oak casks (after having been fermented in stainless steel tanks), and the best wines are actually fermented *and* aged in oak. (See Chapter 2 for more information on the use of oak in making white wines.) The oak imparts aromas and flavors of vanilla and spice to the wine, enhancing the wine's flavors and making it more complex; in the best cases, the wine also gains a rich, creamy texture from the oak.

To simulate the effect of aging in oak barrels (at a fraction of the cost of real barrels), producers of inexpensive Chardonnays often let oak chips soak in the wine. A very few California Chardonnays are produced entirely in stainless steel so that you can taste the actual fruit of the wine without any interference from oak.

Other important considerations that influence the style and quality of California Chardonnay include the

- ✔ Size of the crop (high-yielding vines produce more dilute wines)
- ✔ Location of the vineyard
- ✔ Clone (version) of the Chardonnay grape that is used
- ✔ Individual style of the winemaker/winery

Naturally, factors such as low-yielding vines and outstanding vineyard sites increase not only the quality of the wine but also the cost. The Chardonnays we list in Category 3, following — and to some extent those in Category 2 — reflect these quality factors, leading to the unavoidable conclusion: The highest-quality Chardonnays are expensive.

Fortunately, an expensive, intense, high-quality Chardonnay isn't always what the occasion calls for. At simple luncheons, picnics, parties, large gatherings, or even light dinners, a lighter-bodied, straightforward Chardonnay may be far more suitable than a more expensive wine. Turn to Chapter 5 for food-pairing suggestions.

Recommended California Chardonnays

California Chardonnays start at about $4 a bottle and can go up to about $40, with a few even more expensive. And they vary quite a lot in quality and style from one end of the price spectrum to the other. We have divided California Chardonnays into three categories stylistically, according to the price of the wine.

Naturally, our characterizations of each style are generalizations; they don't necessarily apply to every wine in each category — just to most of them. Our categories are

- **Easy-drinking Chardonnays:** Relatively soft, fruity, usually slightly sweet (compared to more expensive Chardonnays) and often quite oaky. Wines in this group range from $4 to $12 a bottle. You should drink them young, as they are not made for aging.

- **Better Chardonnays:** Usually dry and quite oaky, with good flavor concentration and intensity. Wines in this group are in the $12 to $25 price range. You can begin enjoying them as soon as you buy them, but their quality usually holds until about four years after the vintage.

- **California's elite Chardonnays:** Full-bodied, intensely concentrated, and often more subtle (less obviously flavorful) than the less expensive wines. Typically fermented in new oak barrels, these wines often boast a rich, creamy texture. Wines in this group cost over $25, and they usually need a few years of aging to reach their peak quality. Drink them starting about three or four years after the vintage date, for up to about their tenth year (in the really good vintages).

For each category, we name what we believe to be the best wines, alphabetically. Many wineries make more than one Chardonnay wine. They might make a basic Chardonnay, a "reserve," and/or a Chardonnay mix from the grapes of a single, specific vineyard. If a wine is a *reserve* or *single-vineyard* Chardonnay, we indicate that in listing the wine.

Chablis becomes white wine becomes Chardonnay

Although many people still just ask for "a glass of white wine" when they go to a party, bar, or restaurant, more specific language has crept into wine drinkers' vocabularies. Fifteen to twenty years ago, those wine drinkers who specified what kind of white wine they wanted invariably asked for a "Chablis" (not meaning, of course, the super-dry, real thing — French Chablis — but the bland, semi-dry American jug-wine version). Today, those who specify ask for Chardonnay.

✔ **When we give a geographical location for a wine,** the location indicates the origin of the grapes, which is not in every case the location of the winery.

✔ **If two separate locations are mentioned,** we are referring to two separate Chardonnays made by the same producer.

✔ **When no vineyard is named,** the wine is a blend of two or more vineyards, or the producer's basic wine.

✔ **We mark our own personal favorites** with a wine glass ❢ symbol, and wines that are really good values, a ¢.

The following lists — and all the lists of recommended wines in this book — are *not all-encompassing*. Even though these lists are long, they represent only a small fraction of California's wines. *We believe the wines listed are some of California's best;* please forgive us if we have left out one of your favorites.

Easy-drinking Chardonnays

Easy-drinking Chardonnays are relatively soft, usually slightly sweet (compared to more expensive Chardonnays), and often quite oaky. Wines in this group range from $4 to $12 a bottle. You should drink them as soon as they are available (and within their first few years), as they are not made for aging. Table 6-1 lists our recommendations. Our favorites are marked with a ❢; wines that are good values are marked with a ¢.

Second labels

Some wineries have come up with a perfect solution for their less-than-perfect grapes (grapes grown in vineyards that are not the winery's best sites, or grapes from young vines). The solution is to create a *second label* for the wines made from such grapes, and to sell that second label wine at a lower price than their prestigious, primary brand. The winery's high image lends value to the second-label wine. For example, knowing that Stag's Leap Wine Cellars is one of the established stars among Napa Valley wineries, you would expect that winery's second-label wine, Hawk Crest, to be a reliable, inexpensive alternative to the pricier Stag's Leap wines. And you would be right (as long as your expectations are not *too* high!)

Table 6-1 Recommended Easy-Drinking Chardonnay Wines

Producer	*Wine*	*Location of Vineyard*
Arrowood Vineyards	Domaine de Grand Archer Chardonnay	Sonoma County
Beaulieu *(bo l'yuh)* Vineyards (BV)	"Beau Tour" Chardonnay	Napa Valley
Belvedere Winery	Chardonnay	Alexander Valley
Beringer Vineyards	Chardonnay	Napa Valley
Bonterra Vineyards (Fetzer Vineyards' organic wine)	Chardonnay	Mendocino County
♏¢ Chateau Souverain	Chardonnay	Sonoma County
♏¢ Chateau Woltner (their basic wine)	Chardonnay	Howell Mountain
Christophe	Chardonnay	Napa County
Clos du Bois	Barrel Fermented Chardonnay	Alexander Valley
B.R. Cohn Winery	Silver Label Chardonnay	Carneros
¢ Estancia	Chardonnay	Monterey County
Fetzer Vineyards	"Barrel Select" Chardonnay Reserve Chardonnay	Mendocino County Mendocino County
Forest Glen	Barrel Fermented Chardonnay	Sonoma County
Geyser Peak Winery	Chardonnay	Sonoma County
Glen Ellen Winery	Chardonnay "Proprietor's Reserve"	California
♏¢ Guenoc Winery	Chardonnay	California
Hacienda Wine Cellars	"Clair de Lune" Chardonnay	California
Hawk Crest (second-label, Stag's Leap Wine Cellars)	Chardonnay	California
♏ Hess Select (second-label, The Hess Collection)	Chardonnay	California
♏ Husch Vineyards	Chardonnay	Mendocino County

Producer	Wine	Location of Vineyard
Kendall-Jackson	"Vintner's Reserve" Chardonnay	California
Lockwood Vineyard	Chardonnay	Monterey County
J. Lohr Winery	"Riverstone" Chardonnay	Monterey County
Mark West Vineyards	Barrel Fermented Chardonnay	Russian River Valley
Louis M. Martini Winery	Chardonnay	Napa Valley
Meridian Vineyards	Chardonnay	Santa Barbara County
♟ ¢ Mill Creek Vineyards	Chardonnay	Dry Creek Valley
♟ Robert Mondavi Winery	"Coastal" Chardonnay	Central Coast
♟ ¢ Napa Ridge	Chardonnay, all bottlings (Central Coast, North Coast, Napa, and Reserve)	Central Coast; North Coast; Napa
R.H. Phillips Vineyard	"Barrel Cuvée" Chardonnay	Dunnigan Hills
Q.C. Fly (second-label, Bouchaine Vineyards)	Chardonnay	California
Rabbit Ridge Vineyards	Chardonnay	Sonoma County
Raymond Vineyard	"Amberhill Chardonnay"	California
Round Hill Winery	Chardonnay	California
Rutherford Ranch (second-label, Round Hill Winery)	Chardonnay	California
Sebastiani Vineyards	Chardonnay	Sonoma County
Taft Street Winery	Chardonnay	Sonoma County
Ivan Tamas Winery	Reserve Chardonnay ♟ Hayes Ranch Chardonnay	Livermore Valley Livermore Valley
Trefethen Vineyards (second-label)	"Eshcol" Chardonnay	Napa Valley
♟ Villa Mt. Eden	"Cellar Select" Chardonnay	California
Wente Vineyards	Chardonnay, Wente Family Estate Selection	Central Coast

Better Chardonnays

Table 6-2 lists our recommendations for the better Chardonnays, which are usually dry and quite oaky, with good flavor concentration and intensity. They are in the $12 to $25 price range. You can begin enjoying them as soon as you buy them, but their quality will usually hold until about four years after the vintage. Our favorites are marked with a ♟.

Table 6-2 Recommended Better Chardonnay Wines

Producer	Wine	Location of Vineyard
Acacia Vineyards	Reserve Chardonnay	Carneros
Arrowood Vineyards	Chardonnay	Sonoma County
♟ Au Bon Climat	Chardonnay	Santa Barbara County
Bannister Winery	Allen Vineyard Chardonnay	Russian River Valley
Beaulieu *(bo l'yuh)* Vineyards (BV)	Carneros Reserve	Carneros
Belvedere Winery	"Preferred Stock" Chardonnay	Russian River Valley
♟ Beringer Vineyards	Private Reserve Chardonnay	Napa Valley
♟ Bernardus Vineyards	Chardonnay	Monterey County
Burgess Cellars	Chardonnay, Triere Vineyard Reserve	Napa Valley
Byron Vineyards	Estate Chardonnay	Santa Barbara County
	Reserve Chardonnay	Santa Barbara County
Cakebread Cellars	Chardonnay	Napa Valley
Calera Wine Company	Chardonnay	Mount Harlan
	Chardonnay	Central Coast
Cambria Winery	Katherine's Vineyard Chardonnay	Santa Maria Valley
	Reserve Chardonnay	Santa Maria Valley
♟ Chalk Hill Winery	Chardonnay	Chalk Hill
♟ Chateau Montelena Winery	Chardonnay	Napa Valley

Producer	Wine	Location of Vineyard
Chateau St. Jean	Robert Young Vineyard Chardonnay,	Alexander Valley
	Belle Terre Vineyard Chardonnay	Alexander Valley
Chateau Souverain	Chardonnay	Carneros
	Chardonnay (all Single-Vineyard bottlings)	Russian River Valley
♀ Cinnabar Vineyard	Chardonnay	Santa Cruz Mountains
Clos du Bois	Calcaire Vineyard Chardonnay,	Alexander Valley
	Flintwood Vineyard Chardonnay	Dry Creek Valley
Clos Pegase	Chardonnay	Carneros
	Mitsuko's Vineyard Chardonnay	Carneros
Cronin Vineyards	Chardonnay, all bottlings	Napa Valley; Alexander Valley; Santa Cruz Mountains
Cuvaison Winery	Chardonnay	Carneros
	Reserve Chardonnay	Carneros
De Loach Vineyards	O.F.S. Chardonnay	Russian River Valley
Dehlinger Winery	Chardonnay	Russian River Valley
Edmeades Winery	Dennison Vineyard Chardonnay	Anderson Valley
	Estate Chardonnay	Mendocino County
Edna Valley Vineyard	Estate Chardonnay	Edna Valley
	Reserve Chardonnay	Edna Valley
Gary Farrell Wines	Allen Vineyard Chardonnay	Russian River Valley
	Chardonnay	Russian River Valley
Ferrari-Carano Winery	Chardonnay	Alexander Valley
Fisher Vineyards	"Coach Insignia" Chardonnay	Sonoma County
♀ Flora Springs Wine Company	Barrel Fermented Chardonnay	Napa Valley

(continued)

Table 6-2 *(continued)*

Producer	Wine	Location of Vineyard
♟ Forman Vineyard	Chardonnay	Napa Valley
Foxen Vineyard	Chardonnay	Santa Maria Valley
Franciscan Vineyards	Barrel Fermented Oakville Estate Chardonnay	Napa Valley
Gainey Vineyard	♟ Limited Selection Chardonnay	Santa Ynez Valley
	Chardonnay	Santa Barbara County
Gallo-Sonoma	Laguna Ranch Vineyard Chardonnay	Russian River Valley
Geyser Peak Winery	Trione Vineyard Reserve Chardonnay	Alexander Valley
Girard Winery	Old Vines Chardonnay	Napa Valley
Greenwood Ridge Vineyards	Du Pratt Vineyard Chardonnay	Anderson Valley
Guenoc Winery	G. Magoon Vineyard Reserve Chardonnay	Guenoc Valley
	Estate Chardonnay	Guenoc Valley
Handley Cellars	Chardonnay	Dry Creek Valley
	♟ Chardonnay	Anderson Valley
The Hess Collection	Chardonnay	Mount Veeder (Napa Valley)
♟ Jordan Vineyard	Chardonnay	Alexander Valley
Kalin Cellars	Chardonnay, all bottlings	Sonoma County and Livermore Valley
Kendall-Jackson	Camelot Vineyard Chardonnay	Santa Maria Valley
Landmark Vineyards	Damaris Vineyard Chardonnay	Alexander Valley
	Two Williams Vineyard Chardonnay	Sonoma
MacRostie Winery	Chardonnay	Carneros
	Reserve Chardonnay	Carneros
♟ Mayacamas Vineyards	Chardonnay	Napa Valley
Merryvale Vineyards	Reserve Chardonnay	Napa Valley
Robert Mondavi Winery	Chardonnay	Carneros
	Chardonnay	Napa Valley

Producer	Wine	Location of Vineyard
♆ Mount Eden Vineyards	MacGregor Vineyard Chardonnay	Edna Valley
Navarro Vineyards	Chardonnay Reserve Chardonnay	Anderson Valley Anderson Valley
Newton Vineyard	Chardonnay	Napa Valley
Oakville Ranch Vineyards	Vista Vineyard Chardonnay ORV Chardonnay	Napa Valley Napa Valley
Joseph Phelps Vineyards	Chardonnay	Carneros
Qupe Cellars	Sierra Madre Vineyard Chardonnay	Santa Barbara County
Rabbit RidgeVineyards	Rabbit Ridge Ranch Chardonnay	Russian River Valley
Kent Rasmussen Winery	Chardonnay	Napa Valley
♆ Ravenswood	Sangiacomo Vineyard Chardonnay	Carneros
♆ Ridge Vineyards	Chardonnay	Santa Cruz Mountains
♆ J. Rochioli Vineyard	Chardonnay	Russian River Valley
St. Francis Winery	Chardonnay Reserve	Sonoma Valley
Saintsbury	♆ Carneros Reserve Chardonnay Chardonnay	Carneros Carneros
♆ Sanford Winery	Chardonnay	Santa Barbara County
♆ Shafer Vineyards	Red Shoulder Ranch Chardonnay	Carneros
Silverado Vineyards	Chardonnay	Napa Valley
Simi Winery	Chardonnay	Sonoma County
Robert Sinskey Vineyards	Chardonnay	Carneros
Smith-Madrone Vineyard	Chardonnay	Napa Valley
Sonoma-Cutrer Vineyards	Cutrer Vineyard Chardonnay Les Pierres Vineyard Chardonnay	Sonoma Coast Sonoma Coast
Sonoma-Loeb	Private Reserve Chardonnay	Sonoma County

(continued)

Table 6-2 *(continued)*

Producer	Wine	Location of Vineyard
♥ Stag's Leap Wine Cellars	Chardonnay	Napa Valley
Stonestreet	Chardonnay	Sonoma County
Swanson Vineyards	Chardonnay Reserve Chardonnay	Carneros Napa Valley
Talley Vineyards	Chardonnay Oliver's Vineyard Chardonnay	Arroyo Grande Valley Edna Valley
Marimar Torres Estate	Don Miguel Vineyard Chardonnay	Green Valley
♥ Villa Mt. Eden	Grand Reserve Chardonnay	Carneros
Wild Horse Winery	Chardonnay	Central Coast
Zaca Mesa Winery	Chardonnay, all bottlings	Santa Barbara County
ZD Winery	Chardonnay	California

Recent good vintages of California Chardonnay

Most California white wines are best when they are young. For Chardonnay, we recommend that, with a few exceptions, you drink the wines within five or six years of the vintage. You can drink inexpensive California Chardonnays — those costing less than $12 a bottle — as soon as you buy them, which will usually be within two years of the vintage date.

Fortunately, California has had a string of good vintages lately: The last five released vintages (1990, 1991, 1992, 1993, and 1994) have all been fine, with **1990, 1992,** and **1993** being especially fine; also, our preliminary tastings indicate that 1995 will be good.

California's elite Chardonnays

California's elite Chardonnays are full-bodied, intensely concentrated, and often more subtle (less obviously flavorful) than the less expensive wines. Typically fermented in new oak, these wines often boast a rich, creamy texture. Wines in this group cost over $25, and they usually need a few years of aging to reach their peak quality. Drink them starting about three or four years after the vintage date, up to about their tenth year (for the really good vintages). Table 6-3 lists our recommendations among California's elite Chardonnays. Our personal favorites are marked with a ☿. Any wine available by mailing list only is marked with an envelope. You can find the addresses for these mailing lists at the end of this chapter.

Table 6-3 Recommended Elite California Chardonnay Wines

Producer	Wine	Location of Vineyard
☿ Au Bon Climat (oh bahn klee maht)	Chardonnay, Single-Vineyard & Reserve bottlings	Santa Barbara
☿ Beringer Vineyards	Sbragia Limited Release Chardonnay	Napa Valley
Chalone Vineyard	Estate Chardonnay	Chalone (Monterey County)
	Reserve Chardonnay	Chalone
Chateau Potelle	VGS Chardonnay	Mount Veeder
El Molino	Chardonnay	Napa Valley
Far Niente Winery	Chardonnay	Napa Valley
Ferrari-Carano Winery	Reserve Chardonnay	California
☿ Fisher Vineyards	Whitney's Vineyard Chardonnay	Sonoma County
Franciscan Vineyards	"Cuvée Sauvage" Oakville Estate Chardonnay	Napa Valley
Girard Winery	Reserve Chardonnay	Napa Valley
Grgich Hills Cellar	Chardonnay ☿ Carneros Selection Chardonnay	Napa Valley Carneros
☿ Hanzell Vineyards	Chardonnay	Sonoma Valley
☿ Kistler Vineyards	Chardonnay, all Single-Vineyard bottlings	Russian River Valley and Sonoma

(continued)

Table 6-3 *(continued)*

Producer	Wine	Location of Vineyard
♟ Long Vineyards	Chardonnay	Napa Valley
♟ ✉ Marcassin Winery	Chardonnay, all bottlings	Carneros and Sonoma
♟ Matanzas Creek Winery	Chardonnay	Sonoma Valley
Merryvale Vineyards	"Silhouette" Chardonnay	Napa Valley
♟ Peter Michael Winery	Chardonnay, all bottlings	Napa and Sonoma
Robert Mondavi Winery	Reserve Chardonnay	Napa Valley
♟ Mount Eden Vineyards	Chardonnay	Santa Cruz Mountains
Newton Vineyard	Unfiltered Chardonnay	Napa Valley
♟ Pahlmeyer	Chardonnay	Napa Valley
Joseph Phelps Vineyards	"Ovation" Chardonnay	Napa Valley
♟ J. Rochioli Vineyard	Reserve Chardonnay	Russian River Valley
Sanford Winery	♟ Barrel Select Chardonnay ♟ Sanford & Benedict Vineyard Chardonnay	Santa Barbara County Santa Barbara County
♟ Silverado Vineyards	Limited Reserve Chardonnay	Napa Valley
♟ Simi Winery	Reserve Chardonnay	Sonoma County
♟ Stag's Leap Wine Cellars	Reserve Chardonnay	Napa Valley
Stony Hill Vineyard	Chardonnay	Napa Valley
Robert Talbott Vineyards	Chardonnay, all bottlings	Monterey County
♟ Villa Mt. Eden	Signature Series Chardonnay	Santa Barbara County
Vine Cliff Cellars	"Proprietress Reserve" Chardonnay	Napa Valley
♟ ✉ Williams & Selyem Winery	Allen Vineyard Chardonnay	Russian River Valley

For information about obtaining by mail some of the wines listed above, see Chapter 16 of *Wine For Dummies*, published by IDG Books Worldwide, Inc.

Where have all the simple wine names gone?

As you see from our lists of recommended California Chardonnays, some wines have names that are longer than most royal titles. Is this pure pretension on the part of the wineries?

Actually, most of the information in wine names is there to help wine drinkers understand exactly what they're drinking.

The grape name (Chardonnay, for example) identifies what grape the wine was made from. The place indicated as part of the wine's name (such as Napa Valley or Russian River Valley or even just California) is the official geographic area where the grapes were grown — useful to know, because the climate and soil of that place affect the nature of the wine. The vineyard name, if any, (such as Whitney's Vineyard or Sangiacomo Vineyard) identifies a more specific place where the grapes were grown; in theory, that more specific name offers wine lovers more specific information on the soil and climate that influenced the grapes — but in practical terms, the more specific place helps to distinguish different wines from the same grape made by the same producer. Terms like "Reserve" and "Barrel Select" have no legal meaning on U.S. wine labels, but they are often tip-offs that the wine is a producer's best and most expensive wine from that particular grape.

 (For the lowdown on which label terms are meaningful and which are meaningless, we recommend that you read Chapters 7 and 8 of *Wine For Dummies*.)

If every winery made only one wine from each grape, of course, wine names would be a lot shorter, and wine buying would be a lot simpler. But many winemakers can't resist the urge to separate their grapes according to where they were grown, making a separate wine from the grapes of each location — or the urge to experiment with different winemaking or aging techniques, resulting in several different wines. Personally, we can't complain. If we were winemakers, that's exactly what we would do!

Addresses for Mail-Order-Only Wineries

Marcassin Winery
P.O. Box 332
Calistoga, CA 94515
Telephone: 707-258-3608
Fax: 707-942-5633
(for all of Marcassin's Chardonnays — Carneros and Sonoma)

Williams & Selyem Winery
6575 Westside Road
Healdsburg, CA 95448-9416
Telephone: 707-433-6425
(for Williams & Selyem's Allen Vineyard Chardonnay —Russian River Valley, Sonoma)

Chapter 7
California Whites, Beyond Chardonnay

Chardonnay is such a popular wine in the U.S. that overlooking the many other good white wines from California is easy. Sauvignon Blanc, for one, has been Chardonnay's maid-in-waiting for a long time. Unfortunately, she has never really obtained the stardom, in the eyes of the wine-drinking public, that her producers had hoped. Other white wines from noble grapes, such as Riesling and Gewürztraminer, enjoy an even smaller share of the market place. Why have these other California white wines not made much of an impact on wine buyers? We discuss these issues in this chapter.

Sauvignon Blanc: California's "Other" White Wine

Sauvignon Blanc from California (that is, California wine that's made with the Sauvignon Blanc grape) holds second place to California Chardonnay in production and sales, but it holds a far-off second place.

As much as we hate to say so, we give California Sauvignon Blanc a barely passing grade in terms of quality. But the good news is that California Sauvignon Blancs are improving. Until a few years ago, Sauvignon Blanc wines from California were generally dull, bland, and neutral in flavor. To experience this grape variety at its best, you had to taste Cloudy Bay Winery's Sauvignon from New Zealand, Mulderbosch's Sauvignon from South Africa, Alois Lageder's Sauvignon from the Alto-Adige

(*AH dee jhay*) in Northern Italy, a good Sancerre or Pouilly Fumé (*pwee foo may*) from France's Loire Valley, or a good white Bordeaux from the Graves region (see Chapters 9, 11, and 13).

Too much of California's Sauvignon Blanc had been overproduced (the grape is a prolific grower) and/or not planted in the best sites — both situations resulting in less than ideal wines. Perhaps Sauvignon Blanc has been a victim of Chardonnay's success: Wineries didn't have to worry too much about Sauvignon Blanc as long as Chardonnay was selling so well.

But in the last several years, some California wineries have finally gotten a handle on Sauvignon Blanc. For one thing, winemakers are getting more particular about the vineyard sites for Chardonnay's "stepchild"; for another thing, growers are discovering how to ripen Sauvignon Blanc grapes more effectively. As a result, many of the wines we recommend below — especially in our second group, wines over $10 — show much more intense Sauvignon Blanc character than in previous years. In short, they now taste like Sauvignon Blancs — rather than imitation Chardonnays (an accusation Sauvignon Blancs have faced in the past from some wine critics).

Sauvignon Blanc at its best is a light-to-medium-bodied, very dry, lively white wine that goes extremely well with many foods, especially poultry, seafood, and fish. It should have crisp, racy flavors of minerals, herbs, various fruits (figs and melons, to name two), and/or green grass. A good Sauvignon Blanc should never be heavy or dull; rather, it should leave a refreshing, clean aftertaste on your palate.

Sauvignon Blanc is often blended with up to 25 percent Sémillon, for added body and complexity. This blending tradition hails from Bordeaux, where most of the dry white wines — especially in the Graves region — are a blend of Sauvignon Blanc and Sémillon. (See "Bordeaux Blanc" in Chapter 11).

Recommended California Sauvignon Blancs

Because we believe that, at present, not many great Sauvignon Blancs are being made in California, we have restricted our recommendations to the wines that we feel are the very best examples.

Fumé Blanc *is* Sauvignon Blanc

Have you ever picked up two white wines from California, noticed that one is called Fumé Blanc while the other is named Sauvignon Blanc, and wondered what the difference is? Basically, there isn't any difference! Fumé Blanc is just another name for Sauvignon Blanc.

 Back in the 1970s, Robert Mondavi renamed his Sauvignon Blanc "Fumé Blanc" (a tribute to the Loire Valley's Pouilly Fumé wine, which is made from the Sauvignon Blanc grape) and, at the same time, started making a dryer, crisper version of the wine. As with most of Mondavi's innovations, the name change and style change worked: sales increased dramatically. Naturally, many other wineries copied Mondavi's name change — and his dryer style of Sauvignon — with varying degrees of success. Today, some wineries (to add to the confusion of the two names) make both a "Sauvignon Blanc" and a "Fumé Blanc" in slightly different styles (one aged in oak, perhaps, and the other not). But there is no particular consistency among wineries regarding which style gets which name.

 Being less popular than Chardonnay, Sauvignon Blanc is relatively inexpensive — and the best wines are among the finest values of any of the world's dry white wines.

Most of the Sauvignon Blancs listed here have been blended with a small percentage of Sémillon. We have grouped the Sauvignon Blancs into two categories (happily, the under $10 group is as large as the $10 to $20 group):

  ✔ **Light- to medium-bodied Sauvignon Blancs:** Wines in this group tend to be light- to medium-bodied, have clear varietal flavor because they are often made without any oak-aging, and are ready to drink immediately when you purchase them, although they can age for a few years. These wines cost under $10.

Figure 7-1: A label from a popular California Sauvignon Blanc.

> ✔ **Better Sauvignon Blancs:** Wines in this group are medium-bodied, often have had some exposure to oak and therefore can have a complexity of flavors associated with oak-aging (see Chapter 3), have concentrated varietal character, and are capable of aging for several years. These wines are in the $10 to $20 price range.

In the sections that follow, we name what we believe to be the best wines, alphabetically within each group. These wines might be called Sauvignon Blanc, or Fumé Blanc, or both (some producers put both names on their labels, just for good measure!). The geographical location mentioned for a wine indicates the origin of the grapes.

Table 7-1 lists a selection of recommended light- to medium-bodied Sauvignon Blancs, which have clear varietal flavor because they are often made without any oak-aging. These wines are ready to drink immediately when you purchase them, although they can age for a few years. These wines cost under $10. Our favorites are marked with ☗; good values are marked with ¢.

Table 7-1   Light- to Medium-Bodied Sauvignon Blancs

Producer	Wine	Location of Vineyard
Beringer Vineyards	Fumé Blanc, "Meritage"	Napa Valley Knights Valley
♈ Bernardus Vineyards	Sauvignon Blanc	Monterey County
Chateau Souverain	Sauvignon Blanc, Barrel-Fermented	Alexander Valley
Chatom Vineyards	Sauvignon Blanc	Calaveras County
Clos du Bois	Sauvignon Blanc	Sonoma County
Dry Creek Vineyard	Fumé Blanc	Sonoma County
Gainey Vineyard	Sauvignon Blanc	Santa Ynez Valley
Geyser Peak Winery	Sauvignon Blanc	Sonoma County
♈ Handley Cellars	Sauvignon Blanc	Dry Creek Valley
Kenwood Vineyards	Sauvignon Blanc	Sonoma County
Lakewood	Sauvignon Blanc	Clear Lake
Murphy-Goode Estate Winery	Fumé Blanc	Alexander Valley
♈ ¢ Napa Ridge	Sauvignon Blanc	North Coast
♈ Navarro Vineyards	Sauvignon Blanc "Cuvée 128"	Mendocino County
♈ Robert Pepi Winery	Sauvignon Blanc, "Two-Heart Canopy"	Napa Valley
Preston Vineyards	Sauvignon Blanc, "Cuvée de Fumé"	Dry Creek Valley
Quivira Vineyards	Sauvignon Blanc Sauvignon Blanc Reserve	Dry Creek Valley Dry Creek Valley
♈ Sanford Winery	Sauvignon Blanc	Santa Barbara County
Seghesio Winery	Sauvignon Blanc	Sonoma County
Simi Winery	Sauvignon Blanc	Sonoma County
Voss Vineyards	Sauvignon Blanc	Napa Valley
Wente Vineyards	Sauvignon Blanc, Wente Family Estate Selection	Livermore Valley

When to drink California Sauvignon Blancs

Most California Sauvignon Blanc wines are at their best in the first three years after the vintage, but some of the better and more expensive versions can live five years or more. Many wine drinkers prefer to drink Sauvignon Blanc when the wine is very young, fresh, and lively. Every California vintage since 1990 — including the 1995 — has been very good. You should have no problem finding Sauvignon Blanc wines that are ready to drink.

The higher quality Sauvignon Blancs are medium bodied, often have had some exposure to oak, and therefore can have the complexity of flavor associated with oak-aging (see Chapter 3). Table 7-2 gives our recommendations among these wines. These wines have concentrated varietal flavor and are capable of aging for several years; they are in the $10 to $20 price range. Wines that cost more than $20 are marked with $$. Our personal favorites are marked with ¶. Good value wines are marked with ¢.

Table 7-2   Better California Sauvignon Blanc Wines

Producer	Wine	Location of Vineyard
Araujo *(ah RAU ho)* Estate	Sauvignon Blanc	Napa Valley
Babcock Vineyards	Sauvignon Blanc, 11 Oaks Ranch	Santa Ynez Valley
Chalk Hill Winery	Sauvignon Blanc	Chalk Hill
Dry Creek Vineyard	Fumé Blanc Reserve	Dry Creek Valley
¶ Duckhorn Vineyards	Sauvignon Blanc	Napa Valley
¶ Gary Farrell	Sauvignon Blanc, Rochioli Vineyard	Russian River Valley
Ferrari-Carano	Fumé Blanc Fumé Blanc Reserve	Sonoma County Sonoma County
Flora Springs	Sauvignon Blanc ¶ "Soliloquy"	Napa Valley Napa Valley
¶ Grgich Hills Cellar	Fumé Blanc	Napa Valley

Producer	Wine	Location of Vineyard
Kalin Cellars	Sauvignon Blanc 🍷 $$ Sauvignon Blanc	Potter Valley Livermore Valley
🍷 Matanzas Creek	Sauvignon Blanc	Sonoma County
🍷 Mayacamas Vineyards	Sauvignon Blanc	Napa Valley
Robert Mondavi	Fumé Blanc 🍷 $$ Fumé Blanc Reserve	Napa Valley Napa Valley
Murphy-Goode Estate Winery	Fumé Blanc Reserve	Alexander Valley
¢ Robert Pepi Winery	Reserve Select Sauvignon Blanc	Napa Valley
J. Rochioli Vineyard	Sauvignon Blanc 🍷 Sauvignon Blanc Reserve	Russian River Valley Russian River Valley
🍷 Selene	Sauvignon Blanc, Hyde Vineyard	Carneros
Signorello Vineyards	Sauvignon Blanc	Napa Valley
🍷 Simi Winery	Meritage "Sendal"	Sonoma County
Spottswoode	Sauvignon Blanc	Napa Valley

Far Back in the Pack: The Magnificent Seven

Bored with Chardonnay? But Sauvignon Blanc isn't your cup of tea? Then you might be a candidate for the ABC/S Club — *anything but Chardonnay or Sauvignon Blanc.*

If Chardonnay is by far the most popular white varietal wine in California and Sauvignon Blanc is a distant second, you can imagine how far back other white varietal wines are in sales. They're all good wines — they just haven't caught the fancy of most wine drinkers yet, for various reasons.

The two white wines that lately are gaining the attention of the ABC/S Club are Viognier (popular in France's Northern Rhône Valley, where it makes a wine called Condrieu; see Chapter 11) and Pinot Gris (popular in Alsace, France, and in Oregon; also known as Pinot Grigio in northeastern Italy; see Chapters 8, 11 and 13).

Seven white varietal wines made in California — besides Chardonnay and Sauvignon (Fumé) Blanc — warrant attention. We discuss these wines in the following sections, in alphabetical order, and we recommend some producers for each variety. Although these wines may be a little more difficult to find than the ubiquitous Chardonnay, any good wine shop should carry most, if not all, of them.

Chenin Blanc

Because the Chenin Blanc grape has so frequently been used as an inexpensive blending grape, Chenin Blanc wine just might be California's most maligned and neglected premium white varietal wine. In fact, most American wine drinkers would probably be surprised to learn what a stellar reputation this grape has in France's Loire Valley, and what magnificent Chenin Blanc wines, such as Vouvray, are made there (see Chapter 11).

At its best, California Chenin Blanc is a soft, easy-drinking, off-dry wine, with generous and pleasant fruity flavors of melon, peach, and/or citrus. California examples do not seem to have the amazing, high acidity of Loire Chenins (which makes those wines so long-lived); therefore, California Chenin Blancs should be consumed young, within two or three years.

If you find Chardonnays and Sauvignon Blancs too dry, the off-dry Chenin Blanc may be just the wine for you. (We had a heck of a time trying to find a white wine that one of our relatives would like, until we offered her a Chenin Blanc.) Even Chenin Blanc wines that are labeled "dry" seem somehow less dry and easier to like than many other white wines.

Table 7-3 lists some Chenin Blancs to try; our personal favorites are marked with ☙.

Table 7-3	Recommended California Chenin Blanc Wines		
Producer	*Wine*	*Location of Vineyard*	*Cost*
Chalone Vineyard	Chenin Blanc	Chalone, Gavilan Mountains	about $15
☙ Chappellet Vineyards	Dry Chenin Blanc	Napa Valley	$7.50
Dry Creek Vineyard	Dry Chenin Blanc	California	$7
Durney Vineyard	Chenin Blanc	Carmel Valley	$7 to $8

Producer	Wine	Location of Vineyard	Cost
♟ Foxen Vineyard	Chenin Blanc	Santa Barbara County	$12 to $13
Daniel Gehrs	Chenin Blanc "Le Chenay"	Monterey County	$8 to $8.50
	Chenin Blanc "Le Cheniere"	Santa Barbara County	$8 to $8.50
Husch Vineyards	Chenin Blanc, La Ribera Ranch	Mendocino County	$8
♟ Mirassou Vineyards	Family Selection Dry Chenin Blanc	Monterey County	$6
R.H. Phillips Vineyard	Dry Chenin Blanc	California	$6
Pine Ridge Winery	Chenin Blanc "La Petite Vigne"	Napa Valley	$10 to $11
Preston Vineyards	Chenin Blanc, Barrel Aged	Dry Creek Valley	$9
♟ White Oak Vineyards	Chenin Blanc	California	$7

Gewürztraminer

The pungent, spicy, floral white wine made from the Gewürztraminer grape is impossible to feel neutral about: You either like its exotic flavors, reminiscent of lychee fruit, or you don't. The variety is at its best in Alsace, France (see Chapter 11), but it can also do well in the cool-climate Anderson Valley in Mendocino County and in Sonoma's Russian River Valley.

If you have tried a California Gewürztraminer and have not been too thrilled with it, we understand and sympathize with you. Gewürztraminer has been a perennial underachiever in the U.S. But a handful of wineries have done quite well with this difficult grape variety. We recommend that you give California Gewürztraminer a second chance with one of the wines we recommend.

Some people like to drink Gewürztraminer with spicy Chinese, Thai, or Indian cuisine, thinking that this flavorful, spicy wine can match such savory foods. Although we personally prefer sparkling wine or Champagne with spicy cuisine, we think that pork, ham, sausages and sauerkraut, or soft cheeses are ideal with Gewürztraminer.

One wine-drinking couple's experience with white wine

It was a warm night. We had been drinking Chardonnays (and occasional Sauvignon Blancs) from various countries just about every night with dinner. Too hot for red wine. We decided to have a different white wine on that particular night with our grilled swordfish. We chose a 1992 Lazy Creek Gewürztraminer from California's Anderson Valley. It was perfect. Such distinctive flavors. So rich and flavorful. So delicious! We vowed to drink more Gewürztraminers — and other non-Chardonnays — with future dinners.

Some California wineries produce a dessert-style ("Late Harvest") Gewürztraminer, made from late-picked grapes — but dessert wines are beyond the scope of this book. You can read about those wines whenever we manage to convince our publisher that the world needs *Dessert Wines For Dummies.*

Well-made Gewürztraminer from grapes grown in a cool climate can be dry, rich in aromas and flavor, and absolutely delicious. We personally avoid the popular, off-dry versions, which usually sell for $5 or $6 (they're nice enough wines, but they're just not what Gewürztraminer is all about) in our book. Table 7-4 lists Gewürztraminers that are real palate-pleasers. Our favorites are marked with 🍷.

Table 7-4 Recommended California Gewürztraminer Wines

Producer	*Wine*	*Location of Vineyard*	*Cost*
Babcock Vineyards	Gewürztraminer	Santa Barbara County	$10 to $11
Bouchaine Vineyards	Dry Gewürztraminer	Russian River Valley	$8.50
🍷 Claiborne & Churchill Vintners	Dry Gewürztraminer	Central Coast	$8 to $9
De Loach Vineyards	Gewürztraminer, Early Harvest	Russian River Valley	$8 to $9
Firestone Vineyard	Gewürztraminer	Santa Barbara County	$8 to $9
🍷 Thomas Fogarty	Gewürztraminer	Monterey County	$9

Producer	Wine	Location of Vineyard	Cost
♟ Handley Cellars	Gewürztraminer	Anderson Valley	$8
Hop Kiln Winery	Gewürztraminer, M. Griffin Vineyards	Russian River Valley	$7 to $8
Husch Vineyards	Gewürztraminer	Anderson Valley	$9
♟ Lazy Creek Vineyards	Gewürztraminer	Anderson Valley	$11
Mark West Vineyards	Gewürztraminer	Russian River Valley	$9
♟ Martinelli Winery	Gewürztraminer	Russian River Valley	$7 to $9
♟ Navarro Vineyards	Dry Gewürztraminer	Anderson Valley	$9 to $10
♟ Z Moore Winery	Barrel Fermented Dry Gewürztraminer*	Russian River Valley	$10 to $11

*Unfortunately, Z Moore Winery, which had been specializing in state-of-the-art California Gewürztraminers, has just gone out of business. Obviously, Gewürztraminer is not popular enough with wine lovers.

If you enjoy Gewürztraminer, try to find a bottle of Z Moore Gewürz — while there are still a few around.

Pinot Blanc

For us, Pinot Blanc (a white mutation of the red Pinot Noir vine) is the most underrated white varietal wine in the U.S. We often prefer it to Chardonnay for its fruity vibrancy and lively assertiveness.

With the exception of a few wineries, such as Chalone Vineyards (which makes a wonderful Pinot Blanc, but in the barrel-fermented, oak-aged style of their Chardonnay), California Pinot Blancs usually are lighter-bodied than Chardonnays but have delicious upfront fruit (pear, apple, tangerine, and citrus) and a honeyed character. They are best enjoyed in their first two or three years, like the fine Pinot Blanc wines of Alsace, France, and Pinot Bianco wines of northeastern Italy (both of these areas are known for their Pinot Blancs; see Chapters 11 and 13).

Actually, some Pinot Blanc wines really aren't Pinot Blanc. In some cases, California vintners are growing another grape variety from France — Melon de Bourgogne (pronounced *mel own deh bor guh nyuh*), also known as Muscadet, from the western Loire Valley — and calling it Pinot Blanc. The two varieties (as they exist in California) are similar in appearance and in taste; only recently have *ampelographers* (botanists specializing in grapes) discovered that some of the so-called Pinot Blanc plants are really Melons. A few wineries are now calling these wines Melon or Muscadet, but most are still using the more familiar Pinot Blanc name. Perhaps sometime in the near future we'll find out which wineries have Pinot Blanc and which ones have Melon!

Table 7-5 lists some good California Pinot Blancs (with maybe a few Melons thrown in). Our personal favorites are marked with a wine glass. Good values are marked with ¢.

Table 7-5   Recommended California Pinot Blanc Wines

Producer	Wine	Location of Vineyard	Cost
♟ Arrowood Vineyards	Sara Lee's Vineyard	Russian River Valley	about $33 or $34
(because of good ratings, the price of this wine has almost doubled in a year)			
♟ Benziger Family Winery	Imagery Series, Pinot Blanc, Skinner Vineyard	Sonoma Mountain	$16
Chalone Vineyards	Pinot Blanc ♟ Pinot Blanc Estate Reserve	Gavilan Mountains Gavilan Mountains	$16 $25 to 26
Chateau St. Jean	Pinot Blanc, Robert Young Vineyard	Alexander Valley	$12 or $13
♟ Étude Wines	Pinot Blanc	Napa Valley	$18
¢ Daniel Gehrs	Pinot Blanc, Carmel Vineyard	Monterey County	$11
♟ ¢ Lockwood Vineyard	Pinot Blanc	Monterey County	$10 or $11
♟ Maison Deutz Winery	Pinot Blanc, "Carpe Diem"	San Luis Obispo County	$17
¢ Mirassou Vineyards	Family Selection Pinot Blanc, "White Burgundy"	Monterey County	$7 or $8

Producer	Wine	Location of Vineyard	Cost
Monte Volpe	Pinot Bianco	Mendocino County	$10 or $11
Murphy-Goode Estate Winery	Pinot Blanc, Barrel-Fermented	Alexander Valley	$13 or $14
Saddleback Cellars	Pinot Blanc	Napa Valley	$10
♟ Steele Wines	Pinot Blanc Bien Nacido Vineyard	Santa Barbara County	$15 to $16
Wild Horse Winery	Pinot Blanc Pinot Blanc, Bien Nacido Vineyard	Santa Barbara County Monterey County	$12 to $14 $12 to $14

Pinot Gris (Pinot Grigio)

Although only a few California wineries presently make Pinot Gris wine, the Pinot Gris grape (another white mutation of Pinot Noir) is being planted experimentally in many California vineyards.

Pinot Gris (or Pinot Grigio, as some winemakers are calling the wine, with a mock Italian accent) may well become the next hot white wine variety in California; it's already a major wine in Oregon. The West Coast edition of this variety (both California's and Oregon's) is typically softer and fruitier than the viscous, lively Pinot Gris that you find in Alsace (see Chapter 11).

West Coast Pinot Gris accompanies food extremely well, especially flavorful fish (such as salmon) or poultry.

Table 7-6 lists some good Pinot Gris (or non-Italian "Pinot Grigios") that are worth trying.

Table 7-6	Recommended California Pinot Gris Wines		
Producer	**Wine**	**Location of Vineyard**	**Cost**
Edmunds St. John	"Pinot Grigio"	El Dorado County	$12 to $13
Étude Wines	Pinot Gris	Carneros	$16
Long Vineyards	"Pinot Grigio"	Napa Valley	$15 to $16

Riesling

What has happened to Riesling *(REES ling)* wine is a doggone shame. When grown in cool climates and not over-cropped, the noble Riesling grape variety can provide us with one of the great white wines of the world. Some of the best examples come from the Mosel-Saar-Ruwer *(MOH zel-zar-ROO ver)* and Rheingau *(RHEIN gow)* regions in Northern Germany, and from Alsace, France (see Chapters 11 and 12).

The aromatic, floral, spicy, lime-citrus qualities of the delicate Riesling shine through in the wine when the grape is grown in unfertile soil and in cool climates with a long growing season. Unfortunately, too many cheap, sweetened Riesling wines have been made in the U.S. In California, three wine regions — the Anderson Valley in Mendocino County, Santa Barbara, and Monterey — have proven to be the best areas, with Sonoma's Russian River Valley up and coming.

A lesser grape variety, whose wines are called "Gray Riesling," (which is not the true Riesling grape), is also produced in California. Actual Riesling (also known in the U.S. as Johannisberg Riesling, or White Riesling) is considered the far superior grape variety.

Delicate fish and chicken dishes, scallops and other seafood, and soft cheeses such as Brie are good accompaniments to dry Rieslings (avoid the inexpensive, sweeter versions of Riesling; they will not enhance your food).

Many wineries, such as Joseph Phelps, Beringer, Handley Cellars, Arrowood, and Château St. Jean, produce rich, sweet (late-harvested) dessert wines from Riesling, with varying degrees of success. However, dessert wines are not the subject of this book.

Table 7-7 lists recommended California Rieslings; our personal favorites are marked with ▼. Good values are marked with ¢.

Table 7-7	Recommended California Rieslings		
Producer	**Wine**	**Location of Vineyard**	**Cost**
Babcock Vineyards	Estate Grown Riesling	Santa Ynez Valley	$14
Beringer Vineyards	Johannisberg Riesling	Central Coast	$6 to $7

Producer	Wine	Location of Vineyard	Cost
Bonny Doon Vineyard	"Pacific Rim" White Riesling	California	$8 to $9
Chateau St. Jean	Johannisberg Riesling	Sonoma County	$8 to $9
Claiborne & Churchill Vintners	Dry "Alsatian Style" Riesling	Central Coast	$8 to $9
Firestone Vineyard	Johannisberg Riesling	Santa Barbara County	$6 to $7
Gainey Vineyard	Riesling	Santa Ynez Valley	$9
♀ ¢ Greenwood Ridge Vineyards	White Riesling	Anderson Valley	$8 to $9
Gundlach Bundschu Winery	Riesling, Rhinefarm Vineyards	Sonoma Valley	$9
Hidden Cellars Winery	Johannisberg Riesling	Mendocino County	$8 to $9
♀ Long Vineyards	Johannisberg Riesling	Napa Valley	$16
♀ ¢ Navarro Vineyards	White Riesling	Anderson Valley	$8 to $9
Renaissance Vineyard	Dry Riesling	North Yuba	$9
♀ Smith-Madrone Vineyard	Johannisberg Riesling	Napa Valley	$8 to $9
♀ Stony Hill Vineyard	White (or Johannisberg) Riesling	Napa Valley	$12
♀ Trefethen Vineyards	Dry White Riesling	Napa Valley	$10 to $11

Sémillon

Although winemakers traditionally use the wine of the Sémillon *(sem ee yohn)* grape mainly to blend with Sauvignon Blanc — a custom that originated in the Bordeaux region of France, but also common in the U.S. — lately we are seeing more and more wineries on the West Coast of the U.S. making actual Sémillon wine. Often they blend a small amount of Sauvignon Blanc (or even Chardonnay!) with Sémillon. Australia and South Africa have long thought of Sémillon as one of their best white wines (see Chapter 9) — although they refuse to give this French grape a French pronunciation; they call it *SEM eh lon.*

Whichever way you pronounce it, Sémillon makes a very interesting dry wine. It is quite viscous, somewhat low in acidity (which is one reason it blends so well with the acidic Sauvignon Blanc), and has subtle aromas and flavors of lanolin, with herbaceous and honeyed overtones. We often find a delicate scent of dry mustard in Sémillons from California. The dry, warm Livermore Valley, east of San Francisco, seems to be one of the best growing regions for Sémillon in California. Kalin Cellars and Wente Vineyards — which both use grapes from the Livermore Valley — have championed this excellent, noble variety, which has yet to see its heyday in the U.S.

Sémillon is a terrific wine to have with shellfish, especially oysters. It is also fine with soft cheeses, such as Brie.

Sémillon surely reaches its zenith in the Sauternes region of Bordeaux, where it is the main grape variety for the magnificent dessert wine, Sauternes, which is produced by the great Château d'Yquem and other wineries (see *Wine For Dummies,* Chapter 14). A dessert Sémillon, made from late-harvested grapes, is also produced by some California wineries.

Table 7-8 lists some good California Sémillons. Our personal favorites are marked with 🍷. Good values rate a ¢.

Table 7-8 Recommended California Sémillons

Producer	*Wine*	*Location of Vineyard*	*Cost*
Benziger Winery	"Tribute" (60% Sémillon, 40% Sauvignon Blanc)	Sonoma Mountain	$15
Chatom Vineyards	Sémillon	Calaveras County	$8
Fenestra Winery	Sémillon	Livermore Valley	$9
🍷 ¢ Geyser Peak Winery	"Semchard" (75% Sémillon 25% Chardonnay)	California	$7 to $8

Producer	Wine	Location of Vineyard	Cost
🍷 Kalin Cellars	Sémillon	Livermore Valley	$22 to $23
Lakewood	Sémillon	Clear Lake, Lake County	$11 to $12
🍷 Signorello Vineyards	Barrel Fermented Sémillon	Napa Valley	$19 to $20
Wente Vineyards	Sémillon, Wente Family Estate Selection	Livermore Valley	$8 to $9

Viognier

A few years ago, Viognier *(vee oh nyay)* was the hot new white wine in California, riding the publicity coattails of the red grape varieties from the Rhône Valley in France. Despite its early hoopla, however, Viognier hasn't really caught on in the U.S. One problem is that wine producers are finding Viognier a difficult grape to grow. As a result of the growers' difficulties, the few Viognier wines that do exist are quite expensive.

Yet Viognier wine, so fragrant and delicious, certainly has its fans. The wine has a wonderful floral, spicy aroma, with rich but delicate flavors of fresh apricot and peach. Viognier is a medium- to full-bodied wine (depending on the winemaker) with rather low acidity; you should drink it within its first two or three years, while it has all of its delicious freshness.

WINE & DINE

Viognier makes a wonderful accompaniment to fresh fish.

TIP

Calera Wine Company, in the Mount Harlan region of San Benito County (south of San Francisco), is probably making California's most full-bodied, intensely flavorful Viognier today. A contrast to Calera's is Alban Vineyards' Viognier, crafted in a more elegant, understated fashion.

AUTHORS' CHOICE

Table 7-9 lists some California Viogniers that you can try. Our personal favorites are marked with 🍷. Good values are marked with ¢.

Table 7-9   Recommended California Viognier Wines

Producer	Wine	Location of Vineyard	Cost
Alban Vineyards	Viognier ♀ Viognier	Central Coast San Luis Obispo County	$18 $25 to $26
Arrowood Vineyards	Viognier, Sara Lee's Vineyard	Russian River Valley	$25
♀ ¢ Beringer Vineyards	Viognier, Hudson Ranch	Carneros	$22
♀ Calera Wine Company	Viognier	Mount Harlan	about $32
♀ Edmunds St. John	Viognier	Knights Valley	$18 to $20
Field Stone Winery	Viognier, Staten Family Reserve	Alexander Valley	$16 to $17
Kunde Estate Winery	Viognier	Sonoma Valley	$18 to $19
La Jota Vineyard	Barrel Fermented Viognier Cold Fermented Viognier	Howell Mountain Howell Mountain	$28 $28
McDowell Valley Vineyards	Viognier	Mendocino County	$15 to $16
♀ Joseph Phelps Vineyards	"Vin du Mistral" Viognier	Napa Valley	$25
¢ R.H. Phillips Vineyard	"EXP" Viognier	Dunnigan Hills, Yolo County	$11 to $12
Preston Vineyards	Viognier	Dry Creek Valley	$18 to $19
♀ Qupé Cellars	Viognier, Los Olivos Vineyard	Santa Barbara County	$25
Ritchie Creek Vineyards	Viognier	Napa Valley	$18 to $19

Chapter 8

The White Wines of Oregon, Washington, and New York

In This Chapter

▶ A state where Chardonnay isn't the only white wine on the block

▶ The emergence of Sémillon in the Northwest

▶ Riesling runs deep in the Finger Lakes

*A*lthough Chardonnay dominates all other domestic white wines in U.S. sales, the dominance of Chardonnay does not necessarily hold true for the wines of other states. For instance, Pinot Gris has become Oregon's fastest-selling white wine and may eventually overtake Chardonnay in total sales of Oregon white wines. And although Chardonnay is still the most popular white wine in Washington, Sémillon and Riesling are also doing quite well, thank you. And among the many different white wines made in New York, the best in quality is Riesling from the Finger Lakes region. There *is* life after Chardonnay.

Oregon, Humming a Different Tune

Oregon prides itself on being an independent-minded state. While its neighbors to the north and south primarily make red wines such as Cabernet Sauvignon and Merlot, with Chardonnay as their main white wine, Oregon has championed Pinot Noir as its red wine (see *Red Wine For Dummies,* published by IDG Books Worldwide, Inc., Chapter 8) and is the only state producing any significant quantities of white Pinot Gris.

Chardonnay is still the leading white varietal wine in Oregon in production and sales, followed by Riesling. But Pinot Gris is the state's fastest-growing white wine in sales, by far. In fact, almost everyone in Oregon who makes a Pinot Noir — Oregon's most popular wine — is now also making a Pinot Gris.

The young and the restless

The Oregon wine industry is really only a little more than 30 years old. Richard Sommer, the first of many California expatriates to try his hand at making wine in Oregon, founded Hillcrest Vineyards in Umpqua Valley (in the southwestern part of the state) in 1962. There he planted Riesling and Gewürztraminer grapes as well as Cabernet Sauvignon.

Four years later, David Lett headed up from California to the Willamette *(wil LAM ette)* Valley in northwest Oregon, where he founded The Eyrie *(EYE ree)* Vineyards. Lett released his first Pinot Gris, along with his first Pinot Noir, in 1970. Other pioneers in Oregon from the early 1970s include Dick Ponzi (Ponzi Vineyards), who made Oregon's second Pinot Gris, Bill Fuller (Tualatin Vineyards), who has always specialized in white wines, Ron Vuylsteke of Oak Knoll Winery, and Dick Erath of Knudsen-Erath Winery (recently renamed Erath Winery). But most of Oregon's wineries are less than 15 years old.

Today, six premium white varietal wines are produced in sizeable quantity in Oregon (in order of production):

- Chardonnay
- Riesling
- Pinot Gris
- Gewürztraminer
- Müller-Thurgau
- Sauvignon Blanc

Chardonnay, Riesling, and Pinot Gris are the big three in sales — and we recommend some of Oregon's best wines from these three grapes in the following sections.

You can't go wrong drinking any of Oregon's white wines when they are young — within three or four years, even though Chardonnay and Pinot Gris are capable of aging for at least five or six years; Oregon's Riesling is best even younger (within two years). Of recent vintages (the best are in bold), **1988** is excellent for Chardonnay, **1989** very good for both Pinot Gris and Chardonnay, **1990** tops for Chardonnay, **1991** excellent for Pinot Gris, 1992 is good for Chardonnay, and **1995** is a fine year for Pinot Gris. The older vintages are difficult to find in retail stores, however.

Recommended Oregon Chardonnays

Because Oregon is a cooler growing region than California, generally speaking, Oregon Chardonnays are usually higher in acidity and lighter-bodied than California Chardonnays, without the ripe tropical fruit flavors that California Chardonnays have. Oregon Chardonnays are typically quite dry, more straightforward in style, and less oaky than California versions. The best wines can compete with California Chardonnays in quality, but at a substantially lower price — $12 to $15 for most of them, with a few reserve or single-vineyard Oregon Chardonnays in the $18 to $20 range. Finding some good Oregon Chardonnays under $10 is also possible. In general, Oregon Chardonnays accompany food well, except for the occasional wine that is over-oaked.

The Oregon Chardonnays that we recommend appear in Table 8-1 in alphabetical order. The geographical location mentioned for a wine indicates the region of origin of the grapes. Wines that are called *reserve* are the producers' best wines. We indicate our personal favorites with the ¶.

Wines that are really good values are marked with ¢.

Table 8-1   Recommended Oregon Chardonnay Wines

Producer	Wine	Location of Vineyard	Cost
Bethel Heights Vineyard	¶ Chardonnay Estate	Willamette Valley	$12
	Reserve Chardonnay	Willamette Valley	$15
Bridgeview Vineyard	Chardonnay	Oregon	$7
	¶ ¢ Barrel Select Chardonnay	Oregon	$10
Cameron Winery	Reserve Chardonnay	Willamette Valley	$15 to $16
Chehalem	Chardonnay, Ridgecrest Vineyard	Willamette Valley	$18 to $20
Cristom Vineyards	Chardonnay	Willamette Valley	$12 to $13
Elk Cove Vineyards	Chardonnay	Willamette Valley	$7
	¶ ¢ La Bohème Vineyard Chardonnay	Willamette Valley	$12

(continued)

Table 8-1 *(continued)*

Producer	Wine	Location of Vineyard	Cost
Erath Winery (formerly Knudsen-Erath)	Chardonnay	Willamette Valley	$10
♀ Evesham Wood Winery	Chardonnay	Willamette Valley	$17
The Eyrie Vineyards	Chardonnay ♀ Reserve Chardonnay	Willamette Valley Willamette Valley	$14 to $15 $22 to $23
Foris Vineyard	Barrel Fermented Chardonnay ♀ Reserve Chardonnay	Rogue Valley Rogue Valley	$10 $15
Montinore	Chardonnay, Winemaker's Reserve "Vineyards Estate" Chardonnay	Willamette Valley Willamette Valley	$10 $14
Oak Knoll Winery	Chardonnay	Willamette Valley	$12 to $13
Panther Creek Cellars	Chardonnay, Celilo Vineyard	Washington State	$21 to $22
St. Innocent Winery	Chardonnay, Seven Springs Vineyard Reserve Chardonnay	Willamette Valley Willamette Valley	$13 $18
Shafer Vineyard Cellars	Chardonnay	Willamette Valley	$8
Sokol Blosser Winery	Yamhill Chardonnay ♀ Redland Vineyard Chardonnay	Willamette Valley Willamette Valley	$11 $16 to $17
♀ Tualatin *(too AHL ah tin)* Vineyards	Chardonnay	Willamette Valley	$11 to $12
Valley View Vineyard	Chardonnay Barrel Select Chardonnay	Rogue Valley Rogue Valley	$8 $10

Producer	Wine	Location of Vineyard	Cost
Willamette Valley Vineyards	Chardonnay	Willamette Valley	$11
	Canary Hill Vineyard Chardonnay	Willamette Valley	$23
	Reserve Chardonnay	Willamette Valley	$23
Ken Wright Cellars	Chardonnay, Celilo Vineyard	Washington State	$19 to $20

A melon in Oregon

We visited Ken Wright, former owner-winemaker of Panther Creek Cellars (he now owns Ken Wright Cellars) and asked to taste his Pinot Gris. Ken told us that he doesn't make a Pinot Gris, but he does make a Melon (*a.k.a.* Melon de Bourgogne or Muscadet; see the Pinot Blanc section in Chapter 7). Frankly, we had our doubts, because Melon doesn't have a great reputation. But we were pleasantly surprised by the delicious, honeyed aromas and flavors of Panther Creek's Melon (about $19).

Panther Creek's Melon is a terrific, distinctive white wine — one worth seeking out. Actually, we shouldn't have been surprised. Ken has always made wonderful wines, both at Panther Creek and now at Ken Wright Cellars.

Recommended Oregon Rieslings

To perform at its best, the Riesling grape needs a long, cool growing season and fairly unfertile soil — and Oregon's growing conditions are therefore ideal. Oregon's Riesling wines are usually labeled "White Rieslings," and most of them — especially the inexpensive ($5 to $6) ones — are consumed within the state. (The most interesting Oregon Rieslings are vinified dry and are usually identified as such on the label.) Lighter-bodied and crisper than California Rieslings, most Oregon Rieslings sell for under $10. You should drink them within two or three years of the vintage.

Table 8-2 alphabetically lists Oregon Rieslings that we recommend. We mark our own personal favorites with ❢. All of these Rieslings sell for less than $10.

Table 8-2	Recommended Oregon Riesling Wines	
Producer	*Wine*	*Location of Vineyard*
Adelsheim Vineyard	Estate Riesling	Willamette Valley
Bridgeview Vineyard	"Blue Moon" Riesling	Oregon
Elk Cove Vineyards	Estate Riesling	Willamette Valley
Kramer Vineyards	Estate Riesling	Willamette Valley
Rex Hill Vineyards	Riesling	Willamette Valley
♈ Tualatin Vineyards	Estate White Riesling	Willamette Valley

Oregon Rieslings have delicate, flowery aromas and flavors; they are an excellent companion to freshwater fish or shellfish.

An Oregon success story: Pinot Gris

Twenty years ago, only The Eyrie Vineyards (see Figure 8-1) and Ponzi Vineyards produced Pinot Gris. Today, well over 30 wineries in Oregon make Pinot Gris wine. The Pinot Gris grape is a favorite among Oregon winemakers because of its many endearing qualities: the grapes mature early; they are disease-resistant; and the wine can be released and ready to drink six to eight months after the harvest, yet the wine ages well and still tastes delicious with five or six years of bottle age.

Most Oregon winemakers make their Pinot Gris entirely in stainless steel rather than in oak to retain the freshness and fruitiness of the grape, while some producers barrel-ferment a small part of their wine (a process which adds some oaky complexity to the flavor; see "Barrel-fermentation" in Chapter 2).

Although the word "gris" means *gray* in French, the color of Oregon's Pinot Gris wine varies — depending on the vintage and where the grapes are grown — from a bright, medium gold hue to a light gold, sometimes tinged with pale pink. With a few years of age, the wine often develops striking copper-gold tones of unusual beauty. Typically well-balanced between its fruitiness and acidity, Pinot Gris has distinct, complex aromas and flavors suggestive of pear, apple and/or melon.

Figure 8-1: The Eyrie Vineyards pioneered the production of Oregon Pinot Gris.

Much of Oregon's Pinot Gris is enjoyed locally because it goes so well with the local fish and seafood. Pinot Gris is a wonderful wine with the specialty of the Pacific Northwest, salmon. Pinot Gris and salmon are a marriage made in gastronomic heaven. But Pinot Gris is also great with all kinds of fish, shellfish, poultry, game birds, pork, and fresh vegetables.

Table 8-3, an alphabetical listing, names the Oregon Pinot Gris wines that we recommend. We mark our personal favorites with ♟; wines that are really good values are marked with ¢.

Almost all of Oregon's Pinot Gris wines are in the $10 to $15 price range.

Table 8-3	Recommended Oregon Pinot Gris Wines	
Producer	*Wine*	*Location of Vineyard*
Adelsheim Vineyard	Pinot Gris	Willamette Valley
Bethel Heights Vineyard	Pinot Gris	Willamette Valley
Bridgeview Vineyard	Pinot Gris	Oregon
Chateau Benoit Winery	Pinot Gris	Willamette Valley
Chehalem	Ridgecrest Vineyard Pinot Gris	Willamette Valley
	♇ Pinot Gris Reserve	Willamette Valley
Cristom Vineyards	Pinot Gris	Willamette Valley
Elk Cove Vineyards	Pinot Gris	Willamette Valley
♇ Evesham Wood Winery	Pinot Gris	Willamette Valley
♇ The Eyrie Vineyards	Pinot Gris	Willamette Valley
Foris Vineyards	Pinot Gris	Rogue Valley
Hinman/ Silvan Ridge Vineyards	Pinot Gris	Oregon
King Estate	Pinot Gris	Oregon
	♇ Reserve Pinot Gris	Oregon
Lange Winery	Pinot Gris Reserve	Willamette Valley
♇ Montinore Vineyards	Pinot Gris	Willamette Valley
Oak Knoll Winery	Pinot Gris	Willamette Valley
♇ Ponzi Vineyards	Pinot Gris	Willamette Valley
Rex Hill Vineyards	Estate Pinot Gris	Willamette Valley
	♇ Pinot Gris Reserve	Willamette Valley
Willamette Valley Vineyards	Pinot Gris	Oregon

Sipping Sémillons and Such in Washington State

Most of Washington's wineries, like Oregon's, did not open until the 1980s. But Washington has overtaken Oregon in wine production and now ranks third in the U.S., behind California and New York State.

Although Chardonnay is Washington's best-selling white wine, we believe that Sémillon and Riesling (in that order) are Washington's best white wines. Not that anything is wrong with Washington Chardonnays: Most of them are of good quality, and they're reasonably priced. It's just that Washington's climate and soil in some places are perfect for Sémillon and Riesling. What's more — these wines are real bargains.

It started with Gewürztraminer

Washington's winemaking history is even briefer than Oregon's. In 1967, a group called Associated Vintners (now owners of three leading wineries) released Washington's first commercial *vinifera* wine, a Gewürztraminer. In the same year, the Chateau Ste. Michelle winery was founded. In 1972, Chateau Ste. Michelle achieved its first fame in the wine world when its Riesling captured first place in a huge comparative tasting conducted by the *Los Angeles Times*.

Like Oregon, Washington produces six major white varietal wines — but a couple of them are distinctly Washingtonian. In terms of production, the big two are Chardonnay and Riesling, followed by Sauvignon Blanc, Chenin Blanc, Sémillon, and Gewürztraminer.

Chenin Blanc and Gewürztraminer production have been declining rapidly, while Sémillon has become the new darling of Washington winemakers. Sémillon deserves all the attention it gets because it is producing world-class wines in Washington. (Too bad that Chenin Blanc isn't as popular, because the best Chenin Blancs in the U.S. come from Washington; see "A value among values" sidebar.) In the following sections, we recommend some of our favorite Washington Chardonnays, Rieslings, and Sémillons.

Like California, Washington has been blessed with a string of very good vintages for its white wines (the best are in bold). The **1989** vintage has probably been the greatest one in Washington's short history (but wines from this vintage are difficult to find now). 1991, 1992, and 1993 were all good vintages, with **1994** the best of the current years. And 1995 looks promising at this point.

Recommended Washington Chardonnays

Washington's Chardonnays come in all different styles, with the barrel-aged type, á la California, dominant. If Washington Chardonnays can be faulted as a group, we'd say that they lack specific regional character. Also, they have not aged well. On the other hand, the best producers such as The Hogue Cellars, Château Ste. Michelle, and the tiny Woodward Canyon Winery are making excellent Chardonnays at much more competitive prices than the Chardonnays of California.

Washington's powers that be

One company, Stimson Lane, truly dominates the wine scene in Washington. The company owns Chateau Ste. Michelle winery as well as the popular Columbia Crest Winery, Snoqualmie Winery, and two other Washington labels (in addition to Villa Mt. Eden and Conn Creek Winery in California). Stimson Lane brands account for more than 50 percent of all Washington wine sales. To the company's credit, all of its Washington wineries produce wines of high quality.

The Hogue Cellars and Associated Vintners (owners of Columbia Winery, Covey Run Winery, and Paul Thomas Winery) are two other fairly large Washington firms producing high-quality wines. Together with Stimson Lane, these three companies are responsible for more than 90 percent of Washington's total wine production.

In Table 8-4, listed alphabetically, are the Washington Chardonnays that we recommend. If no specific vineyard is named, the wine is a blend of two or more vineyards, or it's the producer's basic wine. We mark our own personal favorites with ▼; wines that are really good values are marked with ¢.

Table 8-4   Recommended Washington Chardonnay Wines

Name of Producer	Wine	Location of Vineyard	Cost
Arbor Crest Wine Cellars	Chardonnay, "Cameo Reserve"	Columbia Valley	$9 to $10
Barnard Griffin Winery	▼ Chardonnay	Columbia Valley	$12

Name of Producer	Wine	Location of Vineyard	Cost
Chateau Ste. Michelle	Chardonnay ♟ all Single-Vineyard and Reserve Chardonnays	Columbia Valley Columbia Valley	$11 to $12 $22 to $24
Columbia Winery	Woodburne Chardonnay Wyckoff Vineyard Chardonnay	Yakima Valley Yakima Valley	$10 $14 to $15
Columbia Crest Winery	Chardonnay ♟ ¢ "Estate" Chardonnay	Columbia Valley Columbia Valley	$8 to $9 $10 to $11
Covey Run Winery	Chardonnay ♟ Celilo Vineyard Reserve Chardonnay	Yakima Valley Yakima Valley	$9 $12
Gordon Brothers Cellars	Chardonnay	Washington	$9
The Hogue Cellars	Chardonnay ♟ ¢ Reserve Chardonnay	Columbia Valley Columbia Valley	$9 to $10 $12 to $14
Hyatt Vineyards	Chardonnay	Yakima Valley	$10
Latah Creek Wine Cellars	Chardonnay	Washington	$10
L'Ecole #41	Chardonnay	Washington	$15
Staton Hills Winery	Chardonnay	Washington	$10
Paul Thomas Winery	Chardonnay ♟ Reserve Chardonnay	Columbia Valley Columbia Valley	$10 $15
Washington Hills Cellars	Chardonnay	Columbia Valley	$8 to $9
Waterbrook Winery	Chardonnay ♟ Reserve Chardonnay	Columbia Valley Columbia Valley	$9 $11 to $12
Woodward Canyon Winery	Chardonnay Roza Berge Vineyard Chardonnay ♟ Reserve Chardonnay	Columbia Valley Washington Washington	$21 to $22 $25 to $27 $25 to $27

A value among values

Looking for a good $6 to $8 white wine that has a touch of sweetness balanced by crisp, lively acidity? Try a Washington Chenin Blanc. It's the best white wine value in the U.S. Chenin Blancs are inexpensive because this variety is not "in vogue," but Washington wineries happen to be making some really fine wines from Chenin Blanc.

Some of the best Washington Chenin Blancs come from The Hogue Cellars, Andrew Will Winery (✉12526 S. W. Bank Road; Vashon, WA 98070; 206-463-3290; FAX 206-463-3524), Kiona Vineyards, Washington Hills Cellars, Worden, Blackwood Canyon, Paul Thomas Winery, and Chateau Ste. Michelle.

Recommended Washington Rieslings

Riesling wine isn't very popular in the U.S. at the moment, which is unfortunate for Washington winemakers, because the Riesling grape variety grows well in their state. At least Washington Riesling sells well in its home market, where much of it goes for $5 to $6 per bottle.

Although Washington Rieslings can't compare with the finest Rieslings from Alsace or Germany (see Chapters 11 and 12) in terms of aroma or complexity, they are crisp, delicate, delicious — and affordable! Washington Rieslings accompany fresh fish and light poultry dishes beautifully. They're best when consumed within a few years of the vintage.

Some Washington wineries call their Riesling "Johannisberg Riesling" and some call it "White Riesling" (for further discussion of Riesling's names, see the Riesling section of Chapter 7). Some wineries use the *Johannisberg* name for their drier versions and *White* for their off-dry (sweeter) versions. Then again, some Washington wineries simply use the word *dry* on their labels for their drier Rieslings and just *Riesling* for their off-dry versions. Any Riesling labeled *Late Harvest,* at least, is definitely a dessert wine.

Table 8-5 alphabetically lists the Washington Rieslings that we recommend. We mark our own personal favorites with ❢; wines that are really good values are marked with ¢. All of the Rieslings we recommend, except as noted, cost about $6 a bottle:

Table 8-5	Recommended Washington Riesling Wines	
Producer	*Wine*	*Location of Vineyard*
Arbor Crest Wine Cellars	Dry Riesling, Dionysus Vineyard	Columbia Valley
♀ ¢ Chateau Ste. Michelle	Dry Riesling	Columbia Valley
Columbia Winery	Johannisberg Riesling	Columbia Valley
♀ Columbia Crest Winery	Johannisberg Riesling	Columbia Valley
Covey Run Winery	Johannisberg Riesling	Yakima Valley
The Hogue Cellars	Dry Johannisberg Riesling	Yakima Valley
	♀ ¢ Reserve Riesling ($8)	Yakima Valley
♀ Kiona Vineyards	Dry White Riesling	Yakima Valley
Latah Creek Wine Cellars	Johannisberg Riesling	Washington
Paul Thomas Winery	Johannisberg Riesling	Washington
	♀ Dry Riesling	Washington
Washington Hills Cellars	Johannisberg Riesling	Columbia Valley

Mr. Sémillon goes to Washington

Washington State has become quite well known for its Merlots and Cabernet Sauvignons (see *Red Wine For Dummies*), but we think that Sémillon might be its very best white wine. Sémillon clearly has done better in Washington than in California, so far. This little-known variety has spent most of its time in the U.S. as a second banana to Sauvignon Blanc (see Sémillon in Chapter 3), a silent partner in blending. But in Washington, Sémillon stands proudly on its own.

Sémillon typically has flavors of melon or figs — and most Washington wineries make Sémillon with little or no wood aging in order to capture those fresh fruit flavors. A few of the smaller wineries, such as L'Ecole #41 and Woodward Canyon, oak-age their Sémillon, resulting in a richer, more complex wine. For inexpensive white wines selling for $6 to $7, Washington Sémillons have remarkable longevity; they're probably at their best within five or six years of the vintage, though.

We strongly suggest that you try Washington Sémillon wines now, while they are still relatively unknown. After they become officially discovered, you can be sure that the price will rise dramatically.

Recommended Washington Sémillons

Table 8-6 alphabetically lists Washington Sémillons that we recommend. We mark our own personal favorites with ♟; wines that are really good values are marked with ¢. DeLille Cellars' wine is marked with a ✉, indicating it is only available by mail at P.O. Box 2233, Woodinville, WA 98072; 206-489-0544; Fax: 206-402-9295.

Table 8-6   Recommended Washington Sémillon Wines

Producer	Wine	Location of Vineyard	Cost
♟ Barnard Griffin	Sémillon	Columbia Valley	$8 to $9
♟ ¢ Château Ste. Michelle	Sémillon	Columbia Valley	$6 to $7
♟ Chinook Wines	Sémillon	Yakima Valley	$7 to $8
♟ ¢ Columbia Winery	Sémillon	Columbia Valley	$6 to $7
	♟ Sémillon-Chardonnay	Columbia Valley	$8
♟ ¢ Columbia Crest Winery	Sémillon	Columbia Valley	$6
	♟ Sémillon-Chardonnay	Columbia Valley	$7 to $8
	♟ Sémillon-Sauvignon	Columbia Valley	$7 to $8
♟ ¢ Covey Run Winery	"Caille de Fumé" (Sémillon-Sauvignon)	Yakima Valley	$7 to $8
♟ ✉ DeLille Cellars	Chaleur Estate (Semillon/Sauvignon Blend)	Yakima Valley	$11 to $12
♟ ¢ The Hogue Cellars	Sémillon	Columbia Valley	$8 to $9
	♟ Sémillon-Chardonnay	Columbia Valley	$7.50 to $8

Producer	Wine	Location of Vineyard	Cost
Hoodsport Winery	Sémillon	Washington	$8
♟ L'Ecole #41	Sémillon	Washington	$11 to $12
♟ ¢ Snoqualmie Winery	Sémillon	Columbia Valley	$7
♟ Woodward Canyon Winery	"Charbonneau" (Sémillon-Sauvignon)	Washington	$20 to $23

Enjoy Sémillon with chicken, pork, salmon, seafood, or soft cheeses. It is also excellent with *foie gras*. Serve it chilled, but not cold (about 55° F).

North of the Border

Washington State's neighbor to the north — the Canadian province of British Columbia — boasts nearly three dozen wineries. Production centers on the Okanagan *(oke ah NAH gan)* Valley region, in the southeastern part of the province, and most of the production is white wine. Chardonnay, Gewurztraminer, and Riesling are all grown there, along with the vinifera grape variety Auxerrois (also seen in Alsace, France) and two vinifera crossings that originated in Germany: Bacchus and Ehrenfelser.

New York State's neighbor to the north — the Canadian province of Ontario — produces more wine than British Columbia, most of it also white, and much of it from the same grape varieties. The specialty of the province, however, is a type of sweet dessert white wine known as ice wine. We hate to be teases, but unfortunately we can't go into detail about dessert wines here.

A New York State of White

New York State ranks second to California in total wine production, although quite a bit of New York's wine is made not from *vinifera* grapes (see Chapter 3) but from sturdier hybrid and local grapes that can survive New York's cold winters. Two noble white wine varieties do manage quite well in New York:

Chardonnay, especially along the milder North Fork of Long Island, and the hardy, frost-resisting Riesling, particularly in the Finger Lakes region in western New York.

Vintages in New York have been unusually good lately for white wines (the best are in bold) — especially on milder Long Island — beginning with the great **1988** (difficult to find at this point). 1990, 1991, and 1992 were all good, while **1993** and **1994** (both warm and dry) produced excellent wines, equal to the great 1988. And **1995**, with its long, hot, dry summer, promises to be the best vintage yet.

Chardonnays Up-State and Down

Although many of the better Chardonnays in New York hail from Long Island, a few good Chardonnays are being produced in New York's two other major wine regions: the Finger Lakes and the Hudson Valley.

New York Chardonnays come in two basic styles: a rich, oak-aged wine, resembling a California Chardonnay or an oaked white Burgundy (see Chapters 6 and 10), which wineries frequently designate as their Reserve Chardonnay; and a simpler style, fermented in stainless steel tanks with little or no oak aging, which is more similar to the style of a French Chablis (see Chapter 11). The latter type is usually less expensive than the oak-aged style.

Long Island and Chardonnay — a marriage of convenience

Long Island's wine industry is still small and young. In 1973, Alex and Louisa Hargrave founded Hargrave Vineyard in the small farming community of Cutchogue, on Long Island's North Fork (east of New York City); they released their first wines in 1977. Today, about 15 wineries occupy the North Fork, and a few are on the South Fork (the Hamptons). All of these wineries make Chardonnay for two obvious reasons:

✔ Chardonnay grows well on Long Island; it produces a good-sized crop, and the plants are not damaged by Long Island winters.

✔ Chardonnay is *the* cash-flow wine: If any wine sells in the U.S., it's Chardonnay. Because most Long Island wineries are family-owned and operate on a shoestring, these wineries need the steady sales that Chardonnay brings.

Many of New York's wineries are quite small (producing between 5,000 and 15,000 cases of wine annually). Smaller wineries often sell all of their wine locally, either to visitors at the winery or to customers within the state.

Our recommended wines, listed in Table 8-7, for the most part are available also outside of New York. The geographical location mentioned for each wine indicates the origin of the grapes, which is not in every case the location of the winery. (When two locations are mentioned, we are referring to two separate Chardonnays made by the same producer.) We mark our own personal favorites with ♟; wines that are really good values are marked with ¢.

Table 8-7 Recommended New York Chardonnay Wines

Producer	Wine	Location of Vineyard	Cost
Bedell Cellars	Silver Label Chardonnay	North Fork of Long Island	$12
	♟ Reserve Chardonnay	North Fork of Long Island	$15
Dr. Frank's Vinifera Wine Cellars	Chardonnay	Finger Lakes	$12
	Reserve Chardonnay	Finger Lakes	$15
Gristina Vineyards	♟ Chardonnay	North Fork of Long Island	$15 to $16
Hargrave Vineyard	Chardonnay	North Fork of Long Island	$12
	♟ Lattice Label Chardonnay	North Fork of Long Island	$14 to $15
Lamoreaux Landing Wine Cellars	♟ Chardonnay	Finger Lakes	$15
Lenz Winery	"Vineyard Selection" Chardonnay	North Fork of Long Island	$10
	Barrel Fermented Chardonnay	North Fork of Long Island	$14 to $15
Millbrook Vineyards	Estate Chardonnay	Hudson River Valley	$11
	Estate Reserve Chardonnay	Hudson River Valley	$15 to $16

(continued)

Producer	Wine	Location of Vineyard	Cost
Palmer Vineyards	Chardonnay	North Fork of Long Island	$10
	♀ Barrel Fermented Chardonnay	North Fork of Long Island	$14 to $15
Paumanok Vineyards	Chardonnay	North Fork of Long Island	$12
	♀ Barrel Fermented Chardonnay	North Fork of Long Island	$15
Pelligrini Vineyards	Chardonnay	North Fork of Long Island	$11 to $12
	♀ "Vintner's Pride" Chardonnay	North Fork of Long Island	$18
Pindar Vineyards	Chardonnay	North Fork of Long Island	$8 to $9
	Chardonnay Reserve	North Fork of Long Island	$12 to $14
Sagpond Vineyards	"Domaine Wolffer Reserve" Chardonnay	South Fork of Long Island	$15
Wagner Vineyards	Reserve Chardonnay	Finger Lakes	$10 to $12
Hermann J. Wiemer Vineyard	Chardonnay	Finger Lakes	$7 to $8
	Reserve Chardonnay	Finger Lakes	$12

The Riesling identity crisis

Rieslings in general have an identity problem. Most people know that Riesling wines are made in Germany, and German wines are sweet, right? Well, many — but not all — German wines are sweet, and Riesling can be — and often is — a dry wine.

Unlike California (whose wine regions are generally too warm for Riesling), Washington, Oregon, and especially upper New York State are well-suited to grow Riesling. And when the Riesling grape is grown in the right climate (warm — not hot — dry days, cool nights, with a long growing season), such as in the Finger Lakes region of western New York, one of the greatest, most noble wines in the world can result.

The best Finger Lakes Rieslings compare favorably to those of Alsace, Germany, and Austria. These Rieslings have a delightful, fresh, floral bouquet with subtle, crisp, delicate flavors suggestive of flower blossoms, honey, citrus fruits, and sometimes

Some good NY Gewürztraminers and Pinot Blancs

Everything in life doesn't always fall into neat little categories. Obviously, more good white wines are being made in New York besides the big two, Chardonnay and Riesling.

The cool New York climate lends itself to producing some darn good Gewürztraminers *(gah VERTZ trah mee ners)*, for example, which are among the best in the U.S. New York Gewürztraminers can't compete with the finest Alsace Gewürztraminers in bouquet, richness, and viscosity (see Chapter 11), but the best of them are delicious, delicately structured, and really good values.

 Lenz Winery, on the North Fork of Long Island, makes one of the best Gewürztraminers — a floral, spicy Alsace-style beauty that sells for about $10. Other interesting New York Gewürztraminers to look for are those of Palmer Vineyards; Pindar Vineyards; Bedell Cellars (all from Long Island's North Fork, and $9 to $10); and two Finger Lakes wines, Standing Stone Vineyards and Dr. Frank's Vinifera Cellars, both under $10.

 Our other favorite neglected white wine, Pinot Blanc, has three champions on Long Island's North Fork: Palmer Vineyards, Hargrave Vineyard (they call theirs *Pinot Bianco*), and Lenz Winery. This lively, crisp, lighter-bodied, less-expensive alternative to Chardonnay costs under $10.

peaches or apricots. Like all good Rieslings that come from suitable growing regions, Finger Lakes Rieslings mature remarkably well, developing more complex aromas and flavors with age.

 Dry Rieslings may be the most versatile wines of all with food. Their light-bodied, delicate aromas and flavors and their crisp, well-balanced structure go well with all kinds of dishes, such as poultry, sausage and other pork dishes, and delicate, fresh fish. Off-dry Rieslings go well with spicy Chinese, Thai, Indian, and Cajun cuisine. And Rieslings are also wonderful *apéritif* wines.

 (*Late-Harvest* or dessert Rieslings are among the finest after-dinner wines in the world; but we do not cover dessert wines in this book. For information about dessert wines, see our book, *Wine For Dummies,* from IDG Books Worldwide, Inc.)

Most of the New York Rieslings that we recommend come from the Finger Lakes region, although a few good ones are made on Long Island. As in the rest of the U.S., Rieslings in New York are often called "Johannisberg Riesling" or "White Riesling," synonyms for the true Riesling grape variety.

Table 8-8, an alphabetical listing, names the New York Rieslings that we recommend. (Just about all New York's Rieslings are in the $8 price range.) We mark our own personal favorites with ♟; wines that are really good values are marked with ¢.

Table 8-8   Recommended New York Riesling Wines

Producer	Wine	Location of Vineyard
Bidwell Vineyards	Riesling	North Fork of Long Island
♟ ¢ Fox Run Vineyards	Riesling	Finger Lakes
♟ ¢ Dr. Frank's Vinifera Wine Cellars	Riesling	Finger Lakes
Hunt Country Vineyard	Riesling	Finger Lakes
Knapp Vineyards Winery	Riesling	Finger Lakes
♟ ¢ Lamoreaux Landing Wine Cellars	Dry Riesling	Finger Lakes
McGregor Vineyards	Riesling	Finger Lakes
♟ ¢ Paumanok Vineyards	Dry Riesling	North Fork of Long Island
♟ ¢ Peconic Bay Vineyards	White Riesling	North Fork of Long Island
Pindar Vineyards	Johannisberg Riesling	North Fork of Long Island
♟ ¢ Prejean Winery	Riesling	Finger Lakes
♟ ¢ Standing Stone Vineyards	Riesling	Finger Lakes
Wagner Vineyards	Johannisberg Riesling	Finger Lakes
♟ ¢ Hermann J. Wiemer Vineyard	Dry Johannisberg Riesling	Finger Lakes

Chapter 9

White Wine Down Under — Australia, New Zealand, and South Africa

. . . .

In This Chapter

▶ Chardonnay's new conquest Down Under

▶ Aussies make great Semillon — they just can't pronounce it

▶ World-class Sauvignons from New Zealand

▶ South Africa awakens to Sauvignon and Chardonnay

. . . .

The past 20 to 25 years have brought about remarkable changes in the wines of Southern Hemisphere countries. Modern technology, combined with a worldwide desire for dry wines, has revolutionized winemaking, enabling countries such as Australia, New Zealand, and lately, South Africa, to make the best wines in their history. Many of those wines are white.

Perhaps no other country in the world has embraced high technology winemaking as Australia has. Necessity might very well have been the mother of the Australians' high-tech inventiveness: a warm climate and great distances for grapes to travel require the best technological conditions if the wines are to be fresh and healthy. Australia has proven itself up to the challenge. You rarely (if ever) taste an Australian wine that has not been made well.

Cool New Zealand has experienced enormous success with its crisp white wines — especially Sauvignon Blanc. Now, if only these wines were more readily available! But considering the high quality of the wines, increased availability is inevitable as demand increases worldwide.

South Africa is the latest country to join the Modern Age of White Wine, with its fresh-tasting and cleanly made white wines. Sauvignon Blancs — as well as Chardonnays — have shown remarkable improvement here within the last ten years.

We begin our exploration of these Southern Hemisphere countries with Australia — home of exotic, full-bodied, ripe, buttery Chardonnays.

Australian White Wines — Easy to Like

In 1980, Australia produced practically no Chardonnay. Although wine has been made in Australia since the late 18th century, most early wines were rich, sweet, *fortified* wines (wines with alcohol added), such as sherry and port. The most important dry, quality white wines were Semillon and Riesling — both still popular in Australia today.

But then a wine boom hit Australia. And with the wine boom came Chardonnay. Australians discovered that this adaptable grape variety does very well in their country. Today, Australia is the world's eighth-largest producer of wine; more than 30 percent of their wines are exported, much of it going to the United Kingdom and the United States. And Chardonnay is now their largest-selling white wine.

Australia's formula for success has been simple — produce fruity, cleanly made wines that reflect the ripeness of the country's grapes; then charge a reasonable price for those wines.

Thanks to the warm, dry climate of Australia's wine regions, Australian wines invariably exhibit intense, ripe fruitiness, and their quality is fairly reliable from year to year. Poor vintages don't exist Down Under — just good, better, and even better!

The French concept of *terroir* (that each wine should reflect the unique growing conditions of its grapes) has had little importance in Australia's brief recent history of winemaking. Grapes from vineyards hundreds of miles apart, grown in very different climates and soils, frequently come together in a single wine. For example, many white Australian wines carry the geographic designation, "South Eastern Australia" on their labels; grapes for these wines can come from vineyards that are literally more than a thousand miles apart.

Australia's leading white wines

Chardonnay is now the most popular dry white wine in Australia, and Semillon-Chardonnay is the most popular blended white wine. Riesling and Semillon follow Chardonnay in popularity.

What's in an (Australian) name

In Australia — as in just about all *New World* (non-European) wine countries — wines are generally named after the sole or dominant grape variety of each wine. If only one grape variety is named on an Australian label, that variety constitutes at least 85 percent of the wine.

A common practice in Australia is to blend the grapes or wines of two varieties together and name the wine after both, with the dominant variety listed first. For example, a popular white wine blend in Australia (now catching on in the U.S.) is Semillon with Chardonnay. The wine is labeled Semillon/Chardonnay (or the reverse, depending on which grape is dominant), and the percentages of each grape variety are usually indicated on the label. Wines made from the grapes of a specific Australian region carry that regional name on their label, along with the grape name(s).

Wine drinkers who are accustomed to the French pronunciation of the Sémillon grape *(seh mee yohn)* are often jarred when they hear the unique Aussie pronunciation *(SEM eh lon)* of the same grape. (The Australians even spell it differently, without an accent.)

When Australians speak of Riesling, they usually specify Rhine Riesling, to distinguish their wines as being made from the actual Riesling grape, unlike another type of Australian wine traditionally named Hunter Valley Riesling, which is really Semillon wine. (If this nomenclature is confusing, don't worry: Aussies drink most of their Riesling themselves.)

White wine regions in Australia

Only a fairly small part of Australia is suitable for grape growing. The northern two-thirds of the country is intensely hot and desert-like. Wine grapes, therefore, grow only in more temperate southeastern Australia and in a small area in southwestern Australia.

Most of Australia's wines — both white and red — come from its three southeastern states: South Australia, Victoria, and New South Wales. Each of these states has several individual wine regions that are important sources of grapes for quality white wine. We discuss the major white wine regions of Australia in the next sections. See Figure 9-1 for a label from an Australian wine.

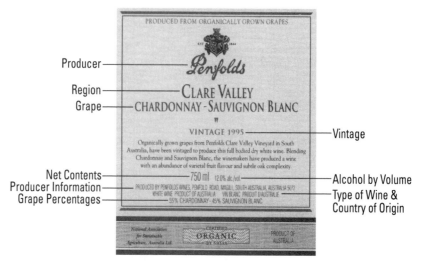

Figure 9-1: A typical Australian wine label.

South Australia

South Australia dominates the viticultural (grapegrowing) scene in Australia, producing about 58 percent of the country's wine grapes.

Of Australia's three major wine-producing states, only South Australia's vineyards remain free of the *phylloxera* louse, an insect that devastated much of the world's vineyards. (For more on phylloxera, refer to Chapter 7 of our book *Wine For Dummies* published by IDG Books Worldwide, Inc.)

Most of South Australia's better white wine regions are in the southern part of the state, near the capital city of Adelaide. The regions known for their white wines are

- ✔ **Adelaide Hills:** Adelaide Hills is a wine region in the suburban hills outside the city of Adelaide, where Rhine Riesling and Chardonnay do well, especially in such subregions as Eden Valley, Pewsey Vale, Mount Pleasant, and Piccadilly.

- ✔ **Barossa Valley:** Barossa Valley, one of Australia's most famous wine regions, is situated north of Adelaide. Most of the large wineries in South Australia make their home in this fairly warm region. Rhine Riesling and Semillon are the white wine specialties of the area.

The style of Australian Chardonnays

Being a huge country with many different microclimates, Australia obviously does not make a single style of Chardonnay. However, most of the Chardonnays that are exported from Australia — especially the less expensive (under $10) wines — do have certain factors in common. Most of those wines come from large wineries and are made from grapes grown in rather warm climates. These Chardonnays usually taste very rich and ripe, with very obvious fruity flavors, often reminiscent of melons, figs, or pears. They characteristically have pronounced oaky flavors (although many producers have been de-emphasizing the oak lately).

In short, Australian Chardonnays tend to be voluptuous, fat wines with conspicuous fruit flavors — quite the opposite of the lean, subtle, unoaked style of Chardonnay that you find in a French Chablis (see Chapter 10 for Chablis).

✔ **Clare Valley:** North of the Barossa Valley; Clare Valley is renowned for its Rhine Rieslings.

✔ **Coonawarra:** A cool region far south, near the South Pacific Ocean, Coonawarra is best known for red wine but is also gaining a reputation for Chardonnay.

✔ **Padthaway:** This cool region in the south, north of Coonawarra, has become Australia's premium white wine region, especially for Chardonnay.

✔ **Southern Vales** (especially **McLaren Vale**): This warm region south of Adelaide is cooled by ocean breezes; Chardonnay and Sauvignon Blanc do well here.

Victoria

Although Victoria produces only 14 percent of Australia's wines, many of the country's finest small wineries are here. Victoria's capital is the charming port city of Melbourne. Regions known for white wine in Victoria are

✔ **Murray River:** A large wine region in northwest Victoria, Murray River, along with its subregions of Mildura and Swan Hill, turns out large quantities of inexpensive wine plus some decent Chardonnay.

✓ **Yarra Valley:** This very cool region to the east of Melbourne is home to many promising, small, new wineries; Chardonnay and Rhine Riesling do well here.

New South Wales

Much of New South Wales is not really very suitable for growing wine grapes: many areas of the state are too hot and too wet, and other places are too dry. As a result, Australia's grape-growing action has shifted in the 20th century away from New South Wales — site of the oldest wine-growing regions in the country — and toward South Australia and parts of Victoria. However, New South Wales still produces 27 percent of Australia's wines, and many of Australia's well-established, large wineries are here.

The finest Semillons have always come from New South Wales.

Regions known for white wine in New South Wales are

✓ **Lower Hunter Valley:** Unquestionably Australia's most famous wine region, Lower Hunter Valley is about a three-hour drive north of the Australian capital city, Sydney. Most of New South Wales' wineries (and wine tourists) are here. Semillon does very well in this region — and if you like your Chardonnays golden, buttery, and opulent, the Chardonnays here are ideal.

✓ **Upper Hunter Valley:** The dryer climate of the upper Hunter Valley suits grape growing better than that of the Lower Hunter Valley. White wines do well here, especially Semillon and Chardonnay.

✓ **Mudgee:** This region, west of the Hunter Valley, is dry and hot and therefore good for red grapes — but voluptuous, full-bodied Chardonnays with melony/fig flavors are also made here.

✓ **Cowra:** Situated west of Sydney, this region is excellent for Chardonnay and, to a lesser extent, Sauvignon Blanc.

Western Australia

This westernmost Australian state makes only a small amount of wine at present, with the best of it coming from two cool regions in the southwestern corner of the country, south of Perth:

✓ **Margaret River:** Margaret River is an up-and-coming region, with fine wine estates such as Leeuwin Estate and Cape Mentelle leading the way; Semillon and Chardonnay do well here.

  ✔ **Lower Great Southern:** Lower Great Southern is a vast, cool region with a big future; Rhine Riesling is particularly good here, with Chardonnay just getting started.

When to drink Aussie whites

Don't worry about the vintage year that you see on a bottle of Australian white wine in terms of its quality, because every vintage is good or better. Notice the vintage for another reason, however: to make certain that the wine is young. Almost all Australian white wines are best when consumed within two years of the vintage. This is certainly the case for Chardonnays, Sauvignon Blancs, Rieslings, and blended wines. Semillons are capable of aging and developing for five to eight years, but can also be consumed when they are young.

Recommended producers of Australian white wines

Most of the wines that we recommend in this section are Chardonnays, clearly Australia's most popular white wine, especially in the U.S. See Figure 9-2 for a label from a popular Australian Chardonnay. We have also included Semillons in our recommendations, because Australia does very well with this wine, plus a few Semillon-Chardonnay blends and Sauvignon Blancs.

Figure 9-2: Label from one of the most popular Australian Chardonnays.

We have grouped our recommended wines into two categories —
wines that retail under $10, and wines that retail over $10. In
Tables 9-1 and 9-2, respectively, we list these wines alphabetically, according to producer. We mark our favorites with ♟.

Table 9-1   Recommended Australian White Wines Under $10

Producer	Wines
Barrier Reef	Chardonnay
	Sauvignon Blanc
Black Opal	Chardonnay
Brown Brothers	Chardonnay (King Valley)
Cedar Creek	Chardonnay
	Semillon-Chardonnay
Chateau Reynella	Chardonnay
Coldridge	Chardonnay
	Semillon-Chardonnay
Cowra Estate	Chardonnay
David Wynn (Mountadam)	Chardonnay
	Semillon-Chardonnay
Hardy's	Chardonnay (Padthaway)
	Chardonnay, Nottage Hill
Hunter Ridge	♟ Chardonnay, Vanessa's Vale
Leasingham	Chardonnay
Peter Lehmann	♟ Semillon
Lindemans	♟ Chardonnay "Bin 65"
	♟ Semillon-Chardonnay "Bin 77"
	♟ Sauvignon Blanc "Bin 95"
McGuigan Brothers	Semillon-Chardonnay
	Chardonnay
McLarens	Chardonnay
	Semillon-Chardonnay
McWilliams	Chardonnay
	Semillon-Chardonnay
Michelton	Chardonnay, Victorian
	Semillon-Chardonnay

Producer	Wines
Milburn Park	♟ Chardonnay Sauvignon Blanc
Montrose	Chardonnay
Normans	Chardonnay, Family Reserve
Orlando	Chardonnay, "Jacob's Creek" Semillon-Chardonnay Sauvignon Blanc, "Jacob's Creek"
Oxford Landing	Chardonnay Sauvignon Blanc
Penfolds	♟ Chardonnay ♟ Semillon-Chardonnay "Koonunga Hill"
Redbank	Chardonnay Semillon
Rosemount Estate	♟ Chardonnay Semillon-Chardonnay Fumé Blanc
Rothbury Estate	Chardonnay
Seaview	Sauvignon Blanc Chardonnay Semillon-Sauvignon Blanc
Seppelt	♟ Chardonnay "Black Label" Chardonnay "Reserve Bin" Semillon-Chardonnay
Taltarni	♟ Sauvignon Blanc
Tyrells	♟ Chardonnay Chardonnay-Semillon (Long Flat)
Wolf Blass	Chardonnay Semillon-Chardonnay
Wyndham Estates	Chardonnay, Oak Cask Chardonnay "Bin 222" Semillon-Chardonnay "Bin 777"
Yalumba	Chardonnay, Oxford Landing

Table 9-2 alphabetically lists producers of recommended wines costing more than $10. We mark our favorites with ♟.

Table 9-2	Recommended Australian White Wines Over $10
Producer	*Wines*
Tim Adams	Semillon Riesling
Bannockburn	� Chardonnay
Barwang	Chardonnay Semillon
Brands Laira	♟ Chardonnay (Coonawarra)
Cape Mentelle	Semillon Chardonnay
Cold Stream Hills	Chardonnay
Cullens	Chardonnay ♟ Semillon Sauvignon Blanc
Evans and Tate	♟ Semillon ♟ Sauvignon Blanc Chardonnay
Henschke	♟ Semillon Chardonnay Sauvignon Blanc
Hill-Smith Estate	Chardonnay Semillon
Leeuwin Estate	♟ Chardonnay
Lindemans	♟ Chardonnay (Padthaway) ♟ Semillon (Padthaway)
Michelton	Chardonnay, Victoria Reserve
Moss Wood	Semillon Chardonnay
Mountadam	Chardonnay
Mount Pleasant	Semillon Chardonnay
Petaluma	Chardonnay
Pierro	Chardonnay
Rosemount Estate	♟ Chardonnay, Roxburgh Estate ♟ Chardonnay, Show Reserve

Producer	Wines
Rothbury Estate	♟ Chardonnay Reserve
Scotchman's Hill	Chardonnay
Tyrell's	♟ Chardonnay "Vat 47"
Wynns	Chardonnay (Coonawarra)
Yalumba	Chardonnay, Show Reserve (Yarra/Eden Valleys)

New Zealand — White Wine Specialists

In this cool country — considerably more southerly in latitude than its neighbor, Australia — white wine rules, especially the wines of the Sauvignon Blanc grape variety. In fact, New Zealand Sauvignon Blanc wines are among the best Sauvignon Blancs in the world — and some people actually maintain that New Zealand's Sauvignon Blancs are the best of all. (New Zealand's Sauvignon Blancs' rivals are the white wines of France's Bordeaux; Sancerre and Pouilly Fumé wines from France's Loire Valley; and possibly South African Sauvignon Blanc. See Chapter 11 for information on the French Sauvignon Blanc-based wines, and see the section "Out of (South) Africa" later in this chapter for more on that country's Sauvignons.)

One New Zealand Sauvignon Blanc wine — that of Cloudy Bay Winery — has received worldwide recognition and is now difficult to find other than in fine restaurants. But many other good Sauvignon Blancs and some fine Chardonnays and Rieslings are being made in New Zealand. Unfortunately, worldwide availability of New Zealand wines is limited; only if you live in or near a large city will you be fortunate enough to find a few examples.

The hurdle to wider availability of New Zealand wines is the small quantity of fine wine that the country produces — which itself is due to the very late start New Zealand has had in winemaking. Despite having some wonderful conditions for grape growing, New Zealand came late to the fine wine business because of ultraconservative attitudes towards alcohol that have relaxed only recently. In the same year that the U.S. made Prohibition a national law (1919), New Zealand enacted a similar law, which was subsequently overturned by a narrow vote. Not until 1979 was the first wine bar license granted in New Zealand, and not until 1990 were "dry" areas (localities that forbade alcohol sales) abolished in the country and supermarkets allowed to sell wine. For wine lovers living in the U. S., this story has a familiar ring.

And so New Zealand's history of making fine wine is a very recent one. The best region for growing Sauvignon Blanc was discovered only in 1973. Remarkably, the first vintage of the now-famous Cloudy Bay Sauvignon Blanc was as recent as 1985!

New Zealand's white grapes

Four white grape varieties are responsible for most of New Zealand's white wines:

- **Müller-Thurgau** *(MOO ler TER gow)*, Germany's most-planted grape variety, is also New Zealand's most widely planted grape. This grape produces rather common white wine here, as in the rest of the world.

- **Chardonnay**, New Zealand's second most important (and second most-planted) grape variety, produces distinguished wines in this country — to the surprise of no one who has followed Chardonnay's success in almost every other wine-producing country.

- **Sauvignon Blanc**, only third in production at present, is just magical here, especially on New Zealand's cooler South Island. If ever there were a grape-*terroir* marriage made in heaven, the union of Sauvignon Blanc and New Zealand is it.

- **Rhine Riesling**, as the Riesling grape is called here, also grows well in New Zealand's cooler regions. A few New Zealand Rhine Rieslings are dry, while many are off-dry, but labeled *dry.*

Other white wines made in New Zealand, in smaller quantities, include Chenin Blanc, Gewürztraminer, and Pinot Gris.

White wine regions of New Zealand

Generally speaking, red wines do best on New Zealand's warmer North Island, and white wines excel on the cooler South Island. But of course the Chardonnay grape, being so adaptable, does well on both Islands, and Chardonnay wine is made in both places. (A riper, heavier, more melony style predominates on the North Island, while a leaner, more lemony, lively style characterizes the wines of the South Island. Sauvignon Blanc wines differ likewise from the North Island to the South Island.)

The following are New Zealand's important white wine regions on the North Island:

- ✔ **Auckland**: On the northern end of the island, this region is home base to many of New Zealand's largest wineries. Some Chardonnay and Sauvignon Blanc grapes are grown in this area, but most white grapes are brought in from the cooler southern regions.

- ✔ **Hawke's Bay**: This region in the central part of the North Island produces some excellent Chardonnays, but Sauvignon Blancs are less good.

- ✔ **Gisborne/Poverty Bay**: This region is located in the central part of the North Island. Lots of Müller-Thurgau wine and some Chardonnay wines come from here, but the region's best wines are its Gewürztraminers and Rhine Rieslings.

- ✔ **Wairarapa/Martinborough**: Chardonnay does very well in this quality wine region at the southern end of North Island. Pinot Gris, Riesling, and Sauvignon Blanc also come from this region.

The following are New Zealand's important white wine regions on the South Island:

- ✔ **Nelson**: This small region at the north end of the island produces some good Rieslings, Chardonnays, Gewürztraminers, and Sauvignon Blancs.

- ✔ **Marlborough**: Also at the north end of the island, Marlborough is *the* premium Sauvignon Blanc region in New Zealand. Excellent Chardonnays and Rieslings come from here as well.

- ✔ **Canterbury**: This small, cool region in the central part of the South Island produces Chardonnays and Rieslings.

- ✔ **Central Otago**: Situated on the southern end of the island, this small but rapidly growing region is in fact the most southerly wine region in the world. Because it has an interior location, summers here are warmer than you would expect at such a southerly latitude. The Germanic grape varieties do well here, especially Müller-Thurgau and Gewürztraminer (Riesling less so), as does the variety that seldom lets winemakers down — Chardonnay.

Spotlight on New Zealand Sauvignon Blanc

The Montana Winery first planted Sauvignon Blanc grapes in the Marlborough region of the South Island in 1973 and 1974, but did not have enough grapes for its first commercial release of the wine until 1980. That harvest and the 1981 harvest were both minuscule for Montana, however, and it was not until 1982 that the winery could release a viable amount of Sauvignon Blanc — that's how new New Zealand Sauvignon Blanc really is! Subsequently, with Cloudy Bay's first vintage in 1985, wine lovers the world over discovered this "new" wine.

New Zealand Sauvignon Blanc wines — particularly those coming from Marlborough — have intensely pungent aromas and flavors of grassiness, green melon, lime, grapefruit, and asparagus, combined with suggestions of tropical fruit and various herbs. They are very lively, assertive, crisp wines, as their acidity is quite high. Yet at their best, they have enough weight and texture to balance their high acidity.

Most Sauvignon Blancs from the cooler New Zealand regions are fermented in stainless steel, are not aged in oak, and are bottled early to retain their maximum freshness.

Enjoying New Zealand Whites

Because much of New Zealand has a maritime climate and quite a bit of rain falls during the growing season, vintages are somewhat variable — unlike Australia. Early reports indicate that the 1996 vintage is a good one, but not great (great vintages are in bold). The 1995 vintage was fair, at best (too much rain), but **1994** was a great year. Fine older vintages include the **1988** and **1989**. If you can find New Zealand white wines, our advice is to pass up the 1995s and buy the 1994s.

All of New Zealand's white wines, including the Sauvignon Blancs, can be consumed immediately upon release to the market, which is usually the year following the vintage. Some winemakers, however, suggest that you drink both Chardonnays and Sauvignon Blancs two years after the vintage. In good vintages, New Zealand Chardonnays and Sauvignon Blancs can age well for about eight years.

New Zealanders are rightfully proud of their large, delicious mussels — a perfect match for New Zealand Sauvignon Blanc. But mussels from elsewhere — and other shellfish, such as oysters — would also go well. New Zealand's Sauvignons and Chardonnays are definitely flavorful enough to accompany lobster, too. As for cheese, fresh goat cheese is excellent with New Zealand's Sauvignon Blancs.

Recommended producers of New Zealand white wines

Most of the white wines we recommend are Sauvignon Blancs, clearly New Zealand's best wine. (We believe that some good Rieslings and Chardonnays are also produced in New Zealand — but good Chardonnay wine is made all around the world, and the demand for New Zealand's Rieslings is not great.) Our recommendations are tempered, of course, by availability: We list only wines that are currently being exported from New Zealand.

As you might expect from the fine reputation that New Zealand Sauvignon Blancs enjoy, these tend to be New Zealand's most expensive white wines. Retail prices range from about $8 for the least expensive Chardonnays and Rieslings to about $18 or $20 for Cloudy Bay Sauvignon Blanc (a reasonable price for a wine of this quality).

Table 9-3 lists our recommended producers of New Zealand wines in alphabetical order. Our personal favorites are marked by ♉.

Table 9-3	Recommended Producers of New Zealand White Wines	
Producer	**Wine(s)**	**Region**
Cloudy Bay	♉ Sauvignon Blanc Chardonnay	Marlborough Marlborough
Coopers Creek	♉ Chardonnay Riesling (off-dry)	Hawke's Bay Hawke's Bay
Corbans	Chardonnay	Gisborne
Goldwater Estate	♉ Chardonnay, "Delmore"	Waiheke Island
Hunters	♉ Sauvignon Blanc ♉ Chardonnay	Marlborough Marlborough
Jackson Estate	♉ Sauvignon Blanc Chardonnay	Marlborough Marlborough

(continued)

Table 9-3 (continued)

Producer	Wine(s)	Region
Kumeu River	Chardonnay	Auckland
	Sauvignon Blanc	Auckland
Matua Valley	♟ Sauvignon Blanc Reserve	Auckland
Morton Estate	Chardonnay "White Label"	Hawke's Bay
Palliser Estate	♟ Sauvignon Blanc	Martinborough
	Chardonnay	Martinborough
C. J. Pask	♟ Chenin Blanc	Hawke's Bay
	Chardonnay	Hawke's Bay
Selaks	♟ Sauvignon Blanc/Semillon	Marlborough
	Sauvignon Blanc	Marlborough
	Chardonnay Reserve	Marlborough
Stoneleigh	Sauvignon Blanc	Marlborough

The following excellent producers of New Zealand white wine are not currently represented in the U.S., but might be in the near future — in some instances, their wines are available in other countries. We list these producers alphabetically:

- Babich
- Collards
- Delegats
- De Redcliffe
- Grove Mill
- Martinborough Vineyard
- Montana
- Neudorf
- Sacred Hill
- Seifried Estate
- Te Mata
- Vavasour
- Vidal
- Villa Maria

Out of (South) Africa

The Chenin Blanc grape — called Steen in South Africa — is South Africa's largest-producing variety. It makes mainly inexpensive wine and is the reason that South Africa is the world's seventh largest wine-producing country. But that picture is changing, as South Africa emerges from its past.

South Africa has made good dessert wines and fortified wines for centuries. But quality dry wine has been common in South Africa for only about ten years. Today, the white wines of South Africa can rival just about any other country's in quality — with the exception of France's finest white wines from Burgundy and Bordeaux (see Chapters 10 and 11).

South Africa's best white wines today are Sauvignon Blancs and Chardonnays, in that order. But the discrepancy between these two types isn't as great as in New Zealand, where Sauvignon Blanc far outshines its perennial rival.

South Africa happens to be one of the few places in the world where you can find a wine called Sauvignon-Chardonnay (or the reverse), blended from a combination of the two grapes. (That odd combination doesn't taste bad, either.)

The style of South African white wine

South Africa's white wine style is unique, whether the grape variety is Sauvignon Blanc or Chardonnay. On one hand, South African whites have some of the leanness, complexity, and subtlety of European white wines, particularly French whites — but they're not quite the same. On the other hand, they don't have the oakiness, fleshy ripeness, fruitiness, and body of New World whites, say from California or Australia.

South African Sauvignon Blancs are definitely flavorful and assertive, but without the intensity and searing acidity of those from New Zealand.

In short, South African white wines combine features of both traditional European and innovative New World white wines. Their wines, like the beautiful country itself, are somewhere between both worlds.

South Africa's major white wine regions

Most of South Africa's best white wine regions are in Cape Province, within 90 miles of its principal city, picturesque Cape Town. The crescent-shaped Coastal Region stretches west to the Atlantic Ocean and east to the Indian Ocean — the only wine region in the world that's situated between two oceans. Four of South Africa's best wine districts are here, where the generally hot climate is cooled by the prevailing ocean breezes:

- **Constantia:** The oldest wine-producing region in South Africa, Constantia is located south of Cape Town.
- **Stellenbosch:** Stellenbosch, east of Cape Town, is the country's most important wine region in terms of quantity and quality.
- **Paarl:** North of Stellenbosch, Paarl is a warmer region that's home to the KWV (the South African wine-regulating body) and some of South Africa's fine wineries, such as the Nederburg Estate.
- **Franschhoek Valley:** East of Stellenbosch, the Franschhoek Valley is an area with many innovative wineries.

Farther east and south, along the coast of the Indian Ocean, is one other up-and-coming wine region worth noting: **Hermanus/Walker Bay.** Hermanus/Walker Bay is a very cool region that shows promise for Chardonnay, especially when the Chardonnay is from the excellent Hamilton Russell Vineyards.

Recent good vintages, and when to drink them

Vintages in South Africa, as in other dry, warm-climate regions, are consistently good. (The cooler Coastal Region does experience some variable weather, however.)

The best recent vintages for white wine are 1995, 1993, 1992, and especially **1991**. 1988 through 1990 are poor to fair, and you don't want any older vintages than that for white wines in South Africa.

In general, you should drink South African white wines young, within two or three years of the vintage. A few of the best Chardonnays can age for three or four more years.

Recommended producers of South African white wines

Table 9-4 lists our recommended South African producers and their best white wines. Most of the wines are Chardonnays and Sauvignon Blancs. Retail prices for these wines are in the $8 to $16 range — good values for wines of this quality. Producers are listed alphabetically; our favorite wines are indicated with a ♟ symbol.

Table 9-4   Recommended White Wines from South Africa

Producer	Wines	Region
Backsberg Estate	♟ Chardonnay Sauvignon Blanc	Paarl Paarl
Boschendal Estate	♟ Sauvignon Blanc ♟ Semillon Chardonnay	Paarl Paarl Paarl
Fleur du Cap	Sauvignon Blanc	Stellenbosch
Glen Carlou	Chardonnay	Paarl
Groot Constantia Estate	Chardonnay Sauvignon Blanc	Constantia Constantia
Hamilton Russell Vyds.	♟ Chardonnay ♟ Chardonnay- Sauvignon Blanc ♟ Sauvignon Blanc	Walker Bay Walker Bay Walker Bay
Klein Constantia Estate	♟ Sauvignon Blanc ♟ Chardonnay	Constantia Constantia
La Motte Estate	♟ Sauvignon Blanc Chardonnay	Franschhoek Franschhoek
Lievland Estate	Chardonnay Sauvignon Blanc	Stellenbosch Stellenbosch
L'Ormarins Estate	♟ Chardonnay Sauvignon Blanc	Franschhoek Franschhoek
Louisvale	♟ Chardonnay Sauvignon-Chardonnay	Stellenbosch Stellenbosch
Meerlust Estate	♟ Chardonnay	Stellenbosch
Mulderbosch Vyds.	♟ Sauvignon Blanc	Stellenbosch

(continued)

Table 9-4 *(continued)*

Producer	Wines	Region
Nederburg Estate	♆ Sauvignon Blanc	Paarl
	♆ Prelude (73% Sauvignon, 27% Chardonnay)	Paarl
	♆ Chardonnay	Paarl
Neil Ellis	♆ Chardonnay	Stellenbosch
	♆ Sauvignon Blanc	Elgin (Overberg)
Overgaauw Estate	Chardonnay	Stellenbosch
	Sauvignon Blanc	Stellenbosch
Plaisir de Merle	♆ Chardonnay	Franschhoek
	♆ Sauvignon Blanc	Franschhoek
Rustenberg Estate	Sauvignon Blanc	Stellenbosch
Simonsig Estate	Chardonnay	Stellenbosch
	Vin Fumé (Sauvignon)	Stellenbosch
Simonsvlei Winery	Chardonnay/ Sauvignon Blanc	Paarl
Thelema Mountain Vyds.	♆ Sauvignon Blanc	Stellenbosch
	♆ Chardonnay	Stellenbosch
	♆ Rhine Riesling	Stellenbosch
Villiera Estate	♆ Sauvignon Blanc	Paarl
	♆ Chenin Blanc	Paarl
	Chardonnay	Paarl
Warwick Estates	Chardonnay	Stellenbosch
Zonnebloem	♆ Sauvignon Blanc	Stellenbosch
	♆ Chardonnay	Stellenbosch
	Sauvignon Blanc-Chardonnay	Stellenbosch
	Blanc de Blanc (Chenin Blanc)	Stellenbosch

Chapter 10

Vin Blanc Français: The Great White Burgundies

. . . .

In This Chapter
- ▶ The world's greatest dry white wines
- ▶ The French approach to winemaking
- ▶ The "real" Chablis
- ▶ The value of place

. . . .

*F*rance's red wines are so justifiably famous that we sometimes forget that this country produces many of the finest white wines in the world.

For us, there are no finer dry white wines than white Burgundies. We only wish that they weren't so expensive — and difficult to find. In this chapter, we explain how the French have set the world standard for fine wines, and why white Burgundy ranks among the greatest white wines in the world.

The Ups and Downs of Burgundy

Wine drinkers who are accustomed to the fairly simple system of naming wines in the U.S. can easily become overwhelmed when they deal with the wines of Burgundy — the topic of this chapter. But the white wines of Burgundy are fathomable, even to beginners, as long as you keep the Big Picture in mind and don't get bogged down in details.

In the pages of this chapter, however, we do get down to details; we *have* to in order to give you what we hope is practical and valuable advice on buying white Burgundy wines. So right here, before we wander off into the hilly terrain of Burgundy villages, vineyards, and producers, we describe the Big Picture. Some of this information might not make complete sense to you right now, but we hope this sketch will become increasingly valuable as you delve into the details of the individual chapter sections. We elaborate on all the points of this Big Picture in the sections of the chapter that follow.

✔ (Practically) all the white wines of Burgundy are made from the same grape, Chardonnay.

✔ What makes one wine different from the next is the precise place where the grapes grow.

✔ An official hierachy of vineyard land exists.

✔ The broader the area of land from which the grapes come, the less fine the wine (in theory).

✔ The more limited the area of land from which the grapes come, the finer the wine (again, in theory).

✔ The areas of land are divided into categories, from broadest down to most specific:

- region (the whole of Burgundy)
- district (there are four)
- subdistrict
- village (also called a *commune*)
- vineyard
- premier cru vineyard (the better vineyards)
- grand cru vineyard (the best vineyards)

✔ The wines are named for the place where their grapes grow (either the region, the district, the village, or the cru vineyard): The wines are not called Chardonnay.

✔ Wines from broader places cost less than wines from more specific places.

✔ Regardless of the hierarchy of places, the most important issue in buying white Burgundy is the quality of the individual producer.

White Burgundy — Chardonnay at Its Best

If you read our previous chapters dealing with Chardonnay (Chapter 6 and Chapter 9), you may have the impression that we either don't like Chardonnay very much or are very tired of it. Some truth lies in both of those conclusions — until the discussion turns to the white wines of Burgundy.

Yes, Chardonnay is the grape of white Burgundies (most white Burgundies, in fact, are 100 percent Chardonnay). In the Burgundy region, the Chardonnay grape rises to its greatest heights. To experience such fine white Burgundy wines as Corton-Charlemagne *(cor tawn shahr luh mahn)*, Montrachet *(mon rah shay)*, Chablis *(shah blee)*, or Meursault *(muhr so)* is a reverential experience for us. The great novelist Alexandre Dumas once said that Montrachet should be drunk while one is on his knees, with his head uncovered.

Getting off our knees for a moment, we must admit that two tiny catches exist for buyers of really fine white Burgundy: (1) the stuff is expensive, and (2) you have to select a really good producer's wine to experience white Burgundy at its best.

Of course, lower-priced white Burgundies, such as Borgogne Blanc and Mâcon-Villages — described later in the chapter — are readily available in wine shops at $8 to $15 and are certainly worth trying. But don't expect to find the same magic in these less expensive Burgundies that you can find in the very finest types that we've just mentioned.

The Land of White Burgundy

The Burgundy region, known as Bourgogne *(boor guh nyuh)*, is in eastern France, a few hours' drive southeast of Paris and directly north of Lyon, France's gastronomic capital.

Limestone soil — ideal for Chardonnay — predominates in all the areas where the grapes for white Burgundy grow. Climate here is continental — hot summers, cold winters, and the ever-present threat of hailstorms in the summer, especially in the northern districts. The fairly harsh climate results in only a few really good vintages for white Burgundy each decade.

Actually, four distinct districts produce white Burgundy. From north to south, they are

- Chablis
- the Côte d'Or *(coat dor)*, especially the subdistrict of the Côte de Beaune *(coat deh bone)*
- the Côte Chalonnaise *(coat shal oh naze)*
- Mâcon *(mah kon)*

The power of place

The French have a way with wine — conceptualizing it, naming it, classifying it — that is completely different from the countries we cover in Chapters 6 through 9 (non-European, "New World" countries, as they're known). To minimize any potential frustration or confusion regarding French white wines, remember these basic precepts that underlie all the laws, names, and classifications of French wines.

- The French see their wines not as the end-product of specific grape varieties, but as the end-product of specific *places*. Most French wines are therefore named after the place where the grapes grow, not after the grape variety.

- The various places where grapes grow in France have all been drawn up, defined in writing, and named. This information has been incorporated into French law, so that no official place-name can be used by anyone (in France or in any other European Union country) whose grapes come from a different place.

- Many of the larger officially recognized places have been subdivided into smaller places that are also officially recognized. Because specificity of place is the principle behind French wines, a wine from a smaller, more specific place is theoretically finer than a wine from the larger area encompassing that smaller place. (Thus, a white Burgundy from the village of Meursault would be considered a finer wine than one simply identified as being from the Burgundy region.) In decreasing size, the places are usually referred to as regions, districts, subdistricts, villages or communes, and vineyards.

- The French have been making wine for so long that they have discovered exactly which grape varieties grow best in which places. This information is codified into law: National wine laws stipulate exactly which grapes can grow in any particular place. (The place-name of a French wine therefore tells you, indirectly, which grape variety or varieties were used to make that wine.)

 For more information about how French wines are named, the words on French wine labels, and the various official ranks that exist among French wines, refer to Chapters 7, 8, and 10 of our book *Wine For Dummies* (published by IDG Books Worldwide, Inc.).

All four districts' wines are white Burgundies, technically speaking. But when people speak about white Burgundy, they are usually referring specifically to the wines of the Côte de Beaune, which include all the wines of the Montrachet family (see "Village-level Côte d'Or White Burgundies" later in this chapter), Meursault, and Corton-Charlemagne. Wine lovers usually call wine from Chablis simply by its own name, and refer to Mâcon's wines by their own specific names — such as Mâcon-Villages *(mah kawn vee lahj)*, Saint-Véran *(san veh rahn)*, or Pouilly-Fuissé *(pwee fwee say)*. The white Burgundies of the Côte Chalonnaise are the least known of the region, so not many people refer to them at all! Wines from that district are therefore excellent values.

Because each district produces distinctly different wine, we examine each of the four separately, beginning with Chablis.

The Real Chablis

Drive southeast out of Paris, toward the Riviera, and in about two hours you arrive in the small village of Chablis, the first outpost of the Burgundy wine region. The wines of Chablis, like most fine white Burgundies from the Côte d'Or district, are 100 percent Chardonnay — but they are markedly different from Côte d'Or white Burgundies in structure and in flavor, due to differences in growing conditions and wine-making practices between the two areas.

Real Chablis doesn't have jugs

Your neighborhood wine store probably sells some wine in the "California Jug Wine" section (made by large producers such as Gallo, Almaden, Inglenook, Paul Masson, or CK Mondavi) that calls itself "Chablis." Also, many American restaurants and bars serve one of these wines and simply identify it as Chablis. Although these inexpensive, medium-dry white wines are decent enough, they bear no resemblance to the true Chablis from the village of Chablis, France. These wines are definitely not made from the Chardonnay grape but are usually blended from less distinguished grapes grown in industrial-scale vineyards in California's hot, fertile Central Valley. If you want to experience the real thing, look at the label of your "Chablis." Make sure that it comes from France.

How one of us caught the wine bug

Chablis has a special meaning to one of us, because this was the first great wine we tasted, back when we were about 20 years old. Portuguese rosés (such as Mateus and Lancer's), sweet, inexpensive German wines, run-of-the-mill Italian wines, and California jug wines made up our wine repertoire in those days — until that evening when someone handed us a glass of French Chablis. We're not exaggerating when we say that, for us, this was a moment of epiphany. We realized for the first time that wine could be something really special — more than just a beverage to wash down food. That night was the beginning of a personal adventure in wine that is still going strong today.

Chablis is typically light-to-medium-bodied, minerally (some say *stony* or *flinty*), and high in acidity. Most Chablis producers ferment and age their wine in stainless steel rather than in oak casks, believing that oak masks or even overwhelms Chablis' delicate flavor and structure. (On the other hand, two of Chablis' greatest producers, Francois Raveneau and René et Vincent Dauvissat, ferment and age their wines in oak, thus making fuller-styled Chablis wine that nevertheless retains the character of Chablis.)

Chablis is an outstanding wine to drink with seafood, especially oysters, clams, and mussels. Grand cru Chablis (see the following section), which is fuller than basic Chablis, is perfect with lobster or dark-fleshed, meaty fish. Serve Chablis cool (58 to 60° F), but not cold, as with all fine, dry white wines.

Grand cru and premier cru Chablis

French wine law recognizes some vineyards in the Chablis district as superior to the other vineyards of the area. The very finest vineyards are called grand cru vineyards, and their wines are considered to be the best wines of Chablis. At the next level of quality are premier cru *(prem yay croo)* vineyards, whose wines are considered better than basic Chablis wines, but less fine than grand cru Chablis.

Of course, the producer's own personal stamp on his wine can influence this hierarchy. For example, a fine producer's premier cru Chablis might very well be better than an average producer's grand cru Chablis.

Grand cru Chablis wines are usually labeled "Chablis Grand Cru," followed by the name of the individual vineyard (or *cru*). The seven grand cru vineyards of Chablis are

- Blanchot *(blahn shoh)*
- Bougros *(boo groh)*
- Les Clos *(lay cloh)*
- Grenouilles *(greh n'wee)*
- Les Preuses *(lay preuh'z)*
- Valmur *(vahl moor)*
- Vaudésir *(voh deh zeer)*

The vineyard site La Moutonne *(moo tun)* is part of Vaudésir and Les Preuses; wines from this vineyard are entitled to be labeled "Chablis Grand Cru" even though the vineyard is technically not a grand cru in its own right.

Grand cru Chablis wines range in price from about $25 to $65 (the most expensive are produced by Francois Raveneau). Unlike basic Chablis wines that sell in the $10 to $18 range and should be consumed within five or six years, grand cru Chablis wines actually improve with five or six years of aging — and in good vintages (see "White Burgundy vintages" later in this chapter), grand cru Chablis can age for up to 15 years.

Of the 22 premier cru vineyards of Chablis, the six most well- known are

- Fourchaume *(for chahm)*
- Les Forêts *(lay for ay)*
- Mont de Milieu *(mon deh meh lyew)*
- Montée de Tonnerre *(mon tay deh tun nair)*
- Montmains *(mon man)*
- Vaillons *(vye yon)*

The premier cru vineyard name appears on the label; if a wine is made from a combination of premier cru vineyards rather than from a single vineyard, however, only the phrase *premier cru* appears on the label. (The word "premier" is sometimes abbreviated as "1er" on labels of white Burgundy.) Premier cru Chablis wines range in price from $18 to $45, depending on the producer, and can age and improve for up to ten years in good vintage years.

Recommended Chablis producers

The vital issue when you are buying Chablis (and all wines from Burgundy — white or red) is that you must choose a producer who has a good-to-excellent recent track record for making quality wines. The second most important criterion is to select a Chablis from a good vintage. Thirdly, we suggest that you stick to grand cru or premier cru Chablis, if you want the best examples of this wonderful, unique white wine.

We list the following recommended Chablis producers in our rough order of preference, and mark our very, very favorites with a ▼ symbol. They all produce both grand cru and premier cru Chablis; choose whichever quality level you can afford. Naturally, the name of each producer appears on the label of his wine. (We have omitted from this list those producers whose wines are extremely limited in quantity or are almost impossible to obtain.)

- Francois Raveneau ▼
- René et Vincent Dauvissat ▼
- Louis Michel et Fils ▼
- Droin Bertonnieres ▼
- Gérard Duplessis
- Jean-Claude Bessin
- Jean Dauvissat
- J. Moreau et Fils
- Domaine Laroche
- Long-Depaquit
- Billaud-Simon
- Jean Collet
- Robert Vocoret et Fils
- William Fèvre/Domaine de la Maladière

The Golden Burgundies of the Côte d'Or

When you leave Chablis, about an hour's drive to the southeast takes you to the Côte d'Or district, home of Burgundy's finest white and red wines. A narrow strip of 28 villages surrounded by vineyards, the Côte d'Or (Golden Slope) runs north to south for 34 miles, from the outskirts of the city of Dijon in the north to just beyond Santenay in the south.

White Burgundy vintages

1986, **1989,** and 1992 have been the best vintages for white Burgundy during the past decade (although some wines from the 1986 vintage are showing signs of aging). 1985 and 1990 are also good vintages, and are aging well. 1995 shows promise, but it is too early to make a final judgment on this vintage. White Burgundies older than 1985 generally are past their best — with the exception of the very finest wines.

The Côte d'Or district of Burgundy is divided into two subdistricts. The northern part, the Côte de Nuits, produces red wines almost exclusively (see our book *Red Wine For Dummies,* for information on those wines). The southern part, the Côte de Beaune, makes great white Burgundies as well as red Burgundies. The commercial center of the Côte de Beaune is the town of Beaune — where several of the larger wine companies, as well as many hotels and restaurants, are located.

Côte d'Or white Burgundies are barrel-fermented and aged in oak for 12 to 14 months (see Chapter 2 for an explanation of the effects of barrel-fermentation). These Burgundies are medium-to-full-bodied wines with firm acidity; their aromas and flavors are often reminiscent of hazelnuts, almonds, vanilla, apples, and honey. At their best, they are so well-balanced that every element of the wine melts together into a creamy ensemble.

Most Côte d'Or white Burgundies are best when consumed within 8 to 10 years of the vintage, although a few of the very best (from vintages like 1978) can age and improve for 20 years or more.

The Côte d'Or classified

The real estate dictum, "location, location, location," could have been invented by the winemakers of Burgundy. Soil and climate vary so much in Burgundy, especially in the Côte d'Or district, that the quality and character of the wine (and its price) vary considerably according to where the grapes grow:

- ✔ The finest and most expensive wines come from specific, small vineyards.
- ✔ The wines from broader and less pedigreed areas are generally less fine, as well as less costly.

Two kinds of Burgundy producers

The wines of Burgundy have traditionally been sold by *négociant* houses, local companies that buy grapes and/or wine from growers and then produce their own Burgundies, according to their own "house style." Some of well-known *négociant* houses in Burgundy are Louis Jadot, Joseph Drouhin, Louis Latour, Bouchard Père et Fils, and Georges Duboeuf.

During the early part of this century, a few Burgundian growers began bottling their own wine rather than selling their grapes or wine to a *négociant* house. After World War II, more and more growers started making and selling their Burgundy wines in their own name; today, about half of all Burgundy wine is made and sold directly by individual growers.

Although the so-called *grower Burgundies* can often be outstanding, thanks to the unique qualities of small vineyard plots that the growers own, and to the growers' personal care for their wines, most of these growers are very small producers, and their wines are therefore expensive. Almost all *négociant* Burgundies, in comparison, are produced in larger quantity and are therefore less expensive as well as easier to find.

 You usually can't tell which category a producer falls into by studying the wine label, but the producers whose names you see most often are usually *négociants*, because their volume is greater.

Every white Burgundy of the Côte d'Or (every red, too, for that matter) falls into one of five categories, or classifications, according to where its grapes grow. At the broadest level are white Burgundies whose grapes come from anywhere in the Burgundy region; at the most specific level are white Burgundies whose grapes come from a particular vineyard that has been designated one of the finest sites of all. In between are wines whose grapes come not from specific small vineyards but from any vineyards that belong to a specific village, or commune. Table 10-1 lists the five categories, from the broadest to the most specific (that is, from the simplest wines to the finest wines).

Table 10-1	The Burgundy Classification System — Côte d'Or and Côte Chalonnaise
Category	*Examples of Wines in the Category*
Regional Wine	Bourgogne Blanc; Bourgogne-Aligoté
District/Subdistrict Wine	Côte de Beaune Blanc; Hautes Côtes de Beaune Blanc
Commune or Village Wine	Puligny-Montrachet; Meursault
Premier Cru Vineyard Wine	Puligny-Montrachet Les Combettes; Meursault Charmes
Grand Cru Vineyard Wine	Montrachet; Bâtard-Montrachet; Corton-Charlemagne

You can tell the difference between a village Burgundy, a premier cru, or a grand cru by looking at the label (see Figure 10-1):

- ✔ A village-level white Burgundy's name is just the village's name (sometimes a hyphenated word), such as Chassagne-Montrachet, Puligny-Montrachet, or Meursault.

- ✔ A premier cru white Burgundy has the name of the village plus the name of a vineyard on the label, both usually in same-sized letters — such as MEURSAULT (the village) GENEVRIÈRES *(jen ev ree aire,* the vineyard).

Why are the best white Burgundies so expensive?

Many wine drinkers are shocked — on two levels — when they attempt to buy white Burgundies for the first time: (1) the best are very difficult to find, and (2) prices for the really good white Burgundies range from $75 to $150 and up, per bottle!

The reasons for this situation are understandable. Burgundy, as a region, produces very little wine. Many producers are very small — some making as little as 25 to 50 cases of a particularly exceptional white Burgundy in any given year. (That amount must supply the needs of the whole world's wine drinkers!) And white Burgundy is one of the most sought-after wines in the world. The obvious conclusion is that the best white Burgundies (as well as red) are always scarce and expensive.

 ✔ If what appears to be a vineyard name is printed in smaller-sized letters than the village's name, the wine is often not a premier cru (that is, not an officially ranked vineyard), but just a single-vineyard wine from that village.

 ✔ Grand cru white Burgundies carry only the name of the grand cru vineyard on the label — such as Montrachet, Chevalier-Montrachet, or Corton-Charlemagne — without the village name.

Additional Producer Name

Wine Name (in this case, a vineyard name)
Official Rank
Country of Origin

DOMAINES DU CHATEAU DE BEAUNE

Vintage

CHEVALIER-MONTRACHET
GRAND CRU
APPELLATION CHEVALIER-MONTRACHET CONTRÔLÉE
PRODUCE OF FRANCE   WHITE BURGUNDY WINE
ALCOHOL 12.5% BY VOLUME   CONT. 750 ML
PRODUCED AND BOTTLED BY : BOUCHARD PÈRE & FILS, BEAUNE
Mise de Maison Bouchard Père & Fils
Négociant au Château, Beaune, Côte d'Or, France

Statement of Appellation of Origin
Type of Wine
Producer

Figure 10-1: Label of a grand cru white Burgundy wine.

Regional- and district-level Côte d'Or white Burgundies

The simplest white Burgundy wine, Bourgogne Blanc, may come from anywhere in the Burgundy region (not just the Côte d'Or district). Such wines are usually made from Chardonnay, but technically Pinot Blanc can be also used; Bourgogne Blanc is priced in the $10 to $18 range.

Three really fine regional Bourgogne Blanc wines to look for are

 ✔ Bourgogne Blanc "Les Clous" ($18), produced by Domaine A. & P. DeVillaine

 ✔ Bourgogne Blanc "d'Auvenay" ($18), produced by Maison Leroy

 ✔ Bourgogne Blanc "Perrieres" ($15), produced by Simon Bize

DeVillaine (of Domaine de la Romanée Conti fame; see *Red Wine For Dummies*) and Leroy are two of the outstanding producers in Burgundy; even their simplest white Burgundies are well-made and a good value. Simon Bize's Burgundies are always quite reliable.

District white Burgundies, such as Côte de Beaune wine, Hautes Côtes de Beaune wine, and Hautes Côtes de Nuits wine, can also be excellent buys when made by good producers such as Jayer-Gilles, Hudelot, Dufouleur, or Cornu. These wines sell in the $15 to $23 range.

Aligoté *(ah lee go tay)* is a white grape variety used in Burgundy's regional wines and in some district Burgundies (the grape name, Aligoté, always appears on the label to indicate that the wine is not Chardonnay-based). Wines made from Aligoté are generally lighter-bodied and more acidic than Chardonnay-based Burgundies, and are usually very crisp and lively. Many Bourgogne-Aligotés, as they are called, sell in the $10 range.

DeVillaine makes a great Bourgogne-Aligoté (from his home town of Bouzeron in the Côte Chalonnaise) that sells for about $16 to $17. The great white Burgundy producer, Domaine Ramonet, also makes a fine Bourgogne-Aligoté ($15 to $16).

Village-level Côte d'Or white Burgundies

Three villages in the Côte de Beaune subdistrict — Meursault, Puligny-Montrachet *(poo lee nyee mon rah shay),* and Chassagne-Montrachet *(shah san yuh mon rah shay)* — are famous for their great white Burgundies, especially on the premier cru and grand cru level. (Puligny-Montrachet produces only white Burgundy, while Chassagne-Montrachet and Meursault also make red Burgundy). A fourth village, Aloxe-Corton *(ah luss cor ton),* is equally renowned for its red and white Burgundies on the grand cru level.

Lesser-known villages on the Côte de Beaune producing white Burgundy — and therefore, sources of good-value wines — are

- ✓ Pernand-Vergelesses *(pair nahn vair juh less)*
- ✓ Savigny-lès-Beaune *(sah vee nyee lay bone)*
- ✓ Beaune
- ✓ Auxey-Duresses *(awk say deh ress)*
- ✓ Monthélie *(mohn teh lee)*
- ✓ Saint-Romain *(san ro man)*
- ✓ Saint-Aubin *(sant oh ban)*

These village names are also the names of the white Burgundy wines produced from the vineyards surrounding each village.

Most white Burgundies with a village name sell in the $20 to $30 price range — although a few from the lesser-known villages cost as low as $14; a village-level Puligny-Montrachet wine from a renowned producer such as Domaine Leflaive can cost more than $40.

A village-level white Burgundy — white Burgundy at any level, as a matter of fact — is a good buy only if (1) it is made by a good producer, and (2) it is from a good vintage. (The producer is even more important than the vintage.) See our list of recommended Côte d'Or producers in the section "Recommended White Burgundy (Côte d'Or) Producers and Wines."

For a good white Burgundy that's less expensive than a premier cru or grand cru wine, look for village-level wines of producers with excellent reputations for their cru wines. For example,

- Both Domaine Ramonet's or Niellon's Chassagne-Montrachet wines at around $29 to $30 are fine choices and good values for the excellent quality they offer.

- The *négociant* Louis Latour (see the sidebar "Two kinds of Burgundy producers") makes reliable and easier-to-find village Burgundies such as Meursault, Meursault-Blagny (Blagny is a hamlet of Meursault), Chassagne-Montrachet, and Puligny-Montrachet, which sell in the $23 to $28 range.

Premier cru Côte d'Or white Burgundies

Those white Burgundies coming from premier cru vineyards — especially those of Meursault, Puligny-Montrachet, and Chassagne-Montrachet — are unquestionably a big step up in depth, concentration, and complexity from village-level Burgundies. But that step up in quality comes with a price. Most premier cru white Burgundies from these three communes are in the $30 to $65 range (with the producer Domaine Leflaive's Puligny-Montrachet Les Combettes and Les Pucelles, his two best premier cru wines, around $85).

Here are the three communes and their most renowned premier cru vineyards:

- **Meursault:** Les Perrières; Les Genevrières; Les Charmes
- **Puligny-Montrachet:** Les Pucelles; Les Combettes; Les Folatières
- **Chassagne-Montrachet:** Les Caillerets; Les Ruchottes; Les Vergers; Les Chaumées

Almost all vineyards in Burgundy are shared by several producers. This is the reason that you must know the producer's name and reputation for quality — as well as knowing the name and reputation of the vineyard. The vineyard reputation alone is not a justification for shelling out $30 to $65 for a bottle of wine! (We list reliable producers later in this chapter.)

The golden villages

Meursault, Puligny-Montrachet, and Chassagne-Montrachet are the three most important sources for village, premier cru, and grand cru white Burgundies. Because of differences in climate and soil, the wines of each of these places are somewhat different from those of the others — each has its own village style, you could say. We describe these village styles (but remember that each producer superimposes his own winemaking signature on the village style).

- **Meursault:** These wines are straw-gold in color, often with light green tinges; they have rich, buttery, floral aromas and flavors, with characteristic suggestions of hazelnuts, honey, toast, and sometimes peaches; the broadest and distinctly the nuttiest flavors of the three villages' wines.

- **Puligny-Montrachet:** These wines are light-yellow gold in color; they are lean, minerally, floral, subtle in aroma and flavor, often with suggestions of apples, butter-scotch, and honeysuckle; Puligny-Montrachets usually are the steeliest, most subtle, and most complex of the three villages' wines, with the liveliest acidity and the most finesse or elegance.

- **Chassagne-Montrachet:** The white Burgundies of Chassagne are quite similar to Puligny's, except that they are normally more full-bodied (but less sturdy than Meursault), more powerful, less elegant, but richer, earthier, and with riper flavors than those of Puligny; they are also usually less expensive than Puligny-Montrachet.

The premier cru white Burgundies of the lesser-known villages mentioned previously (in the section "Village-level Côte d'Or white Burgundies") offer good values ($18 to $25) but you can't expect the same depth of flavor or complexity that you can find in the premier crus of Meursault, Puligny-Montrachet, or Chassagne-Montrachet. Our favorite two of these so-called lesser villages are the premier crus of Beaune and Savigny-lès-Beaune (see Figure 10-2).

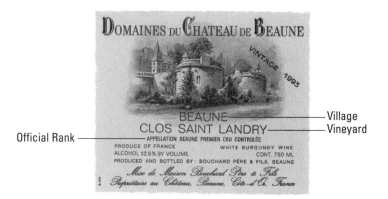

Official Rank

Village
Vineyard

Figure 10-2: Label from a Beaune premier cru wine. Note that the village name and the vineyard name both appear in the same size print.

Look especially for the *négociant* Louis Jadot's premier cru white Burgundy, Beaune-les-Grèves ($25 to $30, depending on the vintage).

Grand cru Côte d'Or white Burgundies

Theoretically, grand cru white Burgundies from the Côte d'Or should be the greatest of all white Burgundies and, arguably, among the greatest dry white wines of the world. Unfortunately, this statement applies only to the wines of the best producers.

Take, for instance, the most famous grand cru vineyard of all, Le Montrachet (part of which is in the village of Puligny-Montrachet, and part of which is in the village of Chassagne-Montrachet). Fifteen different producers make Le Montrachet (usually called simply Montrachet on the label), ranging in price from $200 to $600 per bottle. If you try a Montrachet that is not from one of the vineyard's half-dozen best producers (Domaine Leflaive, Domaine des Comtes Lafon, Domaine Ramonet, Domaine de la Romanée Conti, Domaine Amiot-Bonfils, or Domaine Marc Colin — all of which have very small production) and is not from a good vintage (such as 1992, 1989, or 1986), you might wonder what all the fuss is about.

We advise you to avoid the overrated grand cru, Le Montrachet, unless you are fortunate enough to obtain this fabled wine from one of the producers we recommend in the preceding paragraph, in a good vintage — and then only if you are willing to pay the price that this wine commands.

Other grand cru white Burgundies — such as Bâtard-Montrachet, Chevalier-Montrachet, and Corton-Charlemagne — are less expensive, and often more reliable. Grand crus other than Le Montrachet are mainly in the $75 to $150 range, but a few Corton-Charlemagnes are as low as $50.

See Table 10-2 for a list of all of the grand cru white Burgundies, and the village in which each is situated; some grand cru vineyards are partially in one village and partially in another.

Table 10-2 Grand Cru White Burgundies

Grand Cru Vineyard	Village Location
Corton-Charlemagne	partially in Aloxe-Corton, partially in Pernand-Vergelesses
Le Montrachet	partially in Puligny-Montrachet, partially in Chassagne-Montrachet
Bâtard-Montrachet	partially in Puligny-Montrachet, partially in Chassagne-Montrachet
Chevalier-Montrachet	Puligny-Montrachet
Bienvenues-Bâtard-Montrachet	Puligny-Montrachet
Criots-Bâtard-Montrachet	Chassagne-Montrachet
Corton (Blanc)*	partially in Aloxe-Corton, partially in Ladoix-Serrigny
Musigny (Blanc)* ‡	Chambolle-Musigny (in the Côte de Nuits subdistrict)

Because these two vineyards are more famous for red wine than white, the word "Blanc" always appears on the label of the white version, although that word is not officially part of the vineyard name.

‡ A small amount of excellent Musigny Blanc wine is made from the Pinot Blanc grape by the producer, Comte de Vogüé; it costs about $140 to $150 per bottle.

Recommended white Burgundy (Côte d'Or) producers and wines

Generally speaking, our favorite dry white wines in the world are the white Burgundies of the Côte d'Or district — almost all of which come from the Côte de Beaune subdistrict. Remember: As we stress repeatedly, the producer's reputation for quality is the vital criterion in making your selection. In this section, we mention some of our favorite producers of white Burgundy from the Côte de Beaune — and their most renowned wines.

Table 10-3 lists recommended producers in our rough order of preference. (Our special favorites are indicated with a ♟ symbol.) We have omitted from the list any producers whose wines are extremely limited in quantity or are almost impossible to find.

Table 10-3 Recommended Côte d'Or White Burgundy Producers

Producer	Recommended Wines
♟ Domaine Ramonet	Bâtard-Montrachet Bienvenues-Bâtard-Montrachet any of his Chassagne-Montrachet premier crus
♟ Coche-Dury	Corton-Charlemagne Meursault premier crus (any)
♟ Domaine Comtes Lafon	Meursault Les Perrières Meursault Les Genevrières Meursault Les Charmes
♟ Domaine Leflaive	Chevalier-Montrachet Bâtard-Montrachet Puligny-Montrachet Les Pucelles Puligny-Montrachet Les Combettes
♟ Michel Niellon	Bâtard-Montrachet Chevalier-Montrachet Chassagne-Montrachet Les Vergers
♟ Étienne Sauzet	Bâtard-Montrachet Bienvenues-Bâtard-Montrachet Puligny-Montrachet Les Combettes
Louis Latour	Corton-Charlemagne
Verget	Bâtard-Montrachet Chevalier-Montrachet Meursault premier crus (any)
Colin-Déléger	Chevalier-Montrachet Chassagne-Montrachet Les Chaumées Chassagne-Montrachet Les Chenevottes
Leroy (Dom. d'Auvenay)	Puligny-Montrachet Les Folatières Meursault Les Narvaux Corton-Charlemagne

Producer	Recommended Wines
Louis Jadot	Chevalier-Montrachet "Les Demoiselles" Bâtard-Montrachet Beaune Les Grèves
Louis Carillon	Puligny-Montrachet Les Perrières Puligny-Montrachet Les Champs Canet
Jean-Marc Boillot	Bâtard-Montrachet Puligny-Montrachet Les Combettes
Jean-Noël Gagnard	Bâtard-Montrachet Chassagne-Montrachet Les Caillerets Chassagne-Montrachet Morgeot
Fontaine-Gagnard	Bâtard-Montrachet Chassagne-Montrachet Les Caillerets
Amiot-Bonfils	Chassagne-Montrachet Les Caillerets Puligny-Montrachet Les Demoiselles
Bernard Morey	Chassagne-Montrachet Les Caillerets Chassagne-Montrachet Morgeot
Patrick Javillier	Meursault Les Narvaux Meursault Les Casse Têtes

The Unheralded Côte Chalonnaise

Directly south of the Côte d'Or district, and just before the Mâcon district, is Burgundy's least-known district, the Côte Chalonnaise. The white Burgundies here come primarily from the villages of Rully *(roo ye)* and Montagny *(mon tah nye)*, but a little white wine also comes from Mercurey *(mair coo ray)* and Givry *(jee vree)*. Made from Chardonnay, these wines are typically lighter-bodied than the white Burgundies of the Côte de Beaune and have an earthier, more rustic character, but the price is right: Most cost between $12 and $20. They are best consumed within four or five years of the vintage.

Try the white Burgundies from the Côte Chalonnaise listed in Table 10-4 as your warm-weather whites. These wines are listed in our rough order of preference, with our favorites wines marked by ❢.

Table 10-4	Recommended Côte Chalonnaise White Burgundies	
Producer/Estate Name	*Name of Wine*	*Vineyard*
Antonin Rodet/ Château de Chamirey	♀ Mercurey Blanc	
Domaine de la Folie	Rully Rully	♀ Clos St. Jacques ♀ Clos de Bellecroix
Domaine Bertrand	Montagny	Premier Cru, Les Coeres
René Bourgeon	Givry Blanc	Clos de la Brûlée
Antonin Rodet/ Château de Rully	Rully Blanc Montagny	
Louis Latour	Montagny	La Grande Roche
Olivier Leflaive Frères	Mercurey Blanc Rully Montagny	Premier Cru Premier Cru
Michel Juillot	Mercurey Blanc Mercurey	Les Champs Martins
Château de la Saule	Montagny	Les Burnins
Chartron & Trébuchet	Rully	La Chaume
Joseph Drouhin	Rully	
J. Faiveley	Mercurey Blanc Rully Blanc Montagny	Les Joncs Clos Rochette

The Mâconnais District: Where the Buys Are

When you arrive in the Mâconnais district of Burgundy (directly south of the Côte Chalonnaise district, but north of Beaujolais and the city of Lyon), you notice that the weather is warmer than in Burgundy's more northerly districts. The Côte Mâconnais has a distinct Mediterranean influence; in fact, palm trees grow in the charming city of Mâcon. Because the climate is sunnier here, with less rain, vintages are less important than in the northerly Burgundian districts (those are listed in the "White Burgundy Vintages" sidebar, earlier in this chapter).

Most of the wine in the Mâconnais district is white, and Chardonnay rules. In fact, the village of Chardonnay (possibly the source of the grape name) is in the northern part of this district. The Mâconnais hills contain similar limestone soil to that found in northern Burgundy. But here in the Mâconnais district, stainless steel or glass-lined concrete vats are used almost exclusively for vinification (a few producers who make more expensive Pouilly-Fuissé wines employ oak casks); wines are bottled early, and they are meant to be consumed within two years of the vintage.

The most basic Mâcon wines are simply called Mâcon. Better wines bear the name Mâcon-Villages; these wines come from any of the 43 villages entitled to that name. Often, a village's name appears on the label — such as Mâcon-Lugny or Mâcon-Viré. Most of the wines of Mâcon come from large co-operative wine-producing companies; the wines are reasonably priced in the $7 to $10 range. They usually are fresh and lively — good everyday white wines.

Saint-Véran wine (from the village of the same name) represents a distinct step up from Mâcon-Villages. For us, Saint-Véran wines, priced in the $10 to $13 range, are the best buys of all the Mâcon wines and among France's best wine values. Saint-Véran wines are more concentrated and have more flavor than Mâcon-Villages and are as good as most Pouilly-Fuissés, at a lower cost. We have found that the Saint-Véran of Verget is consistently reliable and flavorful. A best buy!

Pouilly-Fuissé *(pwee fwee say)* is clearly the most renowned wine of the Mâconnais; in fact, it is one of the world's most well-known white wines. Like Saint-Véran, Pouilly-Fuissé comes from the best part of the Mâconnais, the southernmost part, around the villages of Pouilly and Fuissé. Because it is so well-known, Pouilly-Fuissé, 100 percent Chardonnay, is a bit more expensive than it should be (most are in the $15 to $18 range). After all, it is just another Mâcon white wine with its own village name!

Admittedly, however, some producers have brought Pouilly-Fuissé to its greatest heights through restricting the yields of their vineyards, using the fruit of shy-bearing older vines, and aging their wine in oak (sometimes new barrels). Their wines are full, rich, formidable white wines that can compete with Côte de Beaune white Burgundies — in quality if not in style. (Pouilly-Fuissés made in this way are heavier, richer, and more honeyed, but not so elegant as Côte de Beaune white Burgundies; Pouilly-Fuissés tend to have lower acidity.) These oak-aged, fuller-styled Pouilly-Fuissés often have single-vineyard names or the words *Vieilles Vignes,* pronounced *vee ae veenyeh* (and translated as *old vines*) on their labels; they range in price from about $18 to $35. Most of them can age and improve for five to seven years or more.

Some recommended producers of the fuller-styled, oak-aged Pouilly-Fuissés include the following, listed in a rough order of preference, with our favorite wine marked by ♈:

Table 10-5	Recommended Producers of Pouilly-Fuissés
Producer	*Wine Name*
Marcel Vincent/Château Fuissé	Pouilly-Fuissé ♈ Pouilly-Fuissé "Cuvée Vieilles Vignes"
Daniel Barraud	Pouilly-Fuissé La Roche Pouilly-Fuissé La Verchère Pouilly-Fuissé "Cuvée Vieilles Vignes"
Domaine Manciat-Poncet	Pouilly-Fuissé Le Crays Pouilly-Fuissé Vieilles Vignes
Dom. J. A. Ferret	Pouilly-Fuissé, any single-vineyard wines
T. Guerin	Pouilly-Fuissé Clos de France Pouilly-Fuissé La Roche Pouilly-Fuissé La Roche Vieilles Vignes
Dom. R. Denogent	Pouilly-Fuissé Cuvée Claude Denogent Pouilly-Fuissé La Croix Vieilles Vignes Pouilly-Fuissé Les Reisses Vieilles Vignes

White Burgundy and Food

Lighter-bodied white Burgundies from the Mâconnais or Côte Chalonnaise districts, or lighter-vintage Côte d'Or white Burgundies go well with delicate fish dishes. Fuller-bodied Côte d'Or white Burgundies, especially premier cru and grand cru wines, go well with heavier fish dishes, lobster, chicken, turkey, and veal. Suggestion: Try your Thanksgiving turkey with Corton-Charlemagne!

As we mentioned earlier, Chablis is ideal with seafood, and grand cru Chablis is perfect with lobster or dark-fleshed, meaty fish. Oysters-and-Chablis is an all-time classic food and wine pairing.

Chapter 11

Vin Blanc Français: Bordeaux and Beyond

· ·

In This Chapter

▶ Bordeaux Blanc — better than ever

▶ Sincerely Sancerre

▶ The "undiscovered" dry white wines of Alsace

▶ Two of the world's greatest white wine values

· ·

*A*lthough we believe that white Burgundies reign supreme over the world of white wines, France's other white wines can also claim royal status and are not nearly so costly.

The white wines of the Bordeaux region are now of better quality than ever. And, for real values in white wines, the wines of France's Loire Valley and Alsace clearly have the best quality-price ratio of the wines from any major wine region in France — if not the world. The Rhône Valley offers us white wines that are distinctively different from any other white wines anywhere — from the lusciously aromatic Condrieu to the earthy white Hermitage.

After exploring the white wines of all these regions, we drop in to Gascony, the land of The Three Musketeers and Armagnac brandy, and to the Bergerac region of southwest France, to nominate our candidates for two of the world's greatest white wine values.

Bordeaux Also Comes in Blanc

Because the Bordeaux region of France produces the most famous red wines in the world, the dry white wines of the region are often overlooked. In fact, 15 percent of all Bordeaux wines are dry whites.

Various quality-levels of white Bordeaux wine exist, roughly corresponding to the various areas where the grapes grow.

- Most of the best white Bordeaux wines come from one small subdistrict of the Graves *(grahv)* district, right around the city of Bordeaux; this subdistrict is called Pessac-Léognan *(pes sac lay oh nyon)*. Figure 11-1 shows a label from one of the district's very fine wines.

- Most of the inexpensive (under $10) white Bordeaux wines come from the huge Entre-Deux-Mers *(on truh duh mair)* district, to the east of the Graves district.

- Other inexpensive white Bordeaux wines carry the names of more obscure districts, or they simply carry the region-wide name *Bordeaux Blanc*.

Figure 11-1: Label from a very good white Bordeaux that's also an excellent value.

The Bordeaux duo: Sauvignon Blanc and Sémillon

Bordeaux is one region where you can forget about the Chardonnay grape. Here, two other white grape varieties dominate — Sauvignon Blanc and Sémillon. Because each of these grapes lends unique characteristics to the finished wine, most white Bordeaux wines are blends of these two varieties in varying proportions.

- ✔ The Sauvignon Blanc component in the blend is crisp and herbaceous and enjoyable early on, when the wine is young.

- ✔ The Sémillon component is fuller-bodied and more viscous, with lower acidity and a honeyed quality; it adds depth to the wine, but it needs time to unfold its charms.

Working together in Bordeaux — especially in Pessac-Léognan — these two grape varieties produce some of the best dry white wines in the world (at least, the very finest of them are truly great). The dry white wines of the Graves, at their best, are crisp and lively when they are young, and develop a honeyed bouquet, richness, and depth as they mature.

Producers of the best white Bordeaux wines use new oak casks to vinify and age their wines, lending toasty nuances to the wines. In good vintages, the best wines require at least ten years to develop fully and will live on for many years afterwards. (To read more about white Bordeaux wine, turn to the section "White Bordeaux: The Beauty of Blending" in Chapter 4.)

A few châteaux (wine estates) in the Médoc district of Bordeaux — the home of the very finest *red* Bordeaux wines — also produce limited quantities of dry white Bordeaux. The best white wine produced in the Médoc district invariably is Pavillon *(pah vee yon)* Blanc de Margaux (Château Margaux's white wine), made from 100 percent Sauvignon Blanc. It sells for $25 to $35, depending on the vintage.

Buying fine white Bordeaux

To enjoy fine white Bordeaux wine when it is properly mature — ten years old or older in the best vintages — you have two options: Buy the wine at retail when it is first released, about two years after the vintage, and age it yourself; or buy an older bottle of the wine from a store that specializes in mature wines, or from an auction house. Whichever your choice, you can find plenty of good advice in our book *Wine For Dummies* (published by IDG Books Worldwide, Inc.): Chapter 15 discusses the conditions for cellaring wines properly, and Chapter 16 covers wine auctions and specialty wine shops across the U.S.

Vintages in Bordeaux (the best are in bold) have been better lately for dry white wines than for red wines because white grapes are generally harvested sooner, before the damaging autumn rains. **1994** looks as if it will be one of the truly great white Bordeaux vintages — definitely one to buy. **1993**, **1987**, and especially **1985** were also excellent vintages. 1992, 1990, and 1988 were all good vintages for dry white Bordeaux wines, and **1989** was superb for Château Haut-Brion Blanc *(oh bree ahn blahnc)* and Château Laville-Haut-Brion *(la veel oh bree ahn)*.

Dry white Bordeaux wines go well with shellfish, especially scallops and shrimp, as well as lobster and grilled fish. Also, goat cheese is particularly friendly with white Bordeaux.

The top twelve white Bordeaux

In this section, we list our top twelve dry white Bordeaux choices, all from the Pessac-Léognan subdistrict, in approximate order of quality. Most of them are blends of Sauvignon Blanc and Sémillon, but the wines of two châteaux, Couhins-Lurton and Smith-Haut-Lafitte, are 100 percent Sauvignon Blanc. We've separated the wines into three categories.

The elite wines

The four wines that follow truly are in a class by themselves, in terms of quality, and their per bottle price reflects that fact — $40 or $45 to $90 and higher, depending on the vintage. Although these prices are steep, remember that these four wines are the very best dry white Bordeaux wines, and among the best dry white wines of the world. If you compare their prices to white Burgundy's most expensive wine, Montrachet, the prices don't seem quite so high.

The dry white Bordeaux, Château de Fieuzal *(fee oo zahl)*, has been on a hot streak since the 1985 vintage, earning a place in the following elite group. At $40 to $45, it is the lowest-priced of the four wines in this group.

- Château Haut-Brion Blanc
- Château Laville-Haut-Brion
- Domaine de Chevalier *(doh main deh sheh vah lyay)*
- Château de Fieuzal

The very good wines

Our next four white Bordeaux wines all represent excellent values, as they are in the $23 to $30 range. And all four of these estates have improved dramatically over the last decade. If we were to expand our list beyond the boundaries of Pessac-Léognan, we would include Pavillon Blanc de Margaux in this category.

> ✔ Château Pape Clément *(pahp cleh mahn)*
>
> ✔ Château Smith-Haut-Lafitte *(smith oh lah feet)*
>
> ✔ Château Couhins-Lurton *(coo ann ler tohn)*
>
> ✔ Château La Louvière *(lah loo vee aire)*

The best values

The following four white Bordeaux wines are in the $18 to $22 price range. As with so many other white wines of Bordeaux, they have shown marked improvement since the early 1980s.

> ✔ Clos Floridene *(clo flor ee den)*
>
> ✔ Château La Tour-Martillac *(la tor mar tee yak)*
>
> ✔ Château Malartic-Lagravière
> *(mah lar teek lah grah vee aire)*
>
> ✔ Château Carbonnieux *(car bun nyew)*

The Crisp White Wines of the Loire Valley

The Loire *(lwahr)* Valley, certainly one of the most beautiful regions in France, stretches for some 600 miles across France's northwest, following the Loire River from central France in the east to the Atlantic Ocean in the west.

The cool climate of the region makes it an ideal summer vacation destination; as a result, magnificent châteaux, once the summer homes of royalty, exist throughout this "garden of France." The rather cool climate (especially in the western part) also contributes to the lively, crisp character of the white wines for which the Loire Valley is known. (Red and rosé wines are made here also, but the whites are the best wines of the Loire.)

Three separate Loire districts produce white wine:

- ✔ The eastern end, just south of Paris, around the towns of Sancerre and Pouilly-sur-Loire: The grape variety here is Sauvignon Blanc, and the major wines are Sancerre *(sahn sair)* and Pouilly Fumé *(pwee foo may)*.

- ✔ The central Loire Valley, near the city of Tours: The grape variety here is Chenin Blanc, and the major wine is Vouvray *(voo vray)*.

- ✔ The western Loire Valley, near the city of Nantes and the Atlantic Ocean: The grape variety here is Muscadet *(moos cah day)*, and the major wine is also called Muscadet.

The Sancerre district

In the center of France, southeast of the city of Orleans, lies a hilly area of chalky soil. This area is probably the world's most renowned region for the Sauvignon Blanc grape; almost all of the wine here is white, made from this grape variety. Figure 11-2 shows a label from one of these wines.

Figure 11-2: The Sancerre district produces crisp, dry, assertive wines from the Sauvignon Blanc grape.

The two most famous wines of this district are Sancerre and Pouilly-Fumé; lesser-known wines of the area include Menetou-Salon *(meh neh too sah lohn)*, Quincy *(can see)*, and Reuilly *(ruh yee)*.

Lean, green, and assertive

In this part of the Loire Valley, Sauvignon Blanc has established a style much imitated all over the world — in New Zealand, South Africa, and parts of California, to name a few places.

- ✔ Sauvignon Blanc-based wines of the Loire, typified by Sancerre, are assertive: They definitely wake up the palate!
- ✔ Sauvignon Blanc-based wines of the Loire are high in acidity, very lively, with aromas and flavors reminiscent of green grass, green beans, and/or grapefruit.
- ✔ Besides the high acidity and typical aromas and flavors of the Sauvignon Blanc grape, the best of these wines also have distinct minerally flavor.

Sancerre and Pouilly-Fumé are each named for towns on opposite sides of the Loire River. Although both wines are made entirely from Sauvignon Blanc, and their vineyards share similar soil — chalk and marl — Sancerre and Pouilly-Fumé are each distinct wines:

- ✔ In general, Sancerre wines are a bit higher in acidity, crisper, dryer, and more assertive.
- ✔ Pouilly-Fumé wines are somewhat more full-bodied, rounder, and creamier, and a bit higher in alcohol; some Pouilly-Fumés have a classic gunflint aroma.

Because of its characteristics, Sancerre is best with shellfish and lighter fish dishes, whereas Pouilly-Fumé is more suitable with meatier fish (such as salmon or turbot), chicken, or veal. Both are excellent with one of the specialties of the region, goat cheese — but especially Sancerre. One of the great matches for Sancerre is a salad with warm chèvre (goat cheese).

Like most Loire white wines, Sauvignon Blanc-based wines drink best when they are young — within five years of the vintage, but preferably within two or three years. (These Loire Valley Sauvignon Blancs are very different from the more subdued, Sémillon-influenced white Bordeaux wines, which can age considerably longer.)

Pouilly-Fumé versus Pouilly-Fuissé

Pouilly-Fumé and Pouilly-Fuissé might sound alike, but they are completely different wines. The more full-bodied Pouilly-Fuissé, from the Mâconnais district in Burgundy (see Chapter 10), is 100 percent Chardonnay, and is often oak-aged. Pouilly-Fumé, 100 percent Sauvignon Blanc, is usually fermented in stainless steel. Buy a bottle of each, compare them, and taste the difference!

The Loire Valley has experienced some of its all-time great vintages lately (indicated in bold), including the exceptional **1995**. Although Loire wines from **1990** and **1989** are difficult to find now, both were classic vintages in the Loire, and their wines were exceptionally good — therefore capable of aging longer. 1993 was also good, but not great. Our strong advice is to buy some 1995 Loire whites while they are available.

Recommended producers of Sancerre and Pouilly-Fumé

As in Burgundy, you must pay attention to producers' names when you select wines from the Loire, because there are great variations in quality. Basic Sancerre and Pouilly-Fumé wines are in the $10 to $15 price range. Single-vineyard and special cuvée wines (that is, a producer's better selection) retail in the $25 to $40 range and higher — especially for a few of the better Pouilly-Fumés.

For Sancerre, we especially recommend the following producers, listed in our rough order of preference:

- Domaine Lucien Crochet
- Domaine Henri Bourgeois
- Domaine Alphonse Mellot
- Cotat Frères
- Domaine Vincent Pinard
- Pascal Jolivet
- Domaine Vincent Delaporte
- Domaine Paul Millerioux
- Château de Maimbray

✔ Domaine Roger Neveu

✔ Domaine Vacheron

✔ Domaine de Montigny

We particularly recommend a few specific, special-selection Sancerre wines from some of these producers. Those wines are listed in Table 11-1.

Table 11-1   **Highly Recommended Sancerre Wines**

Producer	Wine
Domaine Lucien Crochet	♟ Sancerre "Cuvée Prestige"
Domaine Henri Bourgeois	♟ Sancerre "La Bourgeoise"
Domaine Alphonse Mellot	♟ Sancerre "Cuvée Edmond"

For Pouilly-Fumé, we recommend the following producers, who are listed in our rough order of preference:

✔ Didier Dagueneau

✔ De Ladoucette

✔ Michel Redde

✔ Domaine Cailbourdin

✔ Jean-Claude Chatelain

✔ Domaine Serge Dagueneau

✔ Masson-Blondelet

✔ Château de Tracy

✔ Tinel-Blondelet

We also particularly recommend the specific, special-selection Pouilly-Fumé wines listed in Table 11-2.

Table 11-2   **Highly Recommended Pouilly-Fumé Wines**

Producer	Wine
Didier Dagueneau	♟ Pouilly-Fumé "Cuvée Silex"
De Ladoucette	♟ "Baron de L" Pouilly-Fumé
Michel Redde	♟ Pouilly-Fumé "Cuvée Majorum"

Quality-wise, Didier Dagueneau *(dee de ay dag eh no)* is truly in a class by himself; he is considered one of the world's great white-wine makers, and we agree. Long-haired, colorful Dagueneau makes low-yield, intensely concentrated Pouilly-Fumés. His Cuvée Silex *(see lex)*, an old-vine, barrel-fermented, minerally wine, is simply one of the world's finest Sauvignon Blancs. You will find his rather expensive Pouilly-Fumés mainly in fine restaurants.

Vouvray — home of Chenin Blanc

The heart of the Loire Valley, the central part, revolves around the city of Tours. In this region, known as the Touraine, are the greatest expressions of the often overlooked noble grape variety, Chenin Blanc.

Fine Chenin Blanc wines come from vineyards around the town of Vouvray, a short distance east of Tours. (Other good Chenin Blanc wines, although a bit lighter and less concentrated, come from the lesser-known town of Montlouis, pronounced *mon loo wee*, across the Loire River from Vouvray.)

Vouvray wines come in dry, semi-dry, and sweet (labeled *"moelleux"*) versions, depending on the climatic conditions of the vintage, and, to some extent, the desires of the winemaker. Sparkling Vouvrays are also made. (The best wines of Vouvray happen to be the long-lived sweet wines, which can be made only in great vintages — such as 1989, 1990, and 1995 — and which are comparable to Bordeaux's great dessert wine, Sauternes; those dessert wines happen to fall outside the scope of this book.)

Most Vouvrays today are vinified dry and are usually labeled *sec*; you can also find off-dry *(sec-tendre)* and slightly sweeter, semi-dry *(demi-sec)* Vouvrays. All Vouvrays mature extremely well — and improve with age — a prized quality of the Chenin Blanc grape (at least as it expresses itself in the Vouvray vineyards, with its very fine acidity as a preservative). Vouvrays can be found in the $6 to $10 price range, but the better Vouvrays are usually $15 to $17.

Even sec Vouvrays are not as dry as other white wines — such as wines made from Chardonnay or Sauvignon Blanc — because Chenin Blanc-based wines are never really bone-dry. For this reason, we highly recommend Vouvray to wine drinkers who find other white wines to be too dry, yet want a better-than-average quality wine.

All of the better Vouvray producers make a range of wines, varying both in dryness and intensity (from their "basic" Vouvrays to their single-vineyard or "special cuvée" wines). We recommend the dry or sec Vouvrays from the producers listed below, in our in rough order of preference:

- ✔ Gaston Huet-Noël Pinguet
- ✔ Didier et Catherine Champalou
- ✔ Philippe Foreau/Domaine du Clos Naudin
- ✔ Domaine des Aubuisières
- ✔ Domaine Allias (also labeled as Clos du Petit Mont)
- ✔ Monmousseau/Château Gaudrelle
- ✔ Marc Brédif
- ✔ Prince Poniatowski/Clos Baudin

We also particularly recommend the special selection Vouvray wines listed in Table 11-3.

Table 11-3   Highly Recommended Vouvray Wines

Producer	Wine
Gaston Huet-Noël Pinguet	Vouvray "Le Haut Lieu"
Didier et Catherine Champalou	Vouvray "Cuvée des Fondraux" Vouvray "Clos du Bourg"

The citizens of Vouvray enjoy their wine especially with pork dishes and with their wonderful goat cheese, but they also accompany Vouvray with rabbit, duck, goose, chicken, and salmon.

Muscadet — the wine with shellfish

Sometimes a grape variety must find the right home in order to show its stuff. The Muscadet grape, also known as Melon de Bourgogne *(meh lohn deh boor guh nyuh)*, was banished from all the prime vineyards in Burgundy, but found a home in the Nantais *(nahn tay)*, a wine district surrounding the city of Nantes on the western edge of the Loire Valley, just where the mighty Loire River empties into the Atlantic Ocean.

Here, in the coolest part of the Loire Valley, the Muscadet grape makes a dry, crisp, light-bodied, refreshing wine that is the ideal accompaniment to all kinds of shellfish (try it with a plate of steamed mussels or oysters!).

The best Muscadet comes from a region called Sèvre-et-Maine *(sev'r et mehn)*, and those words appear on the wine label. You also often see the term *sur lie* on the label; this indicates that the wine has been aged on its *lees* (fermentation yeasts) and then bottled straight from the tank (see Chapter 2 for information on lees-aging). The *sur lie* process makes the wine more complex and sometimes gives the wine a slight effervescence.

Muscadets remain one of the best bargains of all the world's white wines. You can find fine Muscadets in the $6 to $8 price range. Buy them as young as you can find them (the best vintages are in bold); they do not age well. For example, in late 1996, you should look for the **1995** Muscadets especially, and certainly buy nothing older than a 1993.

As with other Loire wines, the producer's name is of paramount importance when you are buying Muscadets, in order to avoid getting a nondescript, watery, over-produced version of the wine — plenty of which, unfortunately, exist. We recommend the producers in the following list, who appear in our rough order of preference:

- Louis Métaireau
- Guy Bossard
- Chéreau-Carré
- Sauvion et Fils/Château du Cléray
- Château de la Ragotière
- Domaine la Quilla
- Domaine Chiron
- Domaine des Dorices
- Domaine de la Fruitière
- Domaine de la Haute-Févrie
- Domaine de la Louvetrie
- Domaine Pierre Luneau-Papin
- André-Michel Brégeon
- Domaine de la Gautronnière

- ✔ Domaine de la Tourmaline
- ✔ Joseph Hallereau
- ✔ Marquis de Goulaine

We also particularly recommend the specific wines listed in Table 11-4.

Table 11-4	Highly Recommended Muscadet Wines
Producer	*Wine*
Louis Métaireau	Muscadet de Sèvre-et-Maine, Vignerons d'Art cuvées
Guy Bossard	Muscadet de Sèvre-et-Maine, Domaine de l'Ecu Muscadet de Sèvre-et-Maine, Clos de Bazillière
Domaine de la Louvetrie	Muscadet de Sèvre-et-Maine "Le Fief du Breuil"
Domaine Pierre Luneau-Papin	Muscadet de Sèvre-et-Maine "Domaine de la Grange"
Domaine de la Tourmaline	Muscadet de Sèvre-et-Maine, Domaine de la Perrière
Marquis de Goulaine	Muscadet de Sèvre-et-Maine "Cuvée du Millénaire"

The Dry White Wines of Alsace

We emphasize the word *dry* because the wines from Alsace *(al zass)* are commonly thought to be sweet by those who are not familiar with them. Many people are misinformed about these wines for three reasons:

- ✔ Alsace, in northeastern France, is across the Rhine River from Germany and, in fact, has been part of Germany at various times in its history.
- ✔ Alsace uses many of the same grape varieties as Germany — Riesling, Gewurztraminer, and Sylvaner, for instance.
- ✔ Most people associate German wines with sweetness.

In reality, Alsace is part of France, and the wines of Alsace are mainly dry.

As a result of the confusion over their dryness, the wines of Alsace have not done well in the U.S. market. Therefore, they are invariably good buys, *as they are considerably under-valued.*

Climate and grapes

Although the Alsace region is quite northerly in latitude, the climate is surprisingly sunny and warm. In fact, Alsace is one of the driest wine regions in Europe (perfect conditions for grape growing) thanks to the Vosges *(voejhe)* Mountains west of the region, which shelter Alsace's vineyards from rain and harsh weather.

The great majority of Alsace wines — 93 percent — are white (the region also makes a small amount of red Pinot Noir wine). Among French wines, the wines of Alsace are the easiest to understand:

> ✔ Alsace is the only major wine region in France that names most of its wines after grape varieties. (Of course the place-name, Alsace, always appears on the label as well.)
>
> ✔ Alsace wines are immediately identifiable, because they all come in a unique, tall, thin bottle called a flûte.

Each of the grape varieties grown in Alsace gives its own distinct character to the wines made from it. Regardless of grape variety, however, the wines of Alsace share a certain style that sets them apart from other white wines of the world. Some people describe that style as spicy or minerally, while other people describe it as an unusual combination of full body, intense aromas and flavors, and a lack of sweetness. After trying just a few Alsace wines, you will probably be able to detect this trademark Alsace style yourself.

Four different white wines from Alsace are important. Each is named after the grape variety from which the wine derives:

> ✔ **Pinot Blanc:** Normally the lightest and least expensive ($8 to $12) of Alsace's "serious" wines, Pinot Blanc is made in dry and medium-dry styles, depending on the producer; often served as an apéritif, or as the first wine in a dinner; drink Pinot Blancs in their first few years.
>
> ✔ **Tokay-Pinot Gris:** The growers of Alsace call their Pinot Gris wine by this local name. Alsace Pinot Gris is the richest, spiciest, and most full-bodied of all Pinot Gris wines in the world; it has lots of character; goes well with spicy, white meat dishes; a really good value at $10 to $17, it can age well for up to ten years.

✔ **Riesling:** This "king" of Alsace wines is floral, minerally, firm, and dry (almost steely); can be quite full-bodied and complex; and goes well with delicate fish dishes. Although Alsace Rieslings can be consumed young, they age beautifully for 15 to 20 years in good vintages; most are in the $12 to $20 price range.

✔ **Gewurztraminer:** With intense, pungent, spicy aromas and flavors, often reminiscent of lychee fruit, Alsace's Gewurztraminers clearly are the world's best. Low in acidity, but fairly high in alcohol, Gewurztraminer impresses the palate as both soft and spicy; goes best with foie gras and strong cheeses, although some like it with spicy Asian foods; and does not age quite so long as Riesling, but costs the same.

Some of Alsace's best wines are the late-harvest Rieslings, Gewurztraminers, and Tokay-Pinot Gris wines. These wines, made from super-ripe grapes, are labeled *Vendange Tardive* (pronounced *vahn dahnj tahr deev*). Vendange Tardive wines, many of which are vinified completely dry, are rich, complex, intense beauties with enormous aging capacity (25 years or more); they cost $60 and up.

Alsace, like many of France's wine regions, has enjoyed some superlative vintages in recent years (indicated in bold). **1990**, **1989**, and **1983** are all superb (you still might be able to find a few bottles of the 1989 and 1990 around). 1994 and 1985 are also very good, and 1995 looks promising, but at this point, it's too early to make a final judgment.

An Alsace rarity

Domaine Trimbach's premium Riesling, Clos Sainte Hune, is considered by many wine lovers to be not only the greatest dry Riesling in France but also one of the great white wines of the world. Unfortunately, Trimbach makes only 500 to 600 cases in any given vintage. Clos Sainte Hune demands time to develop fully (15 to 20 years) and still drinks well for 30 years or more in good vintages. Probably your best bet to find Clos Sainte Hune would be in a fine restaurant (especially in Paris or Alsace). Clos Sainte Hune is expensive, of course (well over $50 in wine shops, far more in restaurants), but not nearly so expensive as the famous French white Burgundies, such as Montrachet.

Recommended Alsace producers

The region of Alsace does have many vineyards that are officially designated *grand cru,* but some producers refuse to use the term on their labels (believing that their own names are enough of a guarantee of quality).

The following producers are making some of Alsace's best white wines (listed in rough order of preference):

- Marcel Deiss
- Marc Kreydenweiss
- Josmeyer
- Domaine Trimbach
- Domaine Weinbach
- Domaine Schlumberger
- Leon Beyer
- Zind-Humbrecht
- Bott-Geyl
- Domaine Schoffit
- Domaine Albert Mann
- Domaine Ostertag
- Hugel
- Charles Schleret
- Sick Dreyer
- Pierre Sparr

The Earthy White Wines of the Rhône Valley

Although the Rhône Valley is primarily known for its hearty red wines, a few unique, excellent whites, mainly from the northern Rhône, are definitely worth seeking out.

Condrieu (and Château-Grillet)

Made entirely from the Viognier grape, the wines of the Condrieu *(cohn dree uh)* area and those of the Château-Grillet *(pronounced gree yay,* a separate enclave within the Condrieu zone) are some of the most aromatic, delicious white wines in the world.

Viognier has proven to be a difficult grape variety to grow outside the northern Rhône district, even in sunny California. In Condrieu and Château-Grillet, the Viognier grape makes wines that are uniquely fragrant and floral (aromas of honeysuckle!); redolent of peaches, apricots, and honey; with a delicious, long finish. These wines are dry, but rich and viscous.

Because they are rather low in acidity, *you must consume them within a few years of the vintage.* We have been disappointed with older (more than four years old) Condrieus and Château-Grillet over the years and have learned our lesson.

Quantity is small for these wines: All Condrieu producers together make only about 10,000 cases annually; Château Grillet's one producer makes about 1,200 cases. Much of both wines' production is consumed locally.

Recommended Condrieu producers include the following (listed in rough order of preference):

- ✔ Georges Vernay
- ✔ Yves Cuilleron
- ✔ Antoine Montez's Domaine du Monteillet
- ✔ André Perret
- ✔ Guigal (especially his La Doriane)
- ✔ Chapoutier
- ✔ Gilles Barge
- ✔ Delas Frères
- ✔ René Rostaing

These wines are excellent with foie gras, lobster, salmon, or on their own, as a delicious apéritif.

Condrieu's retail price ranges from $35 to $50 per bottle. The rarer Château-Grillet is in the $65 to $85 range, retail, but you're more likely to find it on restaurant wine lists than in retail stores.

Try the 1994, 1993, or **1991** vintages of Condrieu or Château-Grillet — no older! (and 1991 only because it was a superb vintage); 1995 also looks as if it will be super.

Hermitage Blanc

About one-fourth of the vineyards of the Hermitage *(er mee tahj)* area in the northern Rhone — far more famous for its red wine — produce white Hermitage, for an annual production of about 15,000 to 18,000 cases. Hermitage Blanc is a dry, full-bodied, earthy, minerally wine made from the Marsanne and Roussanne grape varieties, two grapes seldom grown outside this area.

Hermitage Blanc is best consumed either quite young (two or three years old) or after it has matured (10 to 15 years) and developed some complexity of aromas and flavors (minerals, earth, roasted nuts, toffee, herbs, and peaches). In between, its flavors can be rather muted. Prices for Hermitage Blanc are in the $30 to $35 range, retail.

Good vintages for white Hermitage have been the 1994, **1991**, **1990**, **1989** (great!), **1988**, and 1985 (and 1995 looks promising).

Try a white Hermitage with full-flavored fish and shellfish dishes (such as lobster), poultry, veal, pork, or strong cheeses.

The two outstanding producers of Hermitage Blanc are Chapoutier (for his "Chante Alouette" and his other-worldly, more expensive "Cuvée de l'Orée," made from 75-year-old vines and costing about $65) and Jean-Louis Chave.

The world's two greatest white wine values

We hereby nominate our candidates for the world's two greatest white wine values:

♟ Domaine de Pouy

Price: $5 to $6

Region: Côtes de Gascogne

Grape Variety: Ugni Blanc (Italy's Trebbiano)

We have been following this wine for quite a few vintages, and it never disappoints; the trick is to drink it when it is young (within two years of the vintage at the most; within one is better) as it is not an ager.

Domaine de Pouy is a zestful, crisp, light-bodied, lively wine with a fragrant, lemony bouquet and lots of fruit flavor. It's our recommendation for your everyday, "house" white wine, especially if you like the slightest suggestion of sweetness in a white wine. Lots of other similarly priced white wines from the overlooked, unheralded Côtes de Gascogne that begin with the word "Domaine" are also worth trying.

♟ Seigneurs du Perigord

Price: $5 to $6

Region: Bergerac (Southwest France)

Grape Varieties: Sauvignon Blanc (50 percent); Sémillon (40 percent); Muscadelle (10 percent)

What a great white wine for $5.00! The little-known Bergerac region, east of Bordeaux, produces many Bordeaux-look-alike wines at lower prices than Bordeaux wines. The Seigneurs du Perigord is a zesty, lemony, fairly intensely flavored wine; it's crisp, quite dry, light-to-medium-bodied, with good acidity and a clean finish. It reminds us of a lighter version of a good white Bordeaux.

Like the Domaine de Pouy, drink this wine young — within two years of the vintage; within the first year, better yet. (We think so much of it and its value that we have chosen it as the white wine for a large family wedding.)

If you can't find Seigneurs du Perigord, try another white Bergerac. Most of them are very inexpensive, and have a similar, white Bordeaux grape blend of Sauvignon Blanc and Sémillon. To insure that you'll be getting the desirable freshness, make sure that you check the vintage of your Bergerac — the younger, the better.

Other fine white Hermitage producers are Paul Jaboulet-Aîné (for his "Chevalier de Stérimberg"), Henri Sorrel (Les Rocoules), J.L. Grippat, and Guigal.

Châteauneuf-du-Pape Blanc

Only a tiny amount (3 percent) of the wine from the Châteauneuf-du-Pape *(shah tow nuff doo pahp)* area of the southern Rhône is white, and much of that is mediocre stuff that must be consumed within two or three years. White Châteauneuf-du-Pape is made from a blend of many grapes, including Grenache Blanc, Roussanne, and Clairette. It is a full-bodied, earthy, light-golden-colored wine that, at its best, has floral, melony aromas and flavors.

Most white Châteauneuf-du-Pape wines are in the $20 to $25 price range, with a few of the better ones priced around $30.

Good vintages for Châteauneuf-du-Pape Blanc have been the 1994, 1993, **1990**, **1989** (these two are exceptional), and 1988, but 1995 also looks promising.

Hearty white Châteauneuf-du-Papes can accompany the same foods as Hermitage Blanc: full-flavored fish and shellfish dishes (such as lobster), poultry, veal, pork, or strong cheeses.

The outstanding producer of white Châteauneuf du Pape is Château de Beaucastel (the one producer whose wine is capable of improving with age — for 10 years or more); Beaucastel also makes a highly-recommended "Roussanne Vieilles Vignes" Châteauneuf du Pape from old Roussanne vines, that can age even longer, priced at $65. Two other good producers of Châteauneuf du Pape Blanc are Château de la Nerthe ("Beauvenir") and Andre Brunel ("Les Cailloux Blanc").

Some good, inexpensive white Côtes du Rhône

About this time, you might be wondering whether any good quality, affordable white Rhône wines exist. We can suggest a few good examples of Côtes du Rhône Blanc from the southern Rhône. The vintages for these wines are similar to those of white Châteauneuf du Pape:

✔ "Coudoulet de Beaucastel": Château de Beaucastel's white Côtes du Rhône ($16 to $18) is about the best in this category; it contains 30 percent Viognier and is capable of aging for five years or more.

✔ Côtes du Rhône "Belle Ruche": Chapoutier's version of this basic Rhône white vies with Beaucastel's and costs about the same.

✔ Guigal Côtes du Rhône Blanc: This solid wine sells at an attractive price of $9 to $10.

✔ Domaine de Fenouillet: Their Côtes du Rhône Blanc is from the village of Beaumes de Venise, a name which appears on the label. It's a good buy at $8 to $10.

Chapter 12

A League of Their Own: Germany's White Wines

*M*any people think of Germany as a beer-drinking country, and they're not wrong. Yet Germany ranks sixth in the world in wine production, and Germany's per capita wine consumption is about four times higher than that of the United States (although well behind the really big wine drinkers: the French, Italians, and Portuguese).

Of all the major wine-producing countries in the world, Germany is the northernmost. Northerly, of course, means cool. And cool climate — in the wine world — means white grapes and white wine (see "Climate as Style" in Chapter 2). In fact, 85 percent of Germany's wines are white.

Germany's northern exposure dictates not only that her wines are white but also which white grape varieties grow there and where they grow. Germany's dominant grape varieties — Riesling, Müller-Thurgau, and Silvaner — are varieties that ripen their fruit adequately in cool growing seasons and can sustain cold winters. Germany's wine regions are all situated along rivers, which temper climatic extremes and thereby help the grapes to ripen.

The weather in Germany is variable from year to year, meaning that vintage variation is considerable. Some years, when a warm autumn drags on (much to the delight of the winemakers), the grapes can ripen more than other years. Generally, though, only a few vintages each decade are really good ones.

How German Wines Are Named

In the wine world, the Germans are the kings of specificity. When you read the label of a fine German wine, you can find out not only the wine region where the grapes grew (French and Italian labels don't always give that information), the village, and the specific vineyard site (*à la* Burgundy), but also the grape variety and even the stage of ripeness at which the grapes were picked (see Figure 12-1).

Figure 12-1: A German wine label tells you how ripe the grapes were when picked.

The reasons for this level of detail on the label explain the facts of life of German grape growing:

- ✔ Of Germany's 13 wine regions, each has its own particular growing conditions (climate pattern, soil types, hilly or flat terrain, and so on).

- ✔ Different parts of each region, naturally, have even more specific growing conditions; the village name identifies in which part of the region the grapes were grown.

- ✔ Certain individual vineyard sites are famous because of their particular soil or sunlight exposure (very important in a cool climate) or other conditions, which affect the quality and style of the wine.

Which word means what?

Unless you happened to memorize the names of the 100 most important wine villages in Germany and the vineyards associated with each, the multisyllablic, multiword names of German wines are sure to be confusing. But here's a clue: Just as English-speakers often append the suffix "er" to places to indicate that someone is from that place (such as "New Yorker"), Germans do the same. The word in a German wine's name that ends in "er" is likely to be the larger location (the village), while the word that follows is likely to be a vineyard from the area of that village. For example, the name Graacher Himmelreich refers to the Himmelreich vineyard from the village of Graach.

✔ In any particular region, village, and vineyard, German grape growers have a wide choice of grape varieties they may plant; the geographic name therefore does not imply a specific grape variety, as it does in most French wines (such as Sancerre, always made from the Sauvignon Blanc grape) and many Italian wines (such as Soave, always made from a blend of certain grapes). Unless the grape variety is indicated on the label of a German wine — which it usually is — you would have no way of determining which grape made that wine (apart from shrewdly identifying it by aroma and taste!).

✔ From any one vineyard, planted with any one grape such as Riesling, a winemaker might make three or four different wines, each distinguished from the next only according to *when the grapes were picked*. Therefore, the information on when the grapes were picked is a necessary part of the wine's name, and this information appears on the label.

This last issue — making different wines according to when the grapes are picked (that is, according to how ripe the grapes are) — is crucial in understanding fine German wine. Read on.

Information overload, unloaded

If your eyes glaze over at all the information on German wine labels, you're not alone. In order to make their wine labels more comprehensible and user-friendly, some producers have simplified their labels down to only the bare facts: brand name, grape variety, and region. (These simplified labels also do not use Gothic script, a traditional impediment on German wine labels.)

In simplifying the label, of course, the producers have simplified the wine, too. Using (expensive) grapes from a famous vineyard is pointless if the producer doesn't capitalize on that vineyard name on the label; therefore, the grapes for these regionally labeled wines come from various vineyards all throughout a particular region. (The labels are more generic, and so are the wines.)

Wine lovers who delve deeply into the intricacies of German vineyard sites probably have little interest in these wines, but for other wine drinkers the simplicity of the labels can be a blessing.

How ripe was my vineyard

Put yourself in the position of a German winemaker at harvest time. Your grapes have reached a minimum acceptable ripeness, but they could use more ripening. The weather could change — for better or for worse. Should you hold out for more ripeness (and better quality wine), or pick now, sacrificing better quality for the security of a crop that at least is as good as it is now? (How do you say "a bird in the hand . . ." in German?)

Frequently, the answer to this dilemma is: Do both. Pick some of the grapes now, vinify them, then watch the weather (and pray!); pick more grapes in a week or so (if your prayers are answered) when they're riper than those already harvested, vinify them, and continue watching the weather; pick more grapes later — and so on. (How do you say "have your cake and eat it, too" in German?)

The wine from each batch of grapes is kept separate, as a separate wine, and the wine from each batch is different from the next. The less ripe grapes make a lighter-bodied wine than the riper grapes, for example, and their flavors are less intense.

(The very ripest grapes, that have begun to shrivel on the vine by the time they are picked, are so sweet that they'll make a sweet dessert wine; Germany's dessert wines are perhaps the finest in the whole world, but we don't cover dessert wines in this book.)

Telling it like it is

When a producer picks the grapes from one vineyard at various stages of ripeness and vinifies each batch of grapes separately, he needs to state on the label which batch of grapes made the wine in each bottle — because each wine carries the same region, village, vineyard, and grape name and thus otherwise appears to be identical. To communicate to wine buyers which wine is which, wine producers use one of several terms on their labels:

✔ Qualitätswein *(KAL ee tates vine)* or Qualitätswein bestimmter Anbaugebeit (a mouthful of a phrase which everyone just shortens to "Qualitätswein") indicates that the grapes were picked at low levels of ripeness. These grapes are so low in sugar and so high in acid that the winemaker usually adds sugar to the grape juice (which turns into alcohol during fermentation; see Chapter 2) in order to increase the alcohol level of the wine and improve the wine's balance.

✔ Kabinett *(KAB ee net)* indicates that the grapes were picked at a slightly higher ripeness; winemakers who designate their wines as kabinett or riper may not increase the wine's alcohol level by adding sugar to the juice.

✔ Spätlese *(SHPATE lay seh)* indicates higher ripeness than kabinett.

✔ Auslese *(OUSE lay seh)* indicates higher ripeness than spätlese. The grapes picked at this point in the harvest often are affected by a beneficial fungus known as *noble rot,* which concentrates their sweetness.

Three additional terms appear on bottles of sweet, dessert wine. They are, in order of ripeness:

✔ Beerenauslese *(BEER en OUSE lay seh)*

✔ Eiswein *(ICE vine);* same ripeness as the preceding category, but made from grapes that have frozen on the vine

✔ Trockenbeerenauslese *(TROH ken BEER en OUSE lay seh)*

Styles of German Wine

The ripeness of the grapes is such a big issue for German wines that one small detail tends to get lost in all the splitting-of-hairs: Even at the highest ripeness levels for nondessert wines — that is spätlese and auslese ripeness — the grapes are not really all that ripe.

A "very ripe" German wine might have enough sugar to ferment naturally (that is, without adding sugar to the juice) to 11 percent alcohol; a typical California white wine, in comparison, has enough sugar to ferment to more than 13 percent alcohol.

The low ripeness of German grapes means that acidity levels are very high in the juice (see the section "Climate as Style" in Chapter 2.) High acidity, low alcohol, no oak influence, and no malolactic fermentation (see Chapter 2 for a discussion of these two winemaking techniques) translate into a very specific style of wine: *crisp, light-bodied wine with vivid aromas and flavors of the grape variety.* Nearly all German white wines are this style.

The sweetness issue

On the issue of sweetness, less consensus exists. Nowadays, German wines are dry, semi-dry, or semi-sweet — not to mention the sweet, dessert wines.

To counteract the naturally high acidity of their grapes, German winemakers sweeten many of their wines by adding unfermented grape juice to their (dry) wine after fermentation. (The juice is called *süssreserve,* or sweet reserve.) The sweet, nonalcoholic juice reduces the wine's alcohol level, often down to only 7 or 8 percent, and it also makes all that acidity taste far less tart. Most best-selling German wines, such as the popular type called Liebfraumilch *(LEEB frow milsh),* are made in this style.

Many of Germany's best winemakers make slightly sweet wines by a different technique: They halt fermentation (through cold temperature and filtering the yeasts out of the wine) before all the grape sugar has been converted into alcohol. Some of the grape's sweetness then remains in the wine.

But Germany has responded to the worldwide demand for dryer wines. Now almost half of all German wine is being made *trocken* (dry) or *halbtrocken* (semi-dry). Both styles come in all different price ranges.

Unfortunately, the words trocken *(TRO ken)* and halbtrocken *(HAHLB tro ken)* don't always appear on the labels. One of the clues to a dryer German wine is that the alcohol level of the wine — which must appear on the label — is somewhat higher, around 10 or 11 percent.

Nobody does it (Riesling) better

The most important grape variety in Germany in terms of quantity grown is Müller-Thurgau. But the most important grape variety in Germany in terms of quality — and not so far behind in quantity, either — is Riesling. (Chapter 3 features a profile of both grapes, and Chapter 4 describes German Riesling in particular.)

The very finest German wines are made from Riesling grapes grown in certain hillside vineyards along the rivers Rhine, Mosel (and its tributaries, Saar and Ruwer), and Nahe, where the vineyards' soils, slopes, and directional orientation all promote high levels of ripeness.

Other grape varieties whose names appear on bottles of German wine include

- ✔ Silvaner, a high-acid grape with fairly neutral flavors
- ✔ Scheurebe *(SHOY reh beh),* a grape with high acidity and flavors of grapefruit and quince
- ✔ Gewürztraminer (see Chapter 3)
- ✔ Pinot Gris, called Rülander in Germany (see Chapter 3)

German vintages

Contrary to its norm, Germany has enjoyed many good vintages in recent years (the best are in bold). These good vintages for German wines include 1995, **1994**, 1993, especially **1990, 1989,** 1988, and **1983.** In general, German wines are best when consumed within five to six years, but German Rieslings — especially from good vintages — can age and improve for 20 years or more.

Germany's Main Wine Regions

Of Germany's 13 wine regions, five clearly are the most important. Just about all of Germany's great wines come from these five regions, and Riesling, as you might expect, is the most important wine. The five regions are

- ✔ Mosel-Saar-Ruwer *(MOH zel-zar-ROO ver)*
- ✔ Nahe *(NAH heh)*
- ✔ Rheingau *(RYNE gow)*
- ✔ Rheinhessen *(RYNE hess ehn)*
- ✔ The Pfalz *(fallz),* formerly known as Rheinpfalz

Of these five regions, the Mosel-Saar-Ruwer and the Rheingau have more famous, established wine estates than the others; the Rheinhessen has the most vineyard acreage (much of which makes inexpensive wine); and the Nahe and Pfalz boast many relatively new, small, high-quality producers.

Although all five of these regions produce fine Riesling wines, the Rieslings of the Mosel-Saar-Ruwer and the Rheingau are particularly well known by wine lovers outside of Germany. Generally speaking, Mosel Rieslings are the lightest-bodied of all German Rieslings and are characterized by fresh, delicate aromas and flavors, suggesting mixed fruit salad and flowers. Rieslings from the Rheingau are fuller in body, firmer, and less delicate, with pronounced fruit and earth aromas.

Riesling wines and all other wines from the Mosel-Saar-Ruwer come in green bottles. Other German wines come in brown bottles. One region, Franken, bottles its wines in short, rounded bottles rather than the tall, thin bottles used elsewhere in Germany.

Recommended Producers of German Wines

If quality is your aim, the most important information on a German wine label is the name of the producer. Regardless of grape variety, vineyard, or vintage, the best producers make good (if not great) quality wine.

We recommend our favorite producers from Germany's five major wine regions, listed alphabetically within each region. Because each producer makes so many wines in any one year (wines from different vineyards, different grape varieties, different ripeness levels, and different degrees of dryness), we cannot list specific wines for each producer:

✓ **Mosel-Saar-Ruwer**

- Joh. Jos. Christoffel
- Christoffel-Berres
- Dr. Fischer
- Fritz Haag
- Willi Haag
- von Hövel
- Immich-Batterieberg
- Weingut Karlsmühle
- Karthäuserhof (Christoph Tyrell)
- Heribert Kerpen
- Reichsgraf von Kesselstatt
- Dr. Loosen
- Alfred Merkelbach
- Meulenhof
- Mönchhof
- Egon Müller
- Joh. Jos. Prüm
- Reuscher-Haart
- Willi Schaefer
- von Schubert (Maximin Grünhauser)
- Selbach-Oster
- Bert Simon
- Wwe. Dr. H. Thanisch
- Dr. Heinz Wagner
- Dr. F. Weins-Prüm
- Zilliken

✓ **Nahe**

- Hans Crusius & Sohn
- Schlossgut Diel

- Hermann Dönnhof
- Kruger-Rumpf
- Staatliche Weinbaudomäne

✔ **Rheingau**
- Georg Breuer
- Schloss Johannisberg
- Franz Künstler
- Dr. Heinrich Nagler
- Schloss Reinhartshausen
- Schloss Schönborn
- Langwerth von Simmern
- Schloss Vollrads
- Wegeler-Deinhard
- Domdechant Werner

✔ **Rheinhessen**
- Gunderloch
- Louis Guntrum
- Freiherr Heyl zu Herrnsheim
- Bürgermeister Carl Koch
- Georg Albrecht Schneider

✔ **Pfalz**
- Dr. von Bassermann-Jordan
- Dr. Bürklin-Wolf
- Kurt Darting
- J. F. Kimich
- Koehler-Ruprecht
- Lingenfelder
- Müller-Catoir
- Klaus Neckerauer
- Pfeffingen
- Werlé

Chapter 13

White Wines from Italy: More Than Soave and Pinot Grigio

In This Chapter

▶ Superb Pinot Bianco and Sauvignon

▶ Friuli: recommendations from Italy's best white wine region

▶ Other Italian wines worth trying

*I*taly is certainly more famous for her red wines than her white wines (see *Red Wine For Dummies,* published by IDG Books Worldwide, Inc. for information on Italy's reds). But Italian white wines in general happen to be better than ever, and some are downright excellent.

The stylistic pendulum for Italian white wines has swung from one extreme — the tired, oxidized whites of 30 years ago — to the other — the technically well-made but flavorless wines of 10 to 15 years ago — and it now seems to be settling in the middle (that is, clean and balanced wines). Today's wines have more character, more flavor, and slightly more richness than before.

Compared to other white wines of the world, however, Italian whites still show their own particular style: light-bodied, crisp, high acid wines with subdued aromas and flavors, wines meant to accommodate and not overpower food. Even those white Italian wines that mimic French or California wines — oaky Italian Chardonnays, for example — have the crispness of texture and the moderate weight to accompany food well.

Wine Regions of Italy

Most of Italy's best white wines come from three regions in the cooler, northeastern part of the country — sometimes referred to collectively as the Tre Venezie *(tray veh NETZ ee ay)* or Three Venices. Once part of the great Venetian Empire, this area today encompasses the regions of Veneto *(VEN eh toh),* Trentino-Alto Adige *(tren TEE noh-AHL toh AH dee jhay),* and Friuli-Venezia Giulia *(FREE oo lee-veh NETZ ee ah JOO lee ah).*

Although we concentrate on the white wines of those three regions, we also point out some good white wines from some of Italy's other 17 wine regions.

The Veneto — home of Soave

It's a toss-up which Italian white wine is more famous — Soave *(so AH vay)* or Pinot Grigio *(pee noh GREE joe).* Because Soave has been well known for a longer time, we'd put our money there. This dry, light-bodied wine is seemingly ubiquitous not only on its home turf but also in such large export markets as the United States and the United Kingdom.

Actually, Soave and Pinot Grigio are two very different wines. But what they have in common is that a vast majority of both wines are mass-produced, inexpensive, and rather neutral in aroma and flavor. At that quality level, they are both just simple quaffing wines. But better examples of both wines do exist.

Soave is the name of a village and wine zone outside the beautiful, historic city of Verona (Romeo and Juliet's home town). Soave wine is made from local grape varieties, such as the Garganega *(gar GAH neh gah)* and Trebbiano (Italy's most common white grape variety; see Chapter 3). Soave should always be consumed when it is young (no older than three years after the vintage; younger is better yet), while it is fresh and most refreshing.

Three reliable larger producers of Soave are Bolla, Bertani, and Masi (their Soave wines are in the $6 to $8 range). For a dollar or two more, you can buy a more intense, fuller-flavored Soave from one of the following three producers:

- ✔ Pieropan
- ✔ Anselmi
- ✔ Santa Sofia

Anselmi also makes two better-yet, single-vineyard Soaves from low-yielding vineyards, Anselmi Soave "Foscarino" and Anselmi Soave "Capitel Croce"; both retail for about $16 to $17.

Two alternatives to Soave in the $6 to $8 range, also from the Veneto region, are Bianco di Custoza *(bee AHN coh dee cus TOEZ ah)* and Lugana *(loo GAH nah).* Both of these wines are made in zones directly west of Verona, on the shores of Lake Garda. Bianco di Custoza is a blend of Trebbiano, Gargenaga, and Tocai grapes; Lugana (whose wine zone extends west into the Lombardy region) is entirely Trebbiano. Santi is a leading producer of both wines.

Like Soave wine, both Bianco di Custoza and Lugana should be enjoyed young. Seafood and light fish dishes go well with all three wines.

Pinot Grigio and the ever-present Chardonnay are two other white wines made in abundance by Veneto producers. The huge wineries, Santa Margherita and Torresella, make large quantities of these popular wines for worldwide distribution. Santa Margherita's Pinot Grigio, in particular, has a big following among U.S. wine drinkers.

The lively whites of Trentino-Alto Adige

Trentino-Alto Adige is in the northernmost part of Italy, bordering on Austria. (The hyphenated name reflects two separate regions that are attached politically.) The northern part of the region, Alto Adige (also called the South Tyrol), was part of the Austro-Hungarian Empire before World War I, and most of its citizens still speak German; the southern part, Trentino, is Italian-speaking.

Trentino-Alto Adige is one of Italy's most beautiful regions; the dramatically steep Dolomite Mountains (part of the Alps) run down the middle of the region, providing wonderful scenery, hillsides to grow grapes, and great skiing.

Naming Italian wines

Like all wines from European Union member countries, Italian wines follow a certain name protocol. Every single wine must specify a place as part of its name. Sometimes the place is the very name of the wine itself, such as Orvieto (see "Umbria," later in this chapter), and sometimes the place is just part of the wine name along with a grape variety, such as Vernaccia di San Gimignano (see the section on Tuscany in this chapter). Sometimes the place is an official wine zone recognized under Italian law, such as the Collio zone in Friuli, and sometimes the place is just one of Italy's 20 "states," such as Tuscany. However large or small, official or unofficial the place is, it's always spelled-out on the label as part of the wine name. (Usually in small print at the bottom, the label also states the location of the winery. But the winery location and the source of the grapes can be two different places.)

Although the Trentino-Alto Adige region makes red wine, most of it is either consumed locally or exported to Austria and Germany. The rest of the world sees Trentino-Alto Adige's white wines, some of which are excellent. Wines here are named as they are in Germany, Austria, and Alsace — after the grape variety. The four most popular wines are the following:

- ✓ Pinot Grigio (Pinot Gris)
- ✓ Pinot Bianco (Pinot Blanc)
- ✓ Chardonnay
- ✓ Sauvignon (Sauvignon Blanc)

For us, the two best white wines of Alto Adige are Pinot Bianco and Sauvignon. Both grape varieties, but especially Pinot Bianco, reach heights in this region that are seldom equaled anywhere else in the world.

Most of the winemakers of the Alto Adige work in or near the thriving city of Bolzano, Alto Adige's capital. Look for the wines of producers Alois Lageder *(la GAY der),* the brilliant Giorgio Grai *(GRYE),* Tiefenbrunner *(TEEF en broon ner),* or Hofstätter (the latter also makes a fine Gewürztraminer and Riesling).

Alois Lageder's single-vineyard wines, Pinot Bianco "Haberlehof," Sauvignon "Lehenhof," and Pinot Grigio "Benefizium" (see Figure 13-1), are particularly fine examples of what heights Italians can achieve with these varieties. Each of these wines costs about $16; we recommend them highly — especially the Pinot Bianco "Haberlehof."

Figure 13-1: A particularly fine example of a white wine from the Alto Adige region.

The Trentino area is the home of two large cooperative wineries, Cavit and MezzaCorona, located near its capital city, Trento. Both wineries produce tons of reliable, inexpensive white wines, especially Pinot Grigio and Chardonnay.

Three smaller producers from Trentino who are making some excellent white wines are

- **Pojer & Sandri:** Chardonnay; Müller-Thurgau; Traminer
- **Elisabetta Foradori:** Pinot Bianco "Sgarzon"; Gewürztraminer
- **Roberto Zeni:** Pinot Bianco "Sortì" or "Seipergole"; Müller-Thurgau "La Croce"; Chardonnay "Zaraosti"; and Pinot Grigio Rosé "Fontane" (Zeni's Pinot Grigio "Fontane" has a pale pink hue, from the pinkish skins of the Pinot Gris grape; highly recommended.)

Neither . . . nor

If you examine the labels of some white wines from northeastern Italy to determine whether the wine comes from the Veneto, from Trentino-Alto Adige, or from Friuli, you might not find the answer. The fact is that many of the less expensive wines from large producers based in these three regions — especially popular types of wine such as Pinot Grigio — come from grapes grown in more than one of the regions. These wines list their origins as the "Tre Venezie" or the "Venezie" or sometimes "northeastern Italy" — meaning they do not come specifically from one region or the other.

The unique white wines of Friuli-Venezia Giulia

Friuli-Venezia Giulia, often simply known as Friuli, gets our vote as Italy's best white wine region, and in fact — after the Burgundy region of France — as one of the world's best regions for white wines. Tucked away in Italy's northeast corner, Friuli borders Slovenia (formerly Yugoslavia) in the east and Austria in the north. The Slovenian border is a rather hazy one; many of Friuli's vineyards extend into Slovenia, while quite a number of Slavic people actually live in Friuli.

Friuli produces three of Italy's best white wines, all named for their grape variety:

- ✔ Tocai Friulano
- ✔ Pinot Bianco
- ✔ Pinot Grigio

Producers in the region also make Chardonnay and Sauvignon, along with two local varieties, Malvasia *(mal va SEE ah)* and Ribolla Gialla *(ree BOHL lah JAHL lah)* and interesting blends of all of the above varieties.

The best of Friuli

Of the seven wine zones in Friuli-Venezia Giulia, two — Collio *(CO lee oh)* and Colli Orientali *(CO lee or ee en TAH lee)*, both on the Slovenian border in the east — are clearly the best areas for white wine. Practically all of Friuli's finest white wines come from these two zones.

We think that Friuli's (and perhaps Italy's) best white varietal wine is Tocai Friulano *(toe KYE free ou LAH noh),* which is often called Tocai (see Figure 13-2).

Neither the grape called Tocai Friulano nor the wine made from it has any relation to Hungary's dessert wine, Tokaji or Tokay *(toe KAY),* or to Alsace's Tokay-Pinot Gris (which is actually the Pinot Grigio grape variety). Tocai Friulano has a rich, somewhat oily texture, a bouquet of pears and hazelnuts, concentrated flavors, and good acidity. In the hands of a good producer, it is one of the great under-$20 white wines in the world.

Mixed heritage

Like Alto Adige, Friuli-Venezia Giulia was also part of the Austro-Hungarian Empire before World War I. The region's heritage explains the importance of such grape varieties as Riesling, Riesling Italico (the Welschriesling grape of Austria; see the section on Austria later in this chapter) and Müller-Thurgau in Friuli today. Friuli-Venezia Giulia has always been at the crossroads of Europe; along with the Alto Adige, it is probably the least typically "Italian" region in the country. (And that is part of the drama and appeal of Italy — every region is so different!)

Figure 13-2: Tocai Friulano is one of Italy's best white varietal wines

Recommended producers of Friuli's white wines

Friuli has more than its share of small, quality-oriented producers. A pioneer in the area is Mario Schiopetto, who was the first to produce clean, well-made white wines in the region, about 25 years ago; his wine estate is in the Collio zone. Nowadays, Friuli — especially the Collio and Colli Orientali zones — probably boasts the highest percentage of quality producers of any of Italy's wine regions.

In the following list, we recommend producers from Friuli, and we mention a few of the better wines from each producer. (When a parenthesis follows a wine name, the grape varieties of that particular wine are enclosed in the parenthesis.)

> ✔ **Abbazia di Rosazzo:** Sauvignon Blanc, Tocai Friulano, Chardonnay, Pinot Grigio, "Ronco delle Acacie" (Tocai, Pinot Grigio, Ribolla Gialla blend), "Ronco di Corte" (Sauvignon/Pinot Bianco blend)

- **Borgo Conventi:** Sauvignon, Tocai, Pinot Bianco, Pinot Grigio, Ribolla Gialla, Chardonnay
- **Castelcosa (Franco Furlan, producer):** Pinot Grigio, Tocai, Chardonnay
- **Eno Friulia:** inexpensive, reliable brand made by Victor Puiatti (Puiatti's own brand is below) — Tocai, Pinot Bianco, Sauvignon, Chardonnay, Pinot Grigio, "Enopinot Cuvée" (Pinot Grigio/Pinot Bianco blend)
- **Livio Felluga:** Tocai, Sauvignon, Pinot Grigio, Chardonnay, "Terre Alte" (Tocai, Pinot Bianco, Sauvignon blend)
- **Marco Felluga:** Tocai Friulano, Pinot Grigio
- **Conti Formentini:** Pinot Grigio, Ribolla Gialla
- **Gravner:** Chardonnay, Sauvignon, Ribolla Gialla
- **Jermann:** "Vintage Tunina" (Sauvignon, Chardonnay, Pinot Bianco, Malvasia, Ribolla blend), Tocai, Sauvignon Blanc, Chardonnay, Pinot Bianco, Pinot Grigio, "Vinnae" (Ribolla, Riesling, Malvasia blend)
- **Francesco Pecorari:** Pinot Grigio "Gris," Chardonnay "St. Jurosa," Sauvignon "Picol," Tocai, "Charisma" (Chardonnay/Sauvignon blend)
- **Pighin:** Pinot Grigio (especially, the Collio DOC), "Soreli" (Tocai, Pinot Bianco, Sauvignon blend)
- **Plozner:** Chardonnay, Pinot Grigio, Tocai
- **Doro Princic:** Tocai Friulano, Pinot Bianco, "Vedute di Pradis" (Tocai, Pinot Bianco, Ribolla blend)
- **Puiatti:** Chardonnay, Pinot Bianco, Tocai, Sauvignon, Pinot Grigio
- **Radikon:** "Slatnik" (Tocai, Chardonnay, Sauvignon blend)
- **Ronco del Gnemiz:** Chardonnay, Müller-Thurgau, Tocai Friulano, Pinot Grigio
- **Russiz Superiore:** Pinot Grigio, "Roncuzv" (Pinot Bianco, Tocai, Sauvignon, Riesling blend)
- **Mario Schiopetto:** Pinot Bianco, Tocai Friulano, Sauvignon Blanc, Pinot Grigio, Ribolla Gialla, "Blanc des Rosis" (Tocai, Pinot Bianco, Ribolla blend)
- **Vigne dal Leon:** Pinot Bianco, Tocai Friulano, Sauvignon Blanc, "Tullio Zamó" (oak-aged Pinot Bianco)
- **Volpe Pasini:** Tocai, Pinot Bianco, Sauvignon, Pinot Grigio, "Le Roverelle" (Tocai, Sauvignon, Pinot Bianco, Verduzzo blend)

Beyond the Big Three: Italy's other white wine regions

Starting in the north and heading down to the island of Sicily, we point out other interesting white wines from Italy's various regions.

Piedmont

The Piedmont region in northwestern Italy, bordering France and Switzerland, is legendary for its red wines, such as Barolo, Barbaresco, and Barbera. But even the Piedmontese like to drink white wine now and then!

Two noteworthy whites from Piedmont are Gavi *(GAH vee)* and Arneis *(ahr NASE)*. The better-known of the two is Gavi (also known as Cortese di Gavi; Gavi is the town in southern Piedmont that is the center of the Gavi wine zone, while Cortese is the grape variety):

✔ Gavi is a very dry, rather delicate wine with quite pronounced acidity. It is best in its first three or four years and is an ideal wine with fish.

Most Gavi wines sell in the $10 to $15 range; Villa Banfi's Principessa Gavi is a leading brand, less dry than some others. Perhaps the most famous — and most expensive — Gavi is made by La Scolca, the estate that first made the wine. La Scolca's two most renowned Gavi wines are the "White Label," which sells for about $16 or $17, and its "Black Label Gavi di Gavi," priced in the $32 to $34 range — which can age longer than other Gavis, up to seven or eight years. (And at that price, it should!)

Italy's finest white wine?

Silvio Jermann's "Vintage Tunina" from Friuli might well be Italy's greatest white wine. A complex, full-bodied, concentrated wine, made from low-yielding vineyards, Vintage Tunina, like a great white Burgundy, requires many years to fully develop. We tried the 1985 Vintage Tunina with ten years of age and discovered that it had matured beautifully. Vintage Tunina retails in the $25 to $35 range, depending on the vintage — not expensive for a wine of this quality.

➤ The Arneis grape variety, from Piedmont's Roero wine zone near the town of Alba, was practically abandoned by Piedmontese winemakers 25 years ago, because it is a low yielding variety and difficult to grow. Two winemakers, Vietti and Bruno Giacosa, kept it alive, and today they make two of the very best Arneis wines. Ceretto also makes a fine Arneis.

Arneis (its full name is Arneis di Roero; Roero is the locality where Arneis grows), a dry to medium-dry wine, with aromas of peaches and pears and a rich texture, sells for about $16. It is best when it is young (drink it within two years of the vintage).

Arneis is especially refreshing as a warm-weather wine; try it as an *aperitivo,* along with prosciutto and melon, or have a cool Arneis to accompany a light pasta dish with vegetables.

A unique white wine from a red grape

The Nebbiolo grape variety is arguably Italy's finest red grape; Barolo and Barbaresco, two outstanding red wines from Piedmont (see *Red Wine For Dummies*), are made exclusively from this variety. One Barolo producer, Carretta, is now making a unique white wine from this red variety, called **Nebbiolo Bianco del Poggio.** We tried the 1993 vintage, which sells for about $11. It was absolutely delicious! It is a dry, medium-bodied wine with straw-yellow color. What we like about it is that it has lots of character and flavor. This is not a wimpy wine!

Carretta's Nebbiolo Bianco accompanies seafood appetizers quite well. We recommend it highly. It well might become one of our favorite Italian white wines.

Tuscany

Just like Piedmont, the Tuscany region is really red wine country — home of two world-famous reds, Chianti and Brunello di Montalcino. But one excellent white wine comes from here — Vernaccia di San Gimignano (*ver NOTCH cha dee san jee mee NYAH noh*). Various other white wines are made in Tuscany, many of them simple, light-bodied wines based on the

Trebbiano grape. And pricey, oak-aged Chardonnay is fairly common among Chianti producers who want to try their hand at making a major league white wine. But Vernaccia, when made by a good producer, is Tuscany's finest white.

Vernaccia di San Gimignano is produced from the native Vernaccia grape grown in vineyards around the medieval, walled town of San Gimignano, a popular stop for tourists. Vernaccia is a refreshing, medium-bodied white wine with a slightly oily texture and flavors suggesting almonds. Like most Italian white wines, Vernaccia is best when it is consumed young, within a few years of the vintage.

The Montenidoli estate of Elisabetta Fagiuoli makes some wonderful Vernaccias; her basic Vernaccia is about $10, and her more intense Vernaccia "Fiore" sells for $12. Two other Vernaccia producers to look for are Teruzzi & Puthod and Falchini; both of these producers' Vernaccias cost about $9, but Teruzzi & Puthod also makes an interesting Vernaccia Riserva (called "Terre di Tufo") that is aged in French oak barrels and sells for $17.

Try Vernaccia di San Gimignano with pasta that has a cream or cheese sauce, or with roast chicken.

Marche

This region on the eastern (Adriatic) coast of Italy produces a dry, inexpensive white wine, Verdicchio *(ver DEE key oh)*, from the grape of the same name. Quality has improved in this region, making Verdicchio a good buy indeed at $6 to $7.

Verdicchio wine has a remarkable affinity with fish dishes and seafood.

Several wine zones exist for Verdicchio, but Verdicchio dei Castelli di Jesi — from the zone around the town of Jesi — is the most commonly found Verdicchio. Two large, reliable producers are Fazi-Battaglia and Umani Ronchi.

Umbria

Locked between Tuscany to the north and west and Marche to the east, beautiful, mountainous Umbria has been producing wine since pre-Roman times. Umbria's most famous wine has always been Orvieto *(or vee AE toh)*, made around the majestic, old village of the same name, perched atop a hill. Traditionally, Orvieto was made as a medium sweet wine, a style called *abboccato*. But modern taste dictates that most Orvieto wine today is dry.

Orvieto is a blend of several grape varieties, with the dominant two being Procanico (a subvariety of Trebbiano) and the local Grechetto. Lately, producers are using more Grechetto in the blend, as this is considered the village of Orvieto's finest variety, and the wines have more flavor as a result.

Most Orvietos retail in the $6 to $8 range; some leading Orvieto producers include Antinori (see Figure 13-3), Bigi, Melini, and Ruffino.

Antinori also produces several other interesting white wines in Umbria, including Chardonnay and Sauvignon Blanc, under the brand name of his Castello della Sala estate.

Figure 13-3: Antinori also produces an interesting Chardonnay.

Lazio

The eternal city, Rome, dominates the Lazio region. Just southeast of Rome lie several large production zones for white wine, the most famous of which is Frascati. All these zones supply large quantities of inexpensive, light-bodied, dry white wine to the citizens of Rome and the rest of the world. Frascati itself is a dry, crisp, rather neutrally flavored white wine made from Trebbiano and Malvasia grapes. It is definitely most enjoyable when consumed within two years of the vintage. Fontana Candida is a major producer; Frascati retails for $4 to $5 a bottle, $8 to $9 for the 1.5 liter size.

Frascati goes best with fish and seafood.

Campania

Some of Italy's most interesting, flavorful white wines come from this southern Italian region, home of Naples, Sorrento, Capri, and Mount Vesuvius. Perhaps nowhere else in the world can you find such distinctive, unique dry white wines as Greco di Tufo and Fiano di Avellino.

The Greco grape is grown around the village of Tufo. It was introduced to the region by the Greeks almost 3,000 years ago. Greco di Tufo is a dry, full-bodied, full-flavored, viscous wine with a nutty flavor suggestive of toasted almonds. Although you can enjoy it beginning about three years from the vintage, Greco di Tufo can age and develop for ten years or more. The leading producer is Mastroberardino *(mas troh ber ar DEE noh),* whose Greco di Tufo retails for about $16 to $17.

Try Greco di Tufo with fish, poultry, or even veal.

Mastroberardino also makes Fiano di Avellino, a popular wine since Roman times. The Fiano grape variety, always low-yielding, grows in the hills north of Avellino, especially around the village of Lapio (some of these wines are also called Fiano di Lapio). Fiano di Avellino (or Lapio) has a complex, floral, subtle aroma, suggesting pear and spice, with lingering flavors of hazelnuts. It does need four to six years to fully develop, but will continue to mature for up to 15 years or more. Mastroberardino's basic Fiano wine retails for about $22, but his finest Fiano, "Vignadora," costs about $34 or $35.

Try Fiano with delicate fish or seafood dishes.

Mastroberardino has also revived a formerly popular wine, Lacryma Christi del Vesuvio, made from several local varieties of grapes growing in the volcanic soils of Mount Vesuvius. Lacryma Christi *(LAH cree mah KRIS tee)* del Vesuvio is a clean, dry wine with a lingering finish; Mastroberardino's is probably the best example of this wine. It retails for $12 to $13.

Sicily

The island of Sicily is Italy's largest region and also has the most vineyard acreage in the country. Three leading producers of white wine here are Corvo, Regaleali, and Donnafugata:

✔ **Corvo:** The Corvo brand, a product of the huge Duca di Salaparuta winery, is one of Italy's most well-known labels. You can find Corvo White — as it is known — in retail stores and in southern Italian restaurants all over the world. (About 10 million bottles a year, white and red, come from this winery, and 40 percent of that quantity is exported.) Corvo White sells for about $7 or $8. It is best consumed within two years of the vintage. A more intensely flavored Corvo white wine, Colomba Platino, sells in the $11 to $12 range.

✔ **Regaleali:** The Regaleali estate, a small, quality property, grows its grapes on cool, steep hillsides 1,500 feet above sea level, thus compensating for the warm climate of such a southerly island. Besides its basic white wine, called Regaleali Bianco (about $8 to $9); Regaleali produces an expensive, barrel-fermented Chardonnay (about $40); a fascinating, dry but very rich, late-harvest Chardonnay ($50 to $53); and a very good, flavorful Sauvignon Blanc with lots of depth, called "Nozze d'Oro," which sells for about $15.

Along with Mastroberardino and D'Angelo, Regaleali is one of southern Italy's great wine producers.

✔ **Donnafugata:** Donnafugata, owned by Gabriella Rallo, also a producer of Marsala wine (a fortified wine), is making clean, well-styled white wines under $10, including her Bianco and single-vineyard "Vigna di Gabri" wines from local grapes, plus a good Chardonnay.

One special white wine from Basilicata

Wild, mountainous Basilicata, the region that forms the in-step of the Italian boot, is yet another Italian region known mainly for red wines. But the leading producer in the area, Fratelli D'Angelo, also happens to make a fascinating white wine, "Vigna dei Pini," which is primarily a blend of Chardonnay and Pinot Bianco. The wine is a crisp, minerally, dry, full-flavored wine with a vaguely floral, piney aroma and earthy flavors more reminiscent of a red than a white wine (somewhat like a white Hermitage from the Rhône — see Chapter 11 — only crisper). Its earthiness is undoubtedly related to where the grapes are grown, in the volcanic soil of Mount Vulture (*VUL toor ay*). Vigna dei Pini currently sells for about $13 to $14.

Try Vigna dei Pini with main-course dishes, such as roast chicken, roast veal, or rabbit.

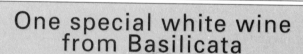

Chapter 14

Spain, Portugal, Austria, and Switzerland

*W*e admit it: European white wines are complicated. Every wine-producing country in Europe grows different white grape varieties. Each European country makes wines that are completely different from the white wines of the country right next door. And then European winemakers name their wines after places, for the most part, and not grapes. How is anyone supposed to remember where all those place are, let alone which grapes grow where?!

In defense of European white wines, however, we hasten to point out the enormous, fascinating variety of wines that exists. Even within one country, such as Germany or Italy, every wine is different. And when the wine is good, each wine tells the unique story of its own place, its own traditions, and its own people.

The white wines of Spain, Portugal, Austria, and Switzerland await you in this chapter, each with its own story.

The White Wines of Sunny Spain

Spain is the third largest wine-producing country in the world, behind Italy and France. And, as in those two countries, red wines in Spain play a more dominant role than white wines. In fact, until about 15 or 20 years ago, Spain's white wines were not thrilling to the non-Spanish palate: they tended to be aged in wood too long, developing tired, oxidized flavors.

Thankfully, those days are over. Today most Spanish white wines are cleanly made wines that usually see very little (if any) aging in wood. Traditionally made white wines that are aged in wood are still produced, but much better (less tired and oxidized) versions exist today.

Traveling from east to west, Spain's four important white wine regions are the following:

- ✔ Penedés *(pen eh DAIS)*, in the province of Catalonia, along Spain's northeastern coast
- ✔ Rioja *(ree OH ha)*, in north central Spain
- ✔ Rueda *(roo AE dah)*, in the province of Castilla y León in northwest Spain
- ✔ Rías Baixas *(REE ahse BYCE ahse)*, in the province of Galicia *(gah LEETH ee ah)* in the extreme northwest corner of Spain

Wines of the Penedés region

Tucked away in the northeast corner of Spain, the province of Catalonia, with its capital of Barcelona and its fast-paced, industrious people, is almost like a different country compared to southern Spain. Catalonia has many up-and-coming wine regions, such as Costers del Segre *(COHS ters del SAY gray)*, Alella *(ah LAY lyah)*, Priorato *(pree oh RAH to)*, and Terra Alta *(TER rah AHL tah)*. But finding the zesty, refreshing white wines from these regions outside of Barcelona is a bit difficult.

Fortunately for wine drinkers in other parts of the world, the Catalonian wines of the Penedés region are available almost everywhere, thanks to one enterprising firm, Torres (see Figure 14-1).

Miguel Torres, Jr., a French-trained winemaker who heads the family business, has made his winery an industry leader in Spain. (Bodegas Torres is Spain's largest family-owned winery.) Torres' formula for success involves using the latest wine-making technology and growing tried-and-true international grape varieties (such as Chardonnay, Sauvignon Blanc, Riesling, Gewürztraminer, and Muscat, among the white grapes). The company has built a fine reputation for its clean, well-made, well-priced wines, and has set up an enviable marketing structure that has enabled Torres' wines to penetrate the globe. The Torres firm now has wineries in Chile, Mexico, and California (Marimar Torres Estate), but the Penedés region remains its home base.

Figure 14-1: Miguel Torres has made Penedés wines available throughout the world.

Torres' most popular white wines are the following:

- ✓ **Viña Sol:** made from the local Parellada grape, clean, with lots of flavor ($6 to $7)

- ✓ **Gran Viña Sol:** made from Parellada and a minimum of 40 percent Chardonnay, with some wood aging; more intensely flavored, more fragrant than the Viña Sol ($10 to $11)

- ✓ **Fransola (green label):** wood-aged blend of Parellada and Sauvignon Blanc; more full-flavored than the Viña Sol; a single-vineyard wine (about $16)

- ✓ **Viña Esmeralda:** a totally unique white wine; made from a blend of Muscat d'Alsace and Gewürztraminer; very fragrant, off-dry, spicy ($10 to $11)

- ✓ **Chardonnay, Milmanda:** Torres' top-of-the-line white wine, from the Milmanda vineyard; a rich and complex Chardonnay barrel-fermented and aged in new French oak (about $40)

Rioja's white wines

Only 10 percent of the wine from Spain's famous (for its red wine) Rioja region is white, and most of it comes entirely from the Viura grape. On the whole, today's white Rioja wines are lively and fresh unoaked wines, with delicate aromas and fruity flavors. Most of them are inexpensive and made to be consumed within a few years.

Some producers still make white Rioja wine in the traditional style, with long periods of wood aging. When well made, these wines are richly flavored and have more character and complexity than the modern style wines; they're also more expensive.

We recommend the following modern white Riojas:

- ✔ **Marqués de Cáceres Rioja White:** modern-style, clean, fruity ($6 to $7)

- ✔ **Conde de Valdemar Blanco Barrique:** fermented in new oak barrels, full-flavored and complex; a modern wine ($15 to $16)

- ✔ **CUNE (also known as CVNE) Blanco Seco Rioja:** modern-style; clean, well-made (about $6)

- ✔ **CUNE "Monopole" Blanco Seco Rioja:** more traditionally made, fuller-bodied than the winery's regular Blanco Seco, but really a compromise between traditional and modern styles (about $8)

The following two wineries make full-blown, traditional white Rioja, aged in wood for several years. The wines are golden-colored, with woody flavors, lots of complexity, and a hint of oxidation; this style is not for everybody, but we happen to love it:

- ✔ R. Lopez de Heredia "Viña Tondonia" White ($11 or $12)

- ✔ Marqués de Murrieta Blanco Reserva ($11 or $12)

Traditional Rioja whites are an excellent accompaniment to popular Spanish dishes, such as paella, and chicken or seafood with rice. Modern-styled white Rioja wines go well with simple fish or poultry dishes.

Wines from the Rueda region

A firm from the Rioja region is the wine pioneer in the Rueda area — Marqués de Riscal. Not satisfied with the white wines

from the local Viura grape in Rioja, Marqués de Riscal opened
its own modern winery in Rueda in the 1970s and, under the
tutelage of the eminent Professor Emile Peynaud of Bordeaux,
began making white wines from the local Verdejo *(ver DAY ho)*
grape. The resulting wine — Verdejo — is richer, spicier, and
more full-flavored than most other Spanish white wines but still
manages to be attractively priced. Marqués de Riscal also
makes an oak-aged Sauvignon Blanc that is more full-bodied
and complex than the Verdejo.

The following two white wines from the Marqués de Riscal are
highly recommended:

- **Rueda Superior:** minimum of 80 percent Verdejo (about $7)
- **Rueda Reserva Limousin** (also known as Sauvignon Blanc
  in some markets): made 100 percent from Sauvignon
  Blanc grapes and matured in mostly new French oak casks
  ($8 to $9)

The exciting wines of Rías Baixas

Spain's most improved and most exciting white wine region is
the Rías Baixas region of Galicia. Modern winemaking arrived in
Rías Baixas just about 10 years ago, and the improvement in
the wines since then has been remarkable.

Rías Baixas is a cool, rather damp region, located next to the
Atlantic Ocean (just north of Portugal). In fact, Rías Baixas
shares with Portugal the really fine white grape variety of the
area, Albariño (called Alvarinho in Portugal). The Albariño *(ahl
bah REE nyoh)* grape variety is quite high in acidity, and its wine
does not appeal to everyone. The better examples of wine made
from Albariño possess a delicate, floral, spicy aroma with an
apricoty, peachy, melony flavor quite similar to the great white
wine from the Rhône Valley of France, Condrieu (see Chapter 11).

You can buy Albariños for $10 or less, but the best examples of
this wine, such as those from the three producers we mention
here, cost about $17 to $18:

- Bodega Morgadío
- Bodegas Marqués de Vizhoja
- Fillaboa

Portugal's "green" white — Vinho Verde

One white wine of note from Portugal (a country that otherwise makes predominantly red wine and dessert wine) is Vinho Verde *(VEEN yo VAIRD)*, which translates as "green wine." Although the wine does have a light greenish tinge, its name apparently derives from the lush green landscape of the Minho region in northwest Portugal, bordering the Atlantic Ocean, where Vinho Verde is made. Lots of rain keeps the Minho green. Another theory about the name is that the wine is meant to be consumed when it's young and still "green."

Two quality levels exist for Vinho Verde:

1. Slightly sweet, slightly effervescent, inexpensive wines that are mainly exported. Aveleda and Casal Garcia are two large brands; these wines sell for $6 to $7.

2. Dry, highly acidic wines with more flavor intensity. The best of these are made from the Alvarinho grape and sell in the $15 to $20 range; these are Portugal's finest white wines. Your best bet to find them is in wine shops or restaurants in Portuguese neighborhoods, or in Portugal itself.

 Vinho Verde is a great white wine for hot summer evenings. Its bracing acidity really wakes up the palate. Try Vinho Verde with grilled fish or seafood.

 Red Vinho Verde also exists, but you must be a genuine native of Portugal (or have at least one Portuguese parent) to handle this wine. It is a *raspingly* acidic wine. Let's just say that it's an acquired taste.

Austria's Crystal Whites

Austria has long enjoyed a reputation for its sweet, dessert wines, but the dryer white wines of Austria are only now becoming known to wine lovers around the world. The fact that they are, is fortunate — because Austria makes some of the finest white wines around.

The white wines of Austria bear certain similarities to German wines. For example, since German is the language of Austria, German words such as *trocken* (dry) and *halbtrocken* (semi-dry) appear on Austrian wine labels. Also, like German wines, Austria's wines are categorized, according to the ripeness level of the grapes, into classifications such as *kabinett, spätlese,* and so on (see "Telling it like it is," in Chapter 12). And grape varieties that are important in Germany, such as Riesling and Müller-Thurgau, are important in Austria, too.

But beyond these superficial similarities, Austrian white wines are quite different from German wines. For one thing, a greater proportion of Austria's non-dessert wines are actually dry. Also, many Austrian white wines are made from grape varieties that are not important in Germany.

Austria's white wines are stylistically quite varied: Some of them are rather full-bodied; a few are made using barrel-fermentation or aging (see Chapter 2); and their aromas and flavors are as diverse as the range of grape varieties grown in Austria. What the best wines have in common, generally speaking, is that they are intensely flavored dry wines with concentration, real substance, and character.

The wine regions of Austria

Austria's vineyards occupy the eastern part of the country only, because western, Alpine Austria is unfit for grape growing (but ideal for skiing). The four wine regions of Austria, from north to south, are

- ✔ Lower Austria (in German, called Niederosterreich, pronounced *nee der OZ ter ryke)*: The largest vineyard region, encompassing eight wine zones, the most famous of which is Wachau *(va COW);* most of the wines from this part of Austria are named Germanically, with village and vineyard names; Riesling is an important grape.

- ✔ Wien *(vee EN)*: The smallest area, encompassing vineyards around the city of Vienna

- ✔ Burgenland *(BURR ghen land)*: Known for its sweet wines; one of the most important regions for red wines, but also the home of many fine dry whites

- ✔ Styria (locally, called Steiermark, pronounced *STY er mark)*: Bordering Slovenia and Italy to the south, an important area for production of white wines from French grapes, such as Chardonnay and Sauvignon Blanc

Original grapes: Grüner Veltliner and Welschriesling

Although many different grape varieties — mainly whites — grow throughout Austria's vineyards, the two most important are grapes seldom seen in the vineyards of western Europe.

The grape that occupies more vineyard land in Austria than any other — by far — is Grüner Veltliner *(GREW ner VELT lee ner)*, a grape thought to be native to Austria. Grüner Veltliner wines vary according to the climate and soil of the vineyard, but they are generally medium- to full-bodied, with crisp acidity and aromas/flavors that range from herbal to spicy and vegetal. Although Riesling is considered globally to be a finer grape than Grüner Veltliner, some critics believe that Austria's finest dry white wines are those from Grüner Veltliner rather than from Riesling.

Welschriesling is Austria's second most important grape variety. Outside of Austria, this grape — unrelated to Riesling — makes pleasant but unremarkable wines; in Austria, it makes good to very good wines with lemon-apple flavors. Many of Austria's Welschriesling wines are dessert wines, but dry Welschrieslings also exist.

Müller-Thurgau and Riesling are the only two additional white grape varieties significant in Austria — and with less than 3 percent of the country's vineyard acreage, Riesling is really important only qualitatively.

Recommended producers of Austrian wine

We list several good producers of Austrian wine in alphabetical order:

- ✔ Willi Bründlmayer
- ✔ Hopler (for Grüner Veltliner)
- ✔ Alois Kracher
- ✔ Martin Nigl
- ✔ Willi Opitz
- ✔ F. X. Pichler
- ✔ Josef Pöckl
- ✔ Franz Prager

- Heidi Shröck
- Georg Steigelmar
- Tement
- Ernst Triebaumer
- Josef Umathum

Switzerland's White Wines

Is there a more beautiful country in which to enjoy wine than Switzerland? No wonder visitors return home wanting to buy Swiss wine. Unfortunately, Switzerland's wine production is not large — in fact, the Swiss drink a lot more wine than they make, importing wines mainly from neighboring France, Italy, and Germany.

Switzerland is one of the few countries in the world in which white wines predominate. (Germany, Austria, and, to a lesser extent, the U.S., also come to mind.) Swiss white wines are ideal for wine drinkers who are tired of heavily oaked Chardonnays. Swiss white wines tend to be crisp, medium-bodied, with minerally and earthy flavors, and, for the most part, made without wood aging.

Most Swiss whites are made from the Chasselas grape, a rather undistinguished performer in Germany and in France's Loire Valley, but at its best in Switzerland's cool wine regions. Most of the wine comes from the French-speaking part of Switzerland: the southwest, around Lake Geneva, Lake Neuchatel, and the Rhône River. Switzerland's most important white wine regions are the following:

- Valais *(vah lay)*, in the south, along the Rhône River
- the Vaud, in the southwest, around Lake Geneva
- Neuchatel *(NOI sha tel)*, in the west, around Lake Neuchatel

Switzerland's best white wines are coming from the Valais region. Here the Chasselas variety (called Fendant, locally, and often on the wine label) reaches its heights, especially around the districts of Sion and Sierre. The Fendant wines of the Valais often have an earthy, and sometimes minerally, complexity of flavors seldom found elsewhere.

The Fendant de Sierre of producer Rouvinez & Fils, at about $14, is a particularly fine example of the Valais style in white wines. Other fine Swiss producers to look for are Robert Gilliard and J. & P. Testuz.

Two particularly interesting grape varieties that you will only find in the Valais, which is Switzerland's sunniest wine region, are the *Petite Arvine* and the *Amigne.* These two grape varieties make especially aromatic, complex white wines with lots of flavor intensity; wines from these grapes are totally unique, completely different in aroma and flavor from any other wines.

Part III
The Part of Tens

In this part . . .

We can think of ten reasons why you should find this part of the book useful:

1. Most people serve white wine too cold.

2. Aging is a myth for most white wines.

3. One Pouilly is not the same as the next.

4. Confusing the taste of oak with the taste of fruit is a common mistake.

5. Sauvignon Blanc doesn't really taste a thing like Chardonnay.

6. Pinot Gris is delicious.

7. You deserve to taste a great Chablis.

8. There's Soave — and then there's Soave.

9. For $6 a bottle, Washington Sémillon is a great buy.

10. Because "dry" doesn't always mean dry.

Chapter 15

Ten Little-Known White Wines Worth Knowing

*R*emember the old television commercial that said, "Try it, you'll like it!"? Keep that in mind when you look over our list of ten unusual white wines in this chapter. We don't guarantee that you will like every one of them, but we're sure you'll find a couple that you're glad you tried.

Some of these wines are widely available, while others are available mainly in major cities and in specialty wine shops and fine restaurants. We don't indicate specific vintages, because we don't know which vintages will be available when you go shopping; instead we offer some specific vintage information in the description of many of the wines.

The wines are identified like this: Name, Producer, Region of Production, Country. (Remember that in the case of most European wines, the name of the wine and the region of production are one and the same.)

Gewürztraminer, Lazy Creek, Anderson Valley (California), U.S.

California doesn't have a great reputation for its Gewürztraminer *(gah VERTZ trah mee ner)* wines among serious aficionados of that type of wine (see Chapter 3 for a description of the Gewürztraminer grape). But the Anderson Valley wine region, in the northern part of the state (Mendocino County), is proving to be an exception.

Lazy Creek Vineyards makes one of the most distinctive Gewürztraminers that we've tasted outside of Alsace, France —

and for about $11, it's a real buy. Really pungent and flavorful, as a Gewürztraminer should be, this dry Gewürztraminer wine shows the rich texture and softness typical of this variety. Buy this wine relatively young and drink it young — no more than five years from the vintage date.

Vigna dei Pini, Fratelli D'Angelo, Basilicata, Italy

A producer known for red wine, Fratelli D'Angelo *(frah TEL lee DAHN jel loh)*, is now also making a fascinating white wine, Vigna dei Pini *(VEE nya day PEE nee)*, which is principally a blend of Chardonnay and Pinot Bianco (Pinot Blanc).

Vigna dei Pini is a crisp, dry, full-flavored wine that has a distinctive, minerally, piney bouquet and earthy flavors. An unusual wine, which sells for about $13 to $14, the Vigna dei Pini is worth seeking out in fine wine shops.

Try Vigna dei Pini with dishes that are earthy and smoky in flavor; we had it with salmon crusted in pine nuts cooked in a wood oven.

Rioja Blanco Reserva, Marqués de Murrieta, Spain

Marqués de Murrieta, one of the oldest wineries in the Rioja *(ree OH ha)* region of Spain, makes an old-style, oak-aged white Rioja, from the Viura grape. The wine has a deep golden color, complex aromas and flavors of wood, honey, and dried fruits, and a hint of oxidation from its long oak-aging.

One of the reasons we like this wine is that it is so unusual: Very few white Riojas are made with so much oak-aging any more — in fact, the majority of white Rioja wines these days are not oaked at all. (Lopez de Heredia's Viña Tondonia is another example of the oaky, old-fashioned style.) We find the Murrieta to be a fascinating wine, although we realize that it might not suit everyone's taste. It costs about $11 or $12. *Generally available.*

Sauvignon Blanc, Mayacamas Vineyards, Napa Valley (California), U.S.

Many California Sauvignon Blancs are so heavily oaked that their varietal character is hidden beneath the toasty, nutty, smoky flavors of oak — with the result that they taste like Chardonnays. Not so with the Mayacamas *(my ah CAH mahs)* Sauvignon Blanc! Mayacamas Vineyards, located high up in the Mayacamas Mountains that separate Napa Valley from Sonoma Valley, makes an intensely varietal Sauvignon Blanc, with pronounced lime and grapefruit flavors, that could never be mistaken for a Chardonnay! It costs about $14 to $15. *Generally available.*

Pinot Gris, The Eyrie Vineyards, Willamette Valley (Oregon), U.S.

David Lett, owner-winemaker of The Eyrie Vineyards in Oregon's Willamette Valley wine region, has consistently been making the best Pinot Gris in the U.S. for many years now. He manages to capture the fruity intensity of the variety (see the description of the Pinot Gris grape in Chapter 3 for more information), and yet keeps his Pinot Gris lively and crisp.

Try this Pinot Gris with shellfish, such as oysters or mussels, or with the Oregon specialty, salmon. It sells for about $13 to $14.

Sémillon, Chateau Ste. Michelle, Columbia Valley (Washington), U.S.

Looking for an inexpensive alternative to Chardonnay? Check out the Sémillons of Washington state. Most of them, such as Chateau Ste. Michelle's, have little or no oak-aging, low to medium acidity, and discreet fruit flavors reminiscent of melon and fig; they sell for $6 to $7. *Generally available.* Also try Columbia Crest's or The Hogue Cellars' Sémillon. (Both are also generally available.)

Sauvignon Blanc/Semillon, Selaks, Marlborough, New Zealand

Although Cloudy Bay Winery has become *the* famous producer of New Zealand Sauvignon Blanc wine, a number of other producers make good examples, such as Selaks Sauvignon Blanc/Semillon blend (here the Semillon helps to tone down the intense vegetal character of the Sauvignon Blanc). Buy it young. Other good producers include Hunters, Jackson Estate, Stoneleigh, Matua Valley Reserve, and Palliser Estate.

Chablis Premier Cru, Montée de Tonerre, Louis Michel, France

What a pleasure it is to taste this exquisite, unoaked premier cru Chablis from Louis Michel! When we opened a bottle from the 1992 vintage, it displayed a wonderful minerally bouquet, combined with gunflint and smoke. It was crisp, yet perfectly balanced. It reminded us that Chablis, when made by a fine producer such as Louis Michel, remains one of the great white wines and white wine values in the world. This wine sells in the

$20 to $25 price range. Refer to the Vintage Chart in Appendix C for recommendations on good vintages for Chablis and their current drinkability.

Bourgogne Blanc Les Clous, A. & P. DeVillaine, France

White Burgundy wines, as a category, are the favorite white wines of many wine lovers. The only problem is that they can be very expensive. The great Burgundy producer, Aubert DeVillaine, of Romanée Conti fame (see *Red Wine For Dummies*) makes two basic white Burgundies that are consistently fine and yet cost under $20:

- Les Clous *(lay clue)*, 100 percent Chardonnay (about $18)
- Bourgogne-Aligoté, from the village of Bouzeron, 100 percent from the Aligoté grape variety (about $16 to $17)

Another excellent basic white Burgundy is Leroy's Bourgogne Blanc d'Auvenay (also 100 percent Chardonnay, and about $18).

Pinot Bianco, Haberlehof Vineyard, Alois Lageder, Alto Adige, Italy

Pinot Blancs have taken a back seat to Chardonnays throughout most of the world's wine regions, but in northeastern Italy, particularly in the Alto Adige *(AHL toh AH dee jhay)* region, Pinot Blanc is a star! The Pinot Bianco that Alois Lageder *(AH loh is lah GAY der)* makes from his Haberlehof vineyard (about $16) is one of the world's greatest Pinot Blancs; it is lively, crisp, and delicious, yet rich and full of character — a perfect expression of this grape variety.

Soave, Pieropan, Italy

Okay, we're cheating; we know this is really #11, but we had to fit all the wines into the Part of Tens, and we didn't have the heart to eliminate any of our favorites.

You may be surprised that we chose a Soave, because this type of wine, which has always been the Veneto region's big-production white wine, admittedly is typically mass-produced from very high-yielding vineyards — with very light, bland, neutral wines as the result. Pieropan's Soave, however, made from the same grape varieties as other Soaves (mainly Garganega and Trebbiano) but from low-yielding vineyards, has much more intensity, concentration, and complexity than most other Soaves. And yet it's only about $8 to $9, just a dollar or two more than the others. Definitely a wine to buy. *Generally available.*

Chapter 16

Ten Frequently Asked Questions about White Wines

. . . .

In This Chapter

▶ First wines

▶ Wines and your health

▶ How dry is dry

▶ What's ready to drink

▶ Chilling out

▶ Matching meats

. . . .

*M*ost people newly-smitten by the wine bug have some nagging questions that need answers before they're willing to deepen the relationship. Here are answers to ten common questions to get you started.

What White Wines Should a Novice Wine Drinker Try First?

Very dry or very tart white wines are likely to put off novice wine drinkers, because they taste so different from the sweetened beverages people tend to drink instead of wine.

We therefore recommend that you start with light-bodied, inexpensive German wines. These fruity, low-alcohol wines are excellent first wines for new wine drinkers, because they're not too dry — and therefore are easy-drinking wines. Specifically, you might try some Riesling wines from the Mosel-Saar-Ruwer region (they come in tall, slender green bottles) or a popular Rhine wine called Liebfraumilch *(LEEB frow milsh)*, which comes in a tall, thin brown bottle. You can find plenty of examples of each for less than $10 in most supermarkets and wine stores. (Turn to Chapter 12 for more information on German wines.)

We suggest that you then try an inexpensive (under $10) Chardonnay wine from California or Australia. Either wine is generally dryer than inexpensive German wines, and yet not that dry. Chardonnay wines are popular wines with many wine drinkers. (Turn to Chapters 6 and 9 for our recommendations on California and Australia Chardonnays, respectively.)

Do Sulfites Cause Headaches?

Because of a mandatory warning, "Contains sulfites," on the labels of wines sold in the U.S., wine drinkers in the U.S. are now very aware of the presence of sulfites in wine — and sulfites end up taking the rap for just about any unpleasant reaction anyone has to wine. The most common sulfur compound in wine is *sulfur dioxide,* a natural by-product of fermentation that's present in all fermented products — not just wine but also breads, pastries, and cheeses. Besides occurring naturally in wine, sulfur dioxide is added to wine in very small quantities as an antibacterial and antioxidant. (Some labels state, "No sulfites added," but those wines probably do contain small amounts of naturally occurring sulfites.)

The sulfites in wine can be detrimental to those who have severe asthma, and to anyone who is under doctor's orders to restrict consumption of sulfites (a relatively small percentage of the population). If you experience headaches after drinking wine, you might be sensitive to other ingredients in wine — such as the alcohol itself. Check with your doctor.

If you do want to reduce your consumption of sulfites in wine, steer toward

- Fully dry white wines
- Finer white wines

The highest sulfite levels tend to appear in wines that are sweet (sulfur dioxide is needed to prevent the sugar in the wine from refermenting) and inexpensive.

How Do I Know How Dry a White Wine Is?

The gamut of sweetness in white wines — excluding sweet dessert wines — ranges from bone-dry to medium-sweet. In decreasing dryness, the terms that apply are *dry, medium-dry,* and *medium-sweet;* often wine people use the term *off-dry* as a generalized descriptor of a wine that is not fully dry.

Many white wines that are not bone-dry nevertheless fall into the category of dry wines because no official classification exists. And anyway, the perception of sweetness or lack of sweetness is very individual. You really are your own best judge of sweetness or dryness in a wine.

Apart from tasting a wine personally to determine how dry you find it, the best way to find out about a wine's level of dryness is to ask a knowledgeable person in your local wine shop. For those times when you are on your own, however, we offer you a few simple guidelines:

- ✔ White wines that have a golden color are often less dry than paler-colored white wines. Sometimes, their sweetness comes from very ripe grapes, which are responsible for the wine's golden color (the ripe, sweet grapes make a higher alcohol wine, and alcohol has a sweet flavor). But the golden color of a white wine can also be caused by the wine's age or maturity, or from oak-aging; color is not a surefire determinant of sweetness.

- ✔ Inexpensive (under $10) white wines tend to be less dry than more expensive white wines. Often, very inexpensive (less than $5) white wines can be quite sweet, even if the label doesn't say so.

- ✔ Inexpensive American white wines that do not indicate a grape variety on the label are usually fairly sweet; sometimes, they have such names as "Sauternes," "Chablis," or "Rhine Wine."

- ✔ Certain grape varieties, such as Chenin Blanc and French Columbard, are usually made into wines that are not totally dry. For example, most Vouvray wines — French white wines made from the Chenin Blanc grape — fall into this category. Because the norm for these wines is off-dry, the dryer versions of these wines are usually clearly labeled "Dry" Chenin Blanc or Vouvray "Sec" *(dry)*.

What's the Difference between a Chardonnay and a Sauvignon Blanc?

Chardonnay and Sauvignon Blanc are two popular grape varieties used in making white wine; these terms are also the names of wines made primarily from each of those grapes. Because each of these grapes has different characteristics, the wines made from them are different — sometimes dramatically so.

What Chardonnay wine and Sauvignon Blanc wine have in common is that both wines, but especially Chardonnay, are frequently made in an oaky style and therefore share certain aromas and flavors (spicy, nutty, toasty, and/or vanilla) that come from the oak.

Other than that, the wines are quite different:

- ✔ Wines made from the Chardonnay grape are normally more full-bodied than Sauvignon Blanc wines.
- ✔ Chardonnay wines are usually dry, with various fruity aromas and flavors ranging from apples (in cooler wine regions) to tropical fruits such as mangos or pineapples (in warmer wine regions).
- ✔ Wines made from Sauvignon Blanc are usually even dryer, lighter-bodied, and are higher in acidity (which makes them taste crisp).
- ✔ Sauvignon Blanc wines often have herbaceous flavors (suggestive of herbs and grass) and are frequently described as grassy. They can also display minerally aromas and flavors and a vegetal character; when the grapes are grown in warmer climates, Sauvignon Blancs can also have fruity aromas and flavors, such as that of ripe melon.

Chapter 3 describes the characteristics of the two grapes. To imprint the differences into your personal experience, try performing Wine-Tasting Exercise #3 in Chapter 17.

How Do I Know When a White Wine Is Ready to Drink?

Almost all white wines are ready to drink when you buy them. They don't require additional aging, and in fact can deteriorate if you let them get too old before drinking them.

Most white wines are made to taste best when they are young and fresh, that is, in their first two or three years; only a very few white wines actually improve with age. The young-and-fresh rule is especially true of inexpensive (under $10) white wines.

Some exceptions to the rule — that is, some white wines that age well and even improve with age — are the following:

- ✔ Better (over $15) white Burgundy wines from France
- ✔ Better (over $20) white Bordeaux wines from France
- ✔ A few of the better (over $15) American Chardonnays
- ✔ A few of the better (over $15) Italian white wines, such as Vintage Tunina, Greco di Tufo, and Fiano di Avellino
- ✔ Better (over $15) German and Alsace Rieslings
- ✔ Better (over $15) Australian Semillons

Are Vintage Years Important for White Wines?

One of the great advantages of a *vintage date* (that is, an indication of the year the grapes were harvested) on white wine bottles is that the vintage date allows you to determine just how old the wine is. For white wines that should be consumed when they are young and fresh (most white wines of the world fall into that category), the vintage date can assure you that your white wine is not too old.

The relative quality of one harvest, or vintage, compared to another is important only for the finest quality white wines — and even then, mainly for wines from those wine regions that experience significant variation in weather from year to year. Vintage-year quality is fairly important, for example, in some European countries such as France, Italy, and Germany.

Consult our vintage chart in Appendix C to learn how we rate vintages of the better white wines from these countries.

How Cold Should I Serve White Wine?

Most white wines are served too cold. (This statement is especially true in many U.S. restaurants where white wine is stored in a refrigerator.) Cold temperatures (as opposed to chilly temperatures) are not ideal because they mute the subtleties of a wine's flavor.

For very inexpensive white wines, cold temperature is less of a handicap than for fine white wines, because really inexpensive whites don't have many subtleties of flavor to begin with; in fact the cold can do the wine a favor by masking the wine's sweetness or hiding any imperfections in the wine. But if you are drinking a better white wine, let's say one that retails for more than $6, you'll be less able to detect the wine's aromas and flavors if the wine is served too cold.

The finer your white wine, the closer it should be to room temperature so that you can appreciate its aroma and flavor. We like to serve very fine white wines, such as Burgundy and Bordeaux, at about 62° F. For less expensive (under $20) but good quality white wines, we recommend a serving temperature of 56° to 60° F.

We are frequently served white wines that are as cold as 35° F in restaurants! In those cases, we ask the server for an unchilled bottle, but one isn't usually available, and we end up being unable to appreciate the wine until we're down to our last sip.

When you are chilling wines at home, remember that you can easily chill down an unchilled white wine by placing the bottle on ice for 10 to 15 minutes — but you can't correct overchilling by putting the bottle in a microwave to warm it up! Less cold is safer.

Can I Drink White Wine with Red Meat?

Although fish and seafood are the traditional accompaniment to white wine, you can definitely enjoy many white wines with meat as well.

Because white wines range from very delicate and light-bodied to very full and flavorful, they suit a wide range of foods. Generally speaking, the lighter-bodied, less flavorful whites (such as Soave, Muscadet, or Sancerre) work best with lighter foods, such as fish, or lighter preparations of light meats and poultry, while fuller-bodied and more flavorful whites are suitable for richer dishes and more flavorful foods.

We have no hard-and-fast rules in matching food and wine. If you want to drink white wine with your steak, do it! You are the best (in fact, the *only*) judge of what tastes good to you.

For more advice on white wine with food, refer to Chapter 5.

Is White Wine (or Just Red Wine) Good for My Health?

Many recent studies have found that wine in general, when consumed in moderation (anywhere from two to five glasses a day, depending on whose advice you choose to follow), seems to promote longevity. Wine appears to be especially beneficial to the cardiovascular system. Studies have not definitively found appreciable differences in the beneficial effects of red wine versus white wine, although most of the studies have focused on red wine.

Wine, both white and red, contains many vitamins and minerals, including the B vitamins, iodine, iron, magnesium, zinc, copper, calcium, and phosphorus. A four-ounce serving of dry white wine contains about 104 calories. Wine contains no fat.

What's the Difference between Fumé Blanc, Pouilly-Fumé, and Pouilly Fuissé?

Fumé Blanc is just another name for Sauvignon Blanc wine. Robert Mondavi originally used the name Fumé Blanc for his Sauvignon Blanc wine from California in the early 1970s; since then, many other producers — as far away as Australia — have adopted the name for their Sauvignon Blancs.

The use of the name Fumé Blanc for wines based on the Sauvignon Blanc grape certainly derives from the fact that one of the most famous Sauvignon Blanc-based wines in the world has the word Fumé (meaning smoky) in its name. That wine is Pouilly-Fumé *(pwee foo may)*, named after the town of Pouilly-sur-Loire in the Loire Valley wine region of France.

The French wine called Pouilly-Fuissé *(pwee fwee say)* is also named after a town called Pouilly — and a town called Fuissé. These two French towns are situated in the Mâcon district of southern Burgundy — a completely different wine region from the Loire Valley.

The only two things that Pouilly-Fumé and Pouilly-Fuissé have in common is that they are both white wines and they both come from France:

- ✔ Pouilly-Fumé is a 100 percent Sauvignon Blanc wine, medium-bodied, crisp, and seldom aged in oak.
- ✔ Pouilly-Fuissé is a 100 percent Chardonnay wine, full-bodied and often aged in oak.

You can purchase both wines in the $12 to $16 range, but the finest examples of both wines can cost over $30. (Oops. That makes three things that the two wines have in common.)

Chapter 17

Ten Palate-Pleasing Exercises for Savoring White Wines

. . . .

In This Chapter

▶ Oaky or fruity

▶ Crisp or fat

▶ Chardonnay versus Sauvignon Blanc

▶ Varietal character

▶ The two Pouillys

▶ Wine quality

▶ New World versus Old

▶ The power of place

▶ A world of Pinot Gris

. . . .

*A*re you tired of reading about how various white wines taste, and ready for a close personal encounter with concepts such as crispness or softness, oakiness, and unctuousness? In this chapter we suggest ten wine-tasting exercises that you can perform at home, to experience various types of wine first-hand and interactively.

We don't recommend specific brands for you to use in your tasting experiments, but only specific types of wine, so that you can buy whichever brand of that type is available to you where you live. The specific wines you taste could vary slightly from our examples, but the general gist of the exercise should come through nevertheless.

Just a bit of advice to start: Be sure that you don't over-chill the white wines that you use in these exercises. If the wines are just cool, rather than really cold, the differences between the wines will be much easier for you to observe.

Exercise #1: Is It Oak? Is It Fruit?

Oaky character is so common in white wines these days that you can easily assume that the oakiness you taste is actually the flavor of the grape. White wine takes on oaky character when it is fermented and/or aged in barrels of oak, or when the winemaker soaks oak chips in the wine. (Turn to Chapter 2 for more on oak in winemaking.) Here's an exercise that helps separate the oak from the fruit.

Buy two wines from the same grape variety, one wine that is oaky and one that isn't. We suggest either two Chardonnay wines or two Sauvignon Blanc wines — and in the latter case, preferably wines that are made entirely from Sauvignon Blanc, just to eliminate the variable of a second grape variety.

To determine whether a wine is oaked or not, ask your retailer, who will be able to discuss the fine points of specific brands with you. For a general idea, however, follow these guidelines:

- Nearly all U.S. and Australian Chardonnays are oaky.
- French white Burgundy wines from Chablis and Mâcon (which are made entirely from the Chardonnay grape) generally are not oaked.
- Inexpensive Italian Chardonnays (under $10 a bottle) usually are not oaked, but pricier Italian Chardonnay wines ($15 and over) usually are very oaky.
- California Sauvignon Blanc wines may or may not be oaky; each producer differs.
- French Sancerre and Pouilly-Fumé wines are generally not oaked.
- New Zealand Sauvignon Blancs are not oaked.

 When you compare the two wines, you are likely to notice the following differences:

- The oaked wine is deeper in color, and the unoaked wine is paler.
- The unoaked wine has a lighter, less intense aroma, and the aroma suggests fruit, herbs or earthy character.
- The aroma of the oaky wine suggests vanilla, toast, smoke, char, butterscotch, or spice (especially cinnamon or cloves).

✔ The oaky wine is probably more flavorful (its flavors are similar to the aromas mentioned just above) and probably has a slight edge of bitterness that you can detect towards the rear of your mouth; it may leave your mouth more dried-out than the unoaked wine.

✔ The unoaked wine probably has less flavor (again, that flavor resembles what you smelled), but it is not bitter; instead, it leaves your mouth feeling clean, and probably makes you salivate.

Depending on which two specific wines you are comparing, you can perhaps detect other differences that may not be attributable to the issue of oak. (For example, one of the wines might be sweeter and richer than the other because it comes from a warmer climate and was made from riper grapes — as explained in Chapter 2.) But the characteristics described earlier relate directly to the use of oak or the lack of it in white wine.

Exercise #2: Crisp White, Fat White

On the spectrum of white wine texture, the two extremes are crisp and fat. (Turn to Chapter 1 to read about wine texture.) Crisp white wines and fat white wines are distinctly different styles, each suitable for different tastes and different foods. Fans of crisp white wines can find fat whites to be . . . well, heavy and fat. Fans of fat white wines can find crisp whites too thin and weak. (Hey, this is starting to sound like social commentary!) But each is a valid style of white wine.

To determine which you prefer — or to get a good grasp of crispness in your wine-tasting vocabulary — try this exercise. Open a bottle of Pinot Grigio from Italy and a bottle of Alsace Pinot Gris (which is probably labeled "Tokay Pinot Gris"), preferably from a producer who favors a full style, such as Hugel or Zind-Humbrecht. Both wines are made from the same grape variety, but the Italian wine is characteristically lean and crisp, while the Alsace style is the opposite.

When you compare the two wines, you're likely to find:

✔ The Italian wine is lighter in body, meaning that it seems less heavy in your mouth; the Alsace wine is the opposite.

✔ The fat Alsace wine feels rich and unctuous in your mouth, not just weightier than the crisp Italian wine, but rounder, too, as if it has no edges.

✔ The Italian wine feels not just lighter but also slightly sharper; it does have edges.

✔ The crisp wine leaves your mouth feeling clean and fresh.

✔ The fat wine leaves your mouth feeling slightly coated with flavor.

To understand the full extent of crispness versus fatness, try each wine with food; notice how the crisp wine refreshes after each bite, while the fatter wine plays a more assertive role in the meal, as if it were another food on the table.

Which style is better? Neither — and both. Decide for yourself which you prefer, and in what circumstances.

Exercise #3: Chardonnay versus Sauvignon Blanc

How much difference can a grape make? This exercise demonstrates what the two most popular white grape varieties each bring of themselves to a wine — in other words, the varietal character of each of the two grapes.

If you choose a Chardonnay wine from anywhere except Italy, Austria, or the Chablis or Mâcon districts of Burgundy, chances are that the wine is oaky. To level the playing field of varietal character, therefore, choose a Sauvignon Blanc wine that is also oaked, and preferably one with only a minimal amount of Sémillon (if any) in its blend. Your retailer should be able to guide you toward a good selection.

Here are some of the differences that you are likely to find when you look at, smell, and taste the two wines side by side:

✔ The Chardonnay is deeper in color than the Sauvignon Blanc; it probably has golden tinges, compared to hints of green color in the Sauvignon.

✔ Both wines smell toasty or smoky or charry from their oak (see Exercise #1 earlier in this chapter), but the underlying aromas differ. The Chardonnay may smell of peaches, ripe apples, pineapple, or various tropical fruits, while the Sauvignon Blanc has an underlying aroma of herbs, green vegetation, tart fruit, or perhaps melon.

✔ Beneath their oak, the two wines should differ likewise in their flavors. The Sauvignon Blanc should have more acidity in your mouth than the Chardonnay, meaning that it will taste somewhat crisper, and less round. Depending on the wines you choose for this exercise, the Sauvignon Blanc may be quite rich and generous due to high alcohol and/ or a slight touch of sweetness, but beneath those characteristics you can probably detect a certain zinginess and zip to the wine, which the Chardonnay doesn't have.

To capture the character of the Sauvignon Blanc grape in its purest form, try an unoaked wine made 100 percent from that grape, such as a Sancerre wine from France, or a New Zealand Sauvignon Blanc. The flavor comes through so loud and clear that you won't need any comparison!

Exercise #4: Varietal Character

Varietal character — that is, the characteristics of a wine that derive from the wine's grape variety — is more than just a fancy term for wine geeks to throw around. Varietal character is real. White wines made from different grapes taste different because of it.

This exercise builds on Exercise #3, comparing Chardonnay wines and Sauvignon Blanc wines. Don't only choose one wine from each of those grapes, also buy a dry wine from the Riesling grape, and a dry wine from the Gewürztraminer grape.

Because Riesling wines and Gewürztraminer wines are seldom oaked, selecting an unoaked example of Sauvignon Blanc and Chardonnay, too, is a good idea. If you can't find an unoaked Chardonnay, however (we offer some suggestions in Exercise #1), have just three of the four wines be unoaked styles:

✔ If the four wines are each true to their grape variety characteristics, you can see color differences among them.

The Sauvignon Blanc and Riesling have greenish glints of color, while the Chardonnay is golden (and deep in color, if it is oaked); the Gewürztraminer is also yellow in hue, without green tones.

✔ In aroma, the Sauvignon Blanc is likely to be herbal, the Chardonnay redolent of tropical fruits and/or earthy smells, the Riesling peachy and limey, and the Gewürztraminer floral — like roses — and exotically fruity, like lychee.

The Sauvignon Blanc and the Riesling wines should have a rather piercing aroma, very fresh and penetrating; the other two wines, especially the Gewürztraminer, have broader, fuller, more down-to-earth smells.

✔ When you taste the four wines, you probably find the Riesling and Sauvignon Blanc light to medium in body, and crisp, while the other two wines are fuller-bodied and softer. (If your Riesling is not fully dry, however, its sweetness will make it feel softer in your mouth than it would otherwise.) The flavors of the four wines should resemble whatever aromas you find in them.

Naturally, you will have a tendency to like one or two of the wines more than the others. For the wines you like less, consider whether certain foods or certain situations (a hot summer day, for example) might make the wine more appealing. Remember: (varietal) variety is the spice of wine!

Exercise #5: Pouilly-Fuissé versus Pouilly-Fumé

The two French wines called Pouilly-Fuissé and Pouilly-Fumé are similar enough in name that many wine drinkers get them confused, but actually they are two completely different wines — as this exercise demonstrates.

Pouilly-Fuissé is a wine from the Burgundy region of France (see Chapter 10), made entirely from the Chardonnay grape; Pouilly-Fumé, in contrast, is a wine from the Loire Valley region of France (see Chapter 11), made entirely from the Sauvignon Blanc grape. (Both regions have towns called Pouilly.) Pouilly-Fuissé — the Chardonnay-based wine — is usually oaked, and Pouilly-Fumé — the Sauvignon Blanc-based wine — is almost never oaked.

When you buy a bottle of each and compare the two wines, you encounter many of the same issues as you do in Exercise #3, comparing Chardonnay and Sauvignon Blanc wines. Besides differences in aroma and flavor, the two wines vary in their weight (Pouilly-Fuissé is heavier and richer, due to its Chardonnay and its warmer growing area) and their texture (the Pouilly-Fumé is particularly crisp).

Exercise #6: Good and Better

What, exactly, is quality in a white wine? What are the standards against which quality is measured? What are the gradations of wine quality?

Unfortunately, the answers to these questions are difficult and complicated. (And to some extent unimportant, because quality apart from personal taste is meaningless.)

In our book, *Wine For Dummies,* we discuss concepts such as length, depth, and balance that professional wine tasters consider when they judge the quality of a wine. The following exercise illustrates some or all of those characteristics, depending on the specific wines that you choose for your comparison.

Buy two wines of the same type that represent different levels of quality — two Chardonnays from Australia, for example, or two German Rieslings, or two white Bordeaux wines.

One sure way to know that the two wines represent different quality levels is to buy two wines from the same producer, such as a producer's "second label" Chardonnay (see Chapter 6) and his primary label wine (or a producer's regular bottling and his reserve bottling), or a QbA-level Riesling from Germany and a spätlese from the same producer (see Chapter 12). Another good clue to quality level is the price of the wine.

For this exercise, be particularly careful to chill the wines only slightly.

Here are some of the observations you are likely to make when you smell and taste the two wines side by side:

- ✔ The less expensive wine is probably more immediately appealing; it offers more aroma and more flavor more readily, while the better wine is more reticent.

- ✔ As you taste the better wine again and again, you begin to notice complexities and subtleties that you didn't notice at first; it holds your interest.

- ✔ The more you taste the less expensive wine, the more you realize that it is somewhat simple and fails to fascinate (even if it is delicious).

✔ The better wine gives you a sense of *depth* when you hold it in your mouth, as if the wine has layers of flavor, compared to the less expensive wine, which operates on the surface only.

✔ The flavors of the better wine probably stretch farther back on your tongue (a characteristic called *length*) than those of the inexpensive wine, which tend to hug the front of your mouth.

✔ Some characteristic or other of the less expensive wine probably sticks out from the rest of the wine — such as sweetness or softness — while the more expensive wine is more of-a-piece, or seamless.

Exercise #7: New World / Old World Sauvignon Blanc

European wines, generally speaking, are fundamentally different in style from non-European wines. (Wine buffs have taken to labeling European wines as *Old World* and non-European wines as *New World.*) European — or Old World — wines tend to be more subdued and understated in their flavors, for example, while New World wines tend to be more flamboyant.

These differences are easily dramatized by a comparison between either a Sancerre or Pouilly-Fumé wine, from France's Loire Valley (see Chapter 11), and a New Zealand Sauvignon Blanc. Both come from the same grape variety (the Sauvignon Blanc) and both are unoaked. But the French wine and the New Zealand wine are two different animals.

✔ When you engage in this exercise, you probably notice that the most salient difference between the two wines is the intensity of aroma and flavor.

Smell the French wine first; its aroma is not shy. But the New Zealand wine, in comparison, is off the charts in its aromatic intensity; it makes the Loire Valley wine seem downright subtle. The flavor intensity of the two wines differs along the same lines.

✔ The nature of the aromas and flavors differs as well.

While the French wine smells and tastes somewhat minerally as well as having herbal characteristics, the New Zealand wine screams, "Fruit!" Lime and grapefruit are probably evident, as well as vegetal aromas and flavors, quite likely asparagus.

What you can extrapolate from the comparison is that Old World, classic European types of wine express their grape variety only incidentally, as that grape variety is interpreted through the growing conditions of the region; the wine itself may end up tasting fruity, or it may not, but it tastes of its type — which is to say, of the place where the wine grows. New World wines express their grape variety as a primary goal, and often in no uncertain terms. What a coincidence that they also tend to be named for their grape!

Exercise #8: New World/ Old World Chardonnay

This exercise builds on Exercise #7, using Chardonnay-based wines rather than Sauvignon Blanc. Buy a white Burgundy wine from the Côte d'Or or the Côte Chalonnais (see Chapter 10), such as a Puligny-Montrachet, a Montagny, or a Bourgogne Blanc (depending on your budget). Pair the wine with a California Chardonnay. For fairness' sake, keep both halves of the comparison in the same price range.

Here's what the comparison is likely to show:

> ✔ The Burgundy is probably much more reserved in its aroma and flavor than the California wine.
>
> ✔ Athough both wines show some oaky character (see Exercise #1), the underlying aromas and flavors of the California wine are quite fruity, suggesting ripe tropical fruits, while aromas and flavors of earth underlie the oakiness in the white Burgundy.
>
> ✔ The Burgundy wine reveals its flavors slowly and gradually in your mouth, subtlety by subtlety; the California Chardonnay delivers the full impact of its flavor in one fell swoop, as soon as you put the wine in your mouth.

Which is better? Whichever you prefer. You may even like both, recognizing each as typical of a different style of wine.

Exercise #9: The Power of Place

After trying Exercise #4 and deciding that, in fact, grape variety does make a big difference in how a wine tastes, try this exercise to understand the importance of place. The growing conditions of the place where the grapes grow definitely influence a wine's taste, as does the typical winemaking style of the place where the wine is made.

Gather five bottles of Chardonnay, each from a different place (call the neighbors: you'll have plenty of wine to go around!): Australia, California, the Tuscan region of Italy, the Côte d'Or district of Burgundy (see Chapter 10), and the Languedoc-Roussillon region of southern France. Line up five wine glasses so that you can compare each wine with the others. Pop the corks, and pour.

Here are some of the differences you are likely to find among the wines:

- ✔ The Burgundy is probably the most subtle in aroma and flavor; you have to swirl your glass a lot and concentrate to pin down the Burgundy aromas: earthiness, maybe some nutty character.

- ✔ The Italian wine, the Californian, and the Australian all show definite signs of oakiness (see Exercise #1); they smell smoky or toasty or woody.

- ✔ The Californian and the Australian wines have the most fruitiness; you can taste ripe, tropical fruit flavors along with the toasty oak. Both wines are very full in your mouth (from their high alcohol level; check the label to see the percentage of alcohol), and they probably give an impression of sweetness — especially the California wine.

- ✔ The Chardonnay from southern France (probably the least expensive of the group) shows ripe, flavorful fruity character, but less so than the wines from California and Australia, and with only a touch of oakiness. The style of this wine is somewhere between the Burgundy and the New World wines.

- ✔ The Italian wine is particularly firm in your mouth, because it is high in acid and oaky, too. (Acid and tannin — which a white wine can take from oak — team up to produce a very firm "mouthfeel."

Pick your favorite styles and then try different brands from the area where your favorite is made. You'll probably like those other brands, too, because their style is similar. That's the power of place.

Exercise #10: Around the World in Three Pinot Gris

When you compare wines made from the Pinot Gris grape in three diffferent parts of the world — northeastern Italy, the Alsace region of France, and Oregon — the differences are more striking than the similarities:

- ✔ The Italian wine, called Pinot Grigio, is pale in color — almost water-pale compared to the other two wines.
- ✔ The American wine has medium color intensity, and the French wine (called Tokay-Pinot Gris) is somewhat deeper.
- ✔ The Italian wine is similarly lacking in intensity in its aroma, compared to the pear/apple/melon aromas of the Oregon wine, and the intense peach-skin and earthy scents of the Alsace wine.

When you taste the three wines, you discover that the Italian version is by far the crispest, freshest, and dryest of the three. The Oregon wine is rather rich and soft on your palate, especially compared to the Italian wine, and may give a slight impression of sweetness. The Tokay-Pinot Gris of Alsace is the highest in alcohol, which expresses itself in a full-bodied character, the opposite extreme of the light-bodied Pinot Grigio; it is also quite firm, however, in contrast to the Oregon wine.

The differences among these three wines are partially attributable to winemaking style; in Italy, for example, winemakers like to harvest their Pinot Gris grapes early so that they are high in acid, even at the expense of ripe flavor. The differences are also due to growing conditions, which influence the flavor of the Alsace wine so uniquely (see Chapter 4 or Chapter 11 for information on the Alsace region).

Part IV
Appendixes

In this part . . .

*I*f you don't take notes while you're reading this book, you probably won't remember exactly where to find the definition of malolactic fermentation, the pronunciation of Puligny-Montrachet, or the best vintages for Alsace wines. So we have gathered together all that information into this handy quick-reference section.

Appendix A

Pronunciation Guide

*T*he different nationalities that contribute terms to the language of wine can make talking about wine somewhat of a challenge to the non-native speaker. This pronunciation guide will help you sound like a native winespeaker wherever you go. Accented syllables, if any, are indicated with capital letters.

Wine Term	Pronunciation
Albariño	ahl bah REE nyoh
Alella	ah LAY lyah
Aligoté	ah lee go tay
Aloxe-Corton	ah luss cor ton
Alsace	al zass
Alto-Adige	AHL toh AH dee jhay
Anjou	ahn jew
Araujo Estate	ah RAU ho
Arneis	ahr NASE
Au Bon Climat	oh bahn klee maht
Auslese	OUSE lay seh
Auxerrois	aus ser whah
Auxey-Duresses	awk say deh res
Batard-Montrachet	bah tar mon rah shay
Beaulieu Vineyards	bo l'yuh

(continued)

Wine Term	Pronunciation
Bianco di Custoza	*bee AHN coh dee cus TOEZ ah*
Blanchot	*blahn shoh*
Bougros	*boo groh*
Bourgogne	*boor guh nyuh*
Burgenland	*BURR ghen land*
Chablis	*shah blee*
Chardonnay	*SHAR doh nay*
Chassagne-Montrachet	*shah san yuh mon rah shay*
Château Carbonnieux	*car bun nyew*
Château Couhins-Lurton	*coo ann ler tohn*
Château de Fieuzal	*fee oo zahl*
Château Grillet	*gree yay*
Château Haut-Brion Blanc	*oh bree ahn blahnc*
Château La Louvière	*lah loo vee aire*
Château La Tour-Martillac	*la tor mar tee yak*
Château Laville-Haut-Brion	*la veel oh bree ahn*
Château Malartic-Lagravière	*mah lar teek lah grah vee aire*
Château Pape Clément	*pahp cleh mahn*
Château Smith-Haut-Lafitte	*smith oh lah feet*
Châteauneuf du Pape	*shah toe nuff doo pahp*
Chenin Blanc	*shen in blahnk*
Chevalier-Montrachet	*sheh vah lyay mon rah shay*
Clos Floridene	*clo flor ee den*
Colli Orientali	*COH lee or ee en TAH lee*
Collio	*COH lee oh*
Condrieu	*cohn dree uh*
Corton-Charlemagne	*cor tawn shahr luh mahn*
Costers del Segre	*COHS ters del SAY gray*
Côte Chalonnaise	*coat shal oh naze*
Côte d'Or	*coat dor*
Côte de Beaune	*coat deh bone*

Wine Term	Pronunciation
Domaine de Chevalier	*doh main deh sheh vah lyay*
Entre-Deux-Mers	*on truh duh mair*
Fourchaume	*for chahm*
Friuli-Venezia Giulia	*FREE oo lee veh NETZ ee ah JOO lee ah*
Galicia	*gah LEETH ee ah*
Gavi	*GAH vee*
Genevrières	*jeh nev ree aire*
Gewürztraminer	*gah VERTZ trah mee ner*
Givry	*jee vree*
Graves	*grahv*
Grenouilles	*greh n'wee*
Grgich	*GHER gitch*
Grüner Veltliner	*GREW ner VELT lee ner*
halbtrocken	*HAHLB tro ken*
Hermitage	*er mee tahj*
Kabinett	*KAB ee net*
La Moutonne	*moo tun*
Les Clos	*lay cloh*
Les Forêts	*lay for ay*
Les Preuses	*lay preuh'z*
Liebfraumilch	*LEEB frow milsh*
Loire	*lwahr*
Lugana	*loo GAH nah*
Mâcon	*mah kon*
Mâcon-Villages	*mah kawn vee lahj*
Malvasia	*mal va SEE ah*
Melon de Bourgogne	*meh lohn deh boor guh nyuh*
Menetou-Salon	*meh neh too sah lohn*
Mercurey	*mair coo ray*
Meursault	*muhr so*

(continued)

Wine Term	Pronunciation
Mont de Milieu	*mon deh meh lyew*
Montagny	*mon tah n'yee*
Montée de Tonnerre	*mon tay deh tun nair*
Monthélie	*mohn teh lee*
Montlouis	*mon loo wee*
Montmains	*mon man*
Montrachet	*mon rah shay*
Mosel-Saar-Ruwer	*MOH zel zar ROO ver*
Müller-Thurgau	*MOO ler TER gow*
Muscadet	*moos cah day*
Muscat	*moos caht*
Nahe	*NAH heh*
Nantais	*nahn tay*
Neuchatel	*NOI sha tel*
Niederosterreich	*nee der OZ ter ryke*
Orvieto	*or vee AE toh*
Pays d'Oc	*pay ee doc*
Penedés	*pen eh DAIS*
Pernand-Vergelesses	*pair nahn vair juh less*
Pessac-Léognan	*pes sac lay oh nyon*
Pfalz	*fallz*
Pinot Bianco	*pee noh bee AHN coh*
Pinot Blanc	*pee noh blahnk*
Pinot Grigio	*pee noh GREE joe*
Pinot Gris	*pee noh gree*
Pouilly-Fuissé	*pwee fwee say*
Pouilly-Fumé	*pwee foo may*
premier cru	*prem yay crew*
Priorato	*pree oh RAH to*
Puligny-Montrachet	*poo lee nyee mon rah shay*
Qualitätswein	*KAL ee tates vine*

Wine Term	Pronunciation
Quincy	*can see*
Reuilly	*ruh yee*
Rheingau	*RYNE gow*
Rheinhessen	*RYNE hess ehn*
Rías Baixas	*REE ahse BYCE ahse*
Ribolla Gialla	*ree BOHL lah JAHL lah*
Riesling	*REESE ling*
Rioja	*ree OH ha*
Rueda	*roo AE dah*
Rully	*roo yee*
Saint-Aubin	*sant oh ban*
Saint-Romain	*san ro man*
Saint-Véran	*san veh rahn*
Sancerre	*sahn sair*
Saumur	*soh muhr*
Sauvignon Blanc	*saw vee nyon blahnk*
Savennieres	*sah ven nyair*
Savigny-lès-Beaune	*sah vee nyee lay bone*
Scheurebe	*SHOY reb beh*
Sémillon	*sem ee yon*
Semillon	*SEM eh lon*
Sèvre-et-Maine	*sev'r et mehn*
Soave	*so AH vay*
Spätlese	*SHPATE lay seh*
St. Veran	*san vehr an*
Steiermark	*STY er mark*
Terra Alta	*TER rah AHL tah*
terroir	*ter WAH*
The Eyrie Vineyards	*EYE ree*
Tocai Friulano	*toe KYE free ou LAH noh*

(continued)

Wine Term	Pronunciation
Tre Venezie	*tray veh NETZ ee ay*
Trebbiano	*treb bee AH noh*
Trentino-Alto Adige	*tren TEE noh AHL toh AH dee jhay*
trocken	*TRO ken*
Vaillons	*vye yon*
Valais	*vah lay*
Valmur	*vahl moor*
Vaudésir	*voh deh zeer*
Vendange Tardive	*vahn dahnj tahr deev*
Veneto	*VEN eh toh*
Verdejo	*ver DAY ho*
Verdicchio	*ver DEE key oh*
Vernaccia di San Gimignano	*ver NOTCH cha dee san jee mee NYAH noh*
vielle vignes	*vee ae veen yeh*
Vinho Verde	*VEEN yo VAIRD*
Viognier	*vee oh nyay*
Vouvray	*voo vray*
Wachau	*va COW*
Weissburgunder	*VICE bur gund er*
Wien	*vee EN*
Willamette Valley	*wil LAM ette*

Appendix B

Glossary

· ·

acidity: A component of wine, generally consisting of tartaric acid (a natural acid in grapes) and comprising approximately 0.5 to 0.7 percent of the wine by volume.

alcohol level: The percentage of alcohol by volume that a wine has; most white wines have an alcohol level between 9 and 14 percent.

American oak: Oak wood from U.S. forests; the barrels made from such wood; some winemakers in certain wine regions (such as Spain and Australia) favor American oak for aging their wines.

AOC: Abbreviation for *Appellation d'Origine Contrôllée,* sometimes shortened to *Appellation Contrôllée* and abbreviated as AC; translates as "protected place name"; France's official category for its highest-ranking types of wine, whose name, origin, grape varieties, and other defining factors are regulated by law.

appellation: An official name; often used to mean the official geographic origin of a wine, which is part of a wine's official name.

aroma: General term for the smell of a wine; more precisely, aroma refers to the youthful scents of a wine, as opposed to bouquet, which refers to a wine's developed scents.

aromatic compounds: Organic substances in grapes responsible for many of the aromas and flavors of wines.

astringent: A descriptor for the mouth-drying, mouth-roughening effect of some wines, mainly red wines, but occasionally whites.

balance: The interrelationship of a white wine's alcohol, residual sugar, and acid; when no one component stands out obtrusively on the palate, a wine is said to be well-balanced; a prized characteristic in wines.

barrel: A relatively small wooden container for fermenting or aging white wine, generally 60 gallons in size and generally made of oak.

barrel-aged: A term that applies to white wines that are fermented in containers of inert material, such as stainless steel, and subsequently placed into wooden barrels for a period of maturation; the term also applies to the maturation period in the barrel of wines that were also fermented in the barrel.

barrel-fermented: A term that applies to white wines that are fermented in oak barrels rather than in containers of inert material, such as stainless steel; the oaky character of such wines is generally more subtle than that of wines that have been merely barrel-aged.

blend: To mix together two or more individual lots of wine, usually wines from different grape varieties; a wine derived from the juice of different grape varieties.

bodega: The Spanish word for winery.

body: The perceived weight of a wine in the mouth, partially attributable to a wine's alcohol content.

bottle-age: Maturation of a wine after it has been bottled; most white wines undergo a very short period of bottle age at the winery before release, but fine white wines can require additional bottle age from the consumer.

bouquet: Evolved, mature aromas of a wine.

cask: A relatively large wooden container for making or storing wine.

castello: Italian for "castle," refers to a winery estate.

château: A French name for a grand winery estate, commonly used in the Bordeaux region as well as other regions.

classico: An Italian term applicable to certain DOC wines whose vineyards are situated in the original, classic part of the territory from which that particular type of DOC wine can be made.

clone: A subvariety of a grape variety, exhibiting characteristics that are specific to it as compared to other manifestations of that grape variety.

colheita: Vintage, in Portuguese.

commune: A village.

complex: Not simple; a complex wine has many different flavors.

cosecha: Vintage, in Spanish.

crisp: A textural term for wines that are high in acidity.

depth: A characteristic of fine wines that give the impression of having underground layers of taste, rather than being flat and one-dimensional.

district: A geographic entity more specific than a region and less specific than a commune.

DO: Abbreviation for *Denominaciónes de Origen,* which translates as "place name"; Spain's official category for wines whose name, origin, grape varieties, and other defining factors are regulated by law.

DOC: Abbreviation for *Denominazione di Origine Controllata,* which translates as "controlled place name"; Italy's official category for wines whose name, origin, grape varieties, and other defining factors are regulated by law; also an abbreviation for Portugal's highest official wine category, *Denominação de Origen Controlada,* translated similarly and having the same meaning.

DOCG: Abbreviation for *Denominazione di Origine Controllata e Garantita,* which translates as "controlled and guaranteed place name"; Italy's official category for its highest-ranking wines.

domaine: A French term for wine estate, commonly used in the Burgundy region.

dry: Not sweet.

estate: A property that grows grapes and produces wines from the grapes of its own vineyards; wines labeled "estate" are made from vineyards owned by (or in some cases, under the direct control of) the same entity that owns the winery and makes the wine; use of the term is regulated by law in most areas.

fermentation: The natural process by which the sugar in grape juice is transformed into alcohol (and the juice is thus transformed into wine) through the action of yeasts.

finish: The final impressions a wine gives after you have swallowed it or spat it out.

firm: A descriptor for white wines whose flavor and texture is not soft, but is not harsh and tough.

flavor compounds: Organic substances in grapes responsible for many of the aromas and flavors of wines.

flavor intensity: The degree to which a wine's flavors are pronounced and easily observable.

flavors: A wine's volatile aromatic compounds as they are sensed in the mouth through the rear nasal passage.

fortified wine: A wine which has had alcohol added to it.

French oak: Oak wood from the forests of France, considered the finest type of oak for aging most white wines; the barrels made from such wood.

grape variety: A genetically individual type of grape.

lees: Grape solids and dead yeast cells, which precipitate to the bottom of a container of white wine following fermentation.

length: A characteristic of fine wines that give a sustained sensory impression across the tongue.

malolactic fermentation: A natural conversion of malic acid into lactic acid, which softens the total acidity of a wine; an optional process in white wine production.

maturation: The aging period at the winery during which a white wine evolves to a state of readiness for bottling; the process of development and evolution which some very fine white wines undergo after they are bottled.

medium-dry: A term to indicate the perceived sweetness of wines that are very slightly sweet.

medium-sweet: A term to indicate the perceived sweetness level of wines that are sweeter than medium-dry, but not fully sweet.

ML: Abbreviation for malolactic fermentation.

new oak: An imprecise term to indicate both oak barrels that are brand new (also called "first year oak") and barrels that have been used approximately one to four times previously.

New World: Collective term for those winemaking countries of the world that are situated outside of Europe.

oak: The type of wood used to make containers for wine in most parts of the world.

oaky: Having characteristics such as aromas, flavors, or tannin attributable to oak.

oenophile: Wine lover.

off-dry: A generalized term for wines that are neither fully dry nor very sweet.

old oak: Oak barrels or casks that are old enough to have lost most of their oaky character, generally five years old and older.

old vines: An unregulated term for grape vines whose fruit quality presumably is quite good due to the fact the vines are old—generally 40 years old or older—and therefore produce very little crop.

Old World: Collective term for the winemaking countries of Europe.

palate: A term used by wine-tasters as a synonym for "mouth," or to refer to the characteristics of a wine that become manifest in the taster's mouth.

phylloxera: An insect parasite that feeds on the roots of vitis vinifera grape vines, resulting in the vines' premature death.

primary aroma: Fresh aromas in a wine that derive from the grapes used to make that wine.

region: A geographical entity less specific than a district, but more specific than a country; when speaking of Italian wines, the term "region" applies to the political entity as well as to the wine zones within that area.

reserva: On a Spanish wine, a wine that has aged longer at the winery (usually in some specified combination of oak-aging and bottle aging) than a non-reserva version of the same type of wine.

reserve: A designation for wines that are presumably finer than the non-reserve, or normal version of the same wine; use of the term is unregulated in the U.S. and in France.

residual sugar: Sugar remaining in the wine after fermentation.

rich: A descriptor of wines that offer an abundance of flavor, texture, or other sensory perceptions.

riserva: Italian word for "reserve," indicating a wine that has aged longer before release from the winery than a non-reserve version of the same type of wine, and suggesting higher quality; the period of time a wine must age before it is entitled to use the term "riserva" (and sometimes the conditions of that aging) is defined by individual DOC regulations for each wine.

second-label wine: A less expensive, second wine or a second brand of wine made by a winery from grapes or wine not considered worthy of the winery's primary label.

serious: A metaphorical descriptor for a wine that is of high quality.

single-vineyard wine: A wine that is made from the grapes of a single (presumably exceptionally good) plot of land and bottled without being blended with wine from other vineyards, and that usually carries the name of the vineyard on its label; the term is unregulated in that the term "vineyard" is not defined as to size or ownership.

skin contact: The process through which the juice of grapes rests in contact with the grapeskins; not normally used in white wine production, but occasionally used to enhance the aromatic character of the wine.

smooth: Descriptor for a wine whose texture is not rough or harsh.

soft: Textural descriptor for a wine whose alcohol and sugar (if any) dominate its acidity, resulting in a lack of hardness or roughness.

structural components: Principally, a white wine's alcohol, acid, and sugar (if any).

structure: That part of the impression a wine conveys that derives from perception of the wine's structural elements (in white wine, mainly alcohol, acid, and sugar).

style: The set of characteristics through which a wine manifests itself.

süssreserve: German for "sweet reserve"; unfermented grape juice that is added to a white wine to increase the wine's residual sugar and sweetness.

sweetness: The impression of a taste of sugar in a wine, which can be due to the presence of residual sugar or other sweet-tasting substances in the wine, such as alcohol.

tannin: A substance in grapes that is uncommon in white wines; white wines that do have perceivable tannic content usually obtained that characteristic from aging in oak barrels.

taste: A general term for the totality of impressions a wine gives in the mouth; more specifically, the primary tastes found in wine: sweetness, sourness, bitterness.

terroir: French word that is collective term for the growing conditions in a vineyard, such as climate, soil, drainage, slope, altitude, topography, and so on.

texture: A wine's consistency or feel in the mouth.

varietal: A wine named for the sole or the principal grape variety from which it was made.

varietal character: The characteristics of a specific grape variety; the characteristics of a wine that are attributable to the grape variety from which it was made.

vegetal: Aromas or flavors that suggest vegetation or vegetables.

vielles vignes: French for "old vines."

vin de pays: French phrase for "country wine"; legally, a category of French wine that holds lower status than AOC wines.

vinification: The activity of making grape juice into wine.

vintage: The year in which a wine's grapes grew and were harvested; sometimes used as a synonym for the grape harvest.

viticulture: The activity of growing grapes.

vitis vinifera: The species to which most of the world's wine grapes belong.

weight: The impression of a wine's volume in the mouth.

wood tannin: Those tannins in a wine that are attributable to the barrels in which the wine aged.

yeasts: One-cell microorganisms responsible for transforming grape juice into wine.

Those Very Good Years: A Vintage Chart

A vintage chart exclusively devoted to white wines is a rare breed, because most of the world's white wines are made for early consumption. We have limited this chart to those regions producing white wines that are known for their ability to age.

Any vintage wine chart must be considered only a rough guide — a general, average rating of the quality of the vintage year in a particular wine region. Some wines will always be exceptions to the vintage's rating. For example, a few exceptional wine producers can find a way to make a decent — or even fine — wine in a so-called *poor* vintage.

The letter ratings (regarding when to drink the various vintages) are also general, or average ratings; for example, you can find some tired 1987 white Burgundies, but the average rating for the vintage must be a "c" (ready to drink), always with the proviso, of course, that the wines have been well-stored. This provision applies to all of the ratings.

Wine Region	1985	1986	1987	1988	1989	1990	1991	1992	1993	1994	1995
Burgundy	85c	90c	80c	80c	90b	85c	70c	90b	75b	85c	90a
Bordeaux	95c	75c	90c	85c	90b	85b	75c	85b	90b	95a	85a
Alsace	90b	80c	75c	85c	95b	95b	75c	85b	80b	90b	85b
Germany	85c	75c	65c	85c	90b	95b	80c	85c	85c	90b	85b
California North Coast											
Chardonnay	85c	90c	75d	85c	75d	90c	85c	90c	90b	85b	85b

Key:

100 = Outstanding	75 = Average	a = Too young to drink
95 = Excellent	70 = Below average	b = May be consumed now, but will improve with time
90 = Very good	65 = Poor	
85 = Good	50-60 = Very poor	c = Ready to drink
80 = Fairly good		d = May be too old

Good Older Vintages of White Wines

Wine Region	Vintage(s)
Burgundy	1978
Bordeaux	1983
Alsace	1983, 1976
Germany	1983, 1976
California North Coast	
Chardonnay	1984 (d)

Index

• G •

• *Z* •

YOUR ONLINE RESOURCE

WWW.DUMMIES.COM

Discover Dummies Online!

The Dummies Web Site is your fun and friendly online resource for the latest information about ...*For Dummies*® books and your favorite topics. The Web site is the place to communicate with us, exchange ideas with other ...*For Dummies* readers, chat with authors, and have fun!

Ten Fun and Useful Things You Can Do at www.dummies.com

1. Win free ...*For Dummies* books and more!
2. Register your book and be entered in a prize drawing.
3. Meet your favorite authors through the IDG Books Author Chat Series.
4. Exchange helpful information with other ...*For Dummies* readers.
5. Discover other great ...*For Dummies* books you must have!
6. Purchase Dummieswear™ exclusively from our Web site.
7. Buy ...*For Dummies* books online.
8. Talk to us. Make comments, ask questions, get answers!
9. Download free software.
10. Find additional useful resources from authors.

Link directly to these ten fun and useful things at
http://www.dummies.com/10useful

WWW.DUMMIES.COM

For other technology titles from IDG Books Worldwide, go to
www.idgbooks.com

Not on the Web yet? It's easy to get started with *Dummies 101*®: *The Internet For Windows*® *95* or *The Internet For Dummies*®, 4th Edition, at local retailers everywhere.

IDG BOOKS WORLDWIDE

Find other ...*For Dummies* books on these topics:

Business • Career • Databases • Food & Beverage • Games • Gardening • Graphics
Hardware • Health & Fitness • Internet and the World Wide Web • Networking
Office Suites • Operating Systems • Personal Finance • Pets • Programming • Recreation
Sports • Spreadsheets • Teacher Resources • Test Prep • Word Processing

Dummies Man and the IDG Books Worldwide logo are trademarks and ...For Dummies is a registered trademark
under exclusive license to IDG Books Worldwide, Inc., from International Data Group, Inc.

IDG BOOKS WORLDWIDE BOOK REGISTRATION

Register
This Book
and Win!

We want to hear from you!

Visit **http://my2cents.dummies.com** to register this book and tell us how you liked it!

- ✔ Get entered in our monthly prize giveaway.

- ✔ Give us feedback about this book — tell us what you like best, what you like least, or maybe what you'd like to ask the author and us to change!

- ✔ Let us know any other ...*For Dummies* topics that interest you.

Your feedback helps us determine what books to publish, tells us what coverage to add as we revise our books, and lets us know whether we're meeting your needs as a ...*For Dummies* reader. You're our most valuable resource, and what you have to say is important to us!

Not on the Web yet? It's easy to get started with *Dummies 101*®: *The Internet For Windows*® *95* or *The Internet For Dummies*,® 4th Edition, at local retailers everywhere.

Or let us know what you think by sending us a letter at the following address:

...*For Dummies* Book Registration
Dummies Press
7260 Shadeland Station, Suite 100
Indianapolis, IN 46256
Fax 317-596-5498

BUSINESS AND
GENERAL
REFERENCE
BOOK SERIES
FROM IDG

COMPUTER
BOOK SERIES
FROM IDG